To Sarah who was all this story

STRICTLY PRIVATE TO PUBLIC EXPOSURE

Series 1: A Plateful of Privilege

BOOK III:
TWO BITES
of THE APPLE

love

ALEXANDER THYNN
THE MARQUESS OF BATH

Alexander

11/IV/05

A

Artnik
London

First published in book form in Great Britain 2003
by Artnik
26 Pont Street
London
SW1X 0AB

ISBN 1 903906 26 1

Layout by Oliver Beesley
Design by Linda Wade

Printed in Bulgaria by Demax PLC

Contents

PART THREE: WOLFENBÜTTEL BARRACKS

❈

PART FOUR: FINAL TRIUMPHS

❈

PART FIVE:
SAVOURING PARIS

PART SIX:
CORONATION TIME

Foreword

NIGEL DEMPSTER

Alexander Thynne is flamboyant, controversial, celebrated, decadent and, at least for a journalist, wonderful copy. In fact, he is a gossip columnist's dream: a wealthy peer with a magnificent stately home who aside from holding eccentric views on virtually everything has acquired a staggering number of wifelets. A harem, in fact, that would cause many a 16th century sultan to eat his heart out. Small wonder that for over twenty-five years he has been regular feature in my *Daily Mail* Dairy.

Actually it was I who dubbed him the "the Loins of Longleat", a tag that has sort of stuck. As he is so colourful, he has attracted a great deal of this kind of press coverage. Yet, having read the first three books of his autobiography, *Strictly Private to Public Exposure*, I rather wish I had looked behind his public image. I can now see there are a lot more facets to his character than the media concedes.

It is very easy, for example, to assume that as Alexander is unconventional and hedonistic he is also indulgent and dissolute. Nothing, as the barest of facts about his full autobiography prove, could be further from the case. So far, this quite monumental chronicle amounts to over 5 million words! Just to produce them would break the back of most professional scribblers. But they are also well-written and informative. These books are a delight to read. His style is elegant, light and, in the best English tradition, gently ironical. It is a rare page that will not draw a wry smile from the reader.

Moreover, in taking readers through the journey of his life and its antecedents, he effortlessly leaves them with a sense of history, an understanding of what made England. Aside from such unexpected delights, my overriding impression from reading his trilogy was to recognise how astonishingly industrious and disciplined he has been and, even in his seventies, continues to be. For all the drinking, eating and wifelet-ing, which we columnists and diarists like to imagine consumes Alexander at Longleat and in his St Tropez villa, he clearly does not let it interfere with his writing.

Aside from the books, though, Alexander is also a poet, prolific artist, sportsman, politician, polemicist, stately home showman... How he has packed it all in defeats me. Who would have thought, for example, that he was an Eton and Army boxing champion? I think if I had known that my more punchy items on his life might have been rather less hard-hitting. I'm sure that the assault on a man in Campden Hill Road in 1994 must have been – as he claims – a case of mistaken identity. But, if it wasn't, well I bet the bounder deserved all he got.

Of course, as those who know him, Alexander is always the perfect English gentleman. He never stands on protocol despite having a bloodline that has a far more aristocratic pedigree than those sticklers for formality, the Windsors. Alexander can be "Your Grace" or "My Lord" as easily as he can be just plain Alexander. The picture that Alexander paints of his upbringing in *A Plateful of Privilege* shows us more elegant, charming, gentler times. The same pattern emerges in his account of his days at Eton and in the army. Those days will never return and only live on in accounts such as his but reading of them made me feel that the world would be a better place if his era had lasted longer. He does not look back at his life through the rose-tinted glasses of nostalgia but with a warm eye that always lights on what it is valuable to record, remember and celebrate.

Alexander often refers to his many murals that adorn the walls of Longleat – some like the Kama Sutra room with explicitly sexual themes – as "keyhole glimpses into my psyche". These first three books, which Artnik has published, open the door on his psyche and reveal a man who is much bigger and far more fascinating than his image.

My overwhelming impression of *A Plateful of Privilege* was the honesty of the narrative. We are often urged to read autobiographies because they are open, frank, candid... yet they can be all that and still self-serving. Most people are cowards when it comes to exposing in print how they know themselves. Alexander is true to himself, which is a rare quality in a man never mind an autobiography. Whatever exception may be taken to Alexander's lifestyle and the causes he holds dear, I defy anyone who reads his memoirs not to enjoy them and end up admiring the person they reveal.

Nigel Dempster
June 2003

TWO BITES
of THE APPLE

PART ONE

BASIC ARMY TRAINING

Chapter 1.1

Career: enlistment in the Brigade of Guards

These were days when all males of school leaving age were required to do a spell of two years National Service in one of the armed forces. I saw this definitely as an intruding imposition – a chore that I must get behind me before I could focus upon matters that were more important to me. But there was another way that I could treat the experience, in that it could be regarded as an opportunity to take a bite from the apple of adult life, before it became necessary to make my final decisions upon what career I would pursue. I had the option of serving my National Service straight away after leaving Eton, or waiting until I had completed my education at Oxford University. On the theory that it might be sensible to postpone the most enjoyable period until the last, I had chosen to get the National Service over and done with.

The choice of regiment had been largely determined for me a couple of years previously, during a dinner conversation at Sturford with my father and sister. Caroline had offered the opinion that, as far as London social life was concerned most of her best friends over that period were officers in the Life Guards and since it was most unlikely that we would actually be going to war with anyone during the crucial two years of my service, it might be wisest to select my regiment for its social advantages, rather than for any particular concern about warfare, or the way it should be fought.

I criticise myself in retrospect for not producing firmer views of my own upon the matter. It should have occurred to me that the choice of an armoured car regiment should presuppose some liking for or interest in the mechanisms and maintenance of cars. The whole idea of cavalry regiments nowadays was of dependence upon such machinery when riding into battle. And even if I took the line that there wouldn't be any real warfare, there would still be the exercises, schemes and manoeuvres with which to contend. It should have occurred to me that I had always felt more at ease when standing upon my own feet. Machinery was an appendage in the control of which I had yet to develop any aptitude – especially if I were to consider this as my battle mode. I was the right material for the Foot Guards, the Rifle Brigade, or even, I dare say, a Parachute Regiment. But it was surely a mistake for me to offer myself for training in either tanks or armoured cars.

But the conversation at Sturford led to my father writing a letter to Ferris St.George, who was currently the Colonel of the Life Guards, asking him (as a friend) to take young Alexander into his regiment for his National Service. And although Henry himself would have been disappointed if I had chosen to sign on for a career in the army – judging it to be the right destiny for aristocrats who couldn't do much else with their lives – the Colonel knew well how there had been many a young officer who, after experiencing the largely leisured life style that was involved, finally opted to sign on. After coming down to Eton to take a look at the various boys on his list, he was therefore happy to accept my application. And it might be added that by Eton standards I had been the most distinguished of the boys thus to present themselves. At this particular stage I have no recollection that any of us were actually rejected.

It flatters me somewhat that Colonel Richard Abel-Smith – who was Ferris St. George's opposite number in the Royal Horse Guards and who had wanted to marry my mother in years long past – had written to Daphne, soon after my acceptance for the Life Guards, to say that it might be more appropriate if I transferred my application to the Blues instead. I mention this to stress how eligible I must have appeared to everyone, which would be in stark contrast to the depths that my general reputation was soon to be plunged. But I declined to transfer my loyalties from one regiment to the other, partly because I was reluctant to change my decision for what seemed inadequate reason and partly because I was looking forward to the prospect of accompanying the Regiment out to West Germany, where they would be stationed in 1952.

Closer to the time when I was due to leave Eton, there were dates when particular batches of us were required to put in an appearance at the local recruiting office in Slough to submit ourselves to a whole variety of rudimentary tests. Naturally the results were never supposed to be made known to us. But I remember how I felt totally lost when it came to the tests for mechanical aptitude. There were six of them in all – of mounting complexity. But the simplest was to assemble the metal handle for a drawer, from a flattened strip of metal and two screws. All that one could possibly do wrong was to assemble it so that instead of the heads of the screws sinking flush into their respective bevelled holes they stood proud of the metal strip. That, of course, is precisely what I did. I noted from the resigned smile on the face of the officer who came up to record my performance that I had done exceptionally badly.

Just how badly I heard a few weeks later, after another batch of Etonians had gone up for their own bouts of testing. When it came to the mechanical aptitude tests, the NCO in charge told them, "You don't need to fret if you feel that you're not much good at these things. In the previous batch that came here for testing from your school, there was someone called Viscount Weymouth. He scored nought out of six. But he still passed!"

Other matters aside, we would no doubt have been sorted out at this stage as to whether we were appropriate recruits for the infantry, the cavalry, the artillery – or whatever. But, then, I had already been selected by Colonel Ferris as a recruit for the Household Brigade. And it was soon to be impressed upon me that the Household Brigade was virtually independent from the rest of the British army. The tests that were devised for others did not necessarily apply to ourselves. So I finally got my papers to report at Combermere Barracks, Windsor, during the first week in January 1951 – while I was still eighteen years old. This was to be the start of my National Service in the Life Guards and what should be regarded as my first taste of life as an adult human being.

Right from the very start, it was a question of watching my sense of self-esteem subjected to such a battering that, at times, I felt that it could never survive. Even when first approaching the barracks, I was foolhardy enough to cut a corner on the parade ground whilst some troop was being drilled there – calling down upon my own head a torrent of abuse from the Corporal of Horse who was drilling them. And that was but a small foretaste of all the indignities to come.

There was a small group of Etonians joining the Life Guards as potential officers on the same day as myself. These were Tim Sainsbury, Patrick Daniel and Jeremy Clay – plus Richard Steele and Milo Devereaux, who were joining the Royal Horse Guards. At Eton, I had not been more than an acquaintance of any of these, although I now befriended Tim in particular. And we were joined as a trio by Laurence Kelly, from Downside, who had spent the last few months being put into (just slightly) more muscular shape with the assistance of a physical training course at Pirbright. But he still looked somewhat puny by the general standard of the Brigade of Guards. And there were two Wykhamists in the same batch as ourselves, of whom Angus McNeill was joining the same regiment as ourselves, whilst Alistair Thompson was going into the Blues – as also was John Margotson from Harrow. Those of us who endured the course were to see a lot of each other over the next few months as we were trained to be Potential Officers.

It should be noted how the entire intake came from public schools with an elitist ring to their names. There was no one at all from one of the lesser public schools, nor anyone from the state sector of education.

Right from the start, I was always aware how I was seen by others as wearing the Old Etonian ticket around my neck. There were stereotype images involved: something about individualism, charm, gentlemanly good manners, and an indomitable conviction about superiority – or arrogance, as the Harrovians viewed it. And unintelligence – the barbed jest thrown in by the Wykhamists. And it is best to leave unstated how Etonians had been brought up to regard the stereotype images of our rivals upon this field of life's battle.

> We **surge** from our **classy kennel, unafraid,**
> while **baying** at **imp**otent **shad**ows, in a **pack gladd**ened
> by **confraternity, eagerly bond**ed to **respond**
> to **all calls** for **mut**ual **aid** and **succour.**
> **Plucked** as the **best ripe fruit** to **suit**
> an **elite pal**ate, we **treat** each **other** to **prom**ises
> of **groom**ing in the **natural leadership** of **men,**
> **sent** on our **way** with the **bless**ings of **divine right.**
> Like **white peacocks** parading on the **social scene,**
> we **preen** our **pale feath**ers with **lan**guid **grace,**
> facing **down** all **lesser** species with **baffling**
> affability – effortless in **lordly charm.**
>> Since **status** has been writ within the stars,
>> you others must accept the world is ours!

Potential Officers were not a popular breed within the eyes of the other ranks. If we made the grade as officers, then they knew only too well how we would soon be lording our authority over them. So this was their opportunity to give us, while we were still without authority, a dose of what we would be soon dishing out. There were sneering comments at every turn. But none of this was in any way comparable to the indignities that were to be foisted upon us after we had been transferred to the Guards' Training Depot at Caterham. We had all heard – from school friends who had gone before us – how this was going to be a memorable, but miserable experience. Their predictions were only too accurate.

I had also found it disheartening to receive a letter shortly before I started my National Service, from Hugh Lawson – who had been the Captain of M'tutor's at Eton when I was first elected into Debate. He wrote to say that he knew that I would soon be arriving at Caterham, where he was currently serving as an officer in the Scots Guards. He warned me, however, not to avail myself of any notion that we had formerly been on friendly terms. He bade me salute him in the same manner as I would any other officer. Only after my training might we resume the notion of friendship, as it once had been. And on the few occasions when I did encounter him, I behaved precisely as I'd been instructed.

Our welfare and happiness over this period was put into the hands of Sergeant McMahon and Trained Soldier Stableford: both of them from the Grenadier Guards, since the recruits from the Household Cavalry had been lumped into the same platoon as those from that regiment. But I was made to feel quite rapidly how there was a special role to be allotted to me in their eyes – which amounted to something in the nature of the squad buffoon.

I saw how I had been singled out for their special attention when we were all first lined up at the foot of our beds in the barrack-hut, for them to make our acquaintance. We were stood to attention, ramrod-fashion, with Sergeant McMahon walking slowly down the line, making the odd sinister comment – just to make us fully aware that our cushy family life was a thing of the past. We each had to state our name and army serial number, while staring straight ahead.

When I had said my piece, he enquired, "Would that be the Viscount Weymouth?" If I had shown the slightest indication of feeling pleased with myself, or flattered that he should know so much about me, I would have been for instant retribution. But I played the situation correctly by just confirming that side of my identity with the minimum of facial expression, and he moved on to take a look at the next in the row. But I had sensed quite distinctly that having a Viscount in their squad – or rather, at this stage, two of us – was something they relished. And I dreaded to think how they might make use of it, or what the traditional line of play in these matters might be.

Potential Officers at Caterham were put into the Brigade Squad, where we were required to absorb within four weeks the disciplinary training that other Guardsmen took in more gradually over a period of months. But during these four weeks, the whole idea was to drain from us every spark of individualism, so that we could be remoulded into the fused identity of a single platoon. The process involved the deliberate destruction, or suspense, of all that had previously amounted to any sense of personal identity. We had to be transformed into automatons before we could be of any use to the Brigade of Guards. And the dehumanising process was focused upon the idea of getting us marching, stamping our feet, pirouetting and twirling to the frenzied bark of Sergeant McMahon.

I had been prepared for a lot when coming into the army, but it involved a greater loss of status than I had been anticipating for a school potentate, of my standing, to be transformed within a few short weeks after leaving Eton into the squad buffoon and butt of all barrack-room jests. I fulfilled the requirements almost perfectly: I was jumpy – because I was highly strung; I remained affable under badinage; I couldn't polish my boots. I had never been required to do such menial tasks before, and it took me ages to get a proper shine even started. I never understood why things were always going wrong, but they invariably did, and Sergeant McMahon relished any opportunity for chasing a viscount up and down the parade-ground. It was, "Deft-doit-deft-doit-deft-doit-deft-turn-doit-turn-baht-turn-deft-doit-deft-doit-deft-doit...." until my feet were flapping like a mechanical duck's. And in the pauses, he would call me all the most opprobrious epithets within his repertoire for vituperation. Anything from a pregnant penguin, to a good-for-nothing donkey-walloper. But I never heard him utter an obscenity. As well as compelling absolute obedience to his commands, the fierceness of his abuse made obscenity redundant.

> As a **blinke**red **robo**t **propelled** on **clockwork boots**,
> and a **new** re**cruit**, I **take** the **brunt** of **pot**
> **shots** from the **barking teeth** of a **loud-mouthed**
> **lout** of a **mili**tant om**nipo**tent **drill-sergeant**.
> **Starting** to **dance** with a **dicky-bird perched**

chirping on my nose, I close my ears to the flurry
of blurred insults, hoping to put hot
rhythm in the steps of my dithering, blinded feet.
I'm greeted as a naked clown, whose nose has grown
overblown, like fallen fruit, frizzled
on a brute, open fire, and prodded with wooden
rods, to the point of slushing to a crushed mush.
  But as I totter round the ordered track,
  there's quite a store of fuel on my back.

Some of us didn't make the grade of course and [A] was the first to fall by
the wayside. He had been totally incapable of adapting himself to the speed
of physical movement demanded by all this square-bashing. I know not
how it was arranged, but he was returned to Combermere Barracks and
soon after this received a medical discharge from his National Service
without even having served his time out in the ranks. The notion of strings
being pulled somewhere within the Old-Boy network sprang naturally to
most of our minds. But we bore him no resentment over this method of
avoiding it all – for he was indeed such a likeable young buffer.

You always had to be so bloody masculine at Caterham. Any departure
from the grin-and-bear-it ideal was liable to be greeted with the fierce abuse
of Sergeant McMahon or the more quiet sarcasm of the Trained Soldier
who had been planted in our barrack-room in order to bite at us whenever
we slackened. One of the initial tests for our masculinity was to see who
fainted during the TAB injections. There were two doses to receive, and we
were all lined up in a long file, with our hands on our hips while the master
of ceremonies came jabbing his way along it like a piston-punching steam-
engine. Since my name began with a W, I had a long time to wait. And on
the first of these occasions, the wretched guardsman in front of me
collapsed in a heap a few seconds before the needle reached him.

Later in the barrack-room, I heard everything they had to say about
that. So by the time I was lined up, waiting for my second dose of these
injections, I was petrified that I might disgrace myself by fainting. Well the
needle arrived and I remained standing. But as soon as it had passed on to
the next man, I began to feel this was about to happen to me. It was a
reaction of relief, I suppose. The walls of my vision closed in on me until
there was only blackness before my eyes. Yet I was now supposed to be
marching off into the adjoining room – which I endeavoured to do.
Marched straight into an invisible pillar in fact. I stood there uncertainly

to attention, waiting for my vision to clear. And as it did so, my first sight was of Sergeant McMahon, now identifiable as the invisible pillar, and glaring at me with a sadistic gleam in his eye.

"You wouldn't be feeling ill, would you Weymouth?"

"No Sergeant, I feel fine."

"Rejoin the squad!"

So on this occasion I had saved myself from ridicule, but there were many others when I did not. I was quite incapable of organising my routine so that all the menial tasks might be completed by the time when lights were put out. As a result of this, I had to spend half the night working by candlelight in the latrines. And I was so bloody tired by morning that I didn't have the resilience to contend with the persecutions of the following day. But it was one of the rules of the game that you had to find this kind of life to be funny. "It's so bloody awful, it's got to be funny. See?" Yes. I saw. And I laughed with the rest of them.

Then one night, on my return from the latrines, I flopped down on my bed for a few seconds and promptly fell asleep. There may have been some idea in the back of my mind that I was pulling a fly move in that I'd be ready-dressed when reveille sounded. Something I deemed might be viewed humorously by the rest of the squad. But I had miscalculated. The Trained Soldier observed that I was dressed before the others and guessed how this had come about. I was put on a charge for idle sleeping.

On being marched into the presence of my Company Commander, who was Captain Gow of the Scots Guards, I was sentenced to the anticipated punishment parade. But I was also greatly perturbed to hear that a copy of a letter from my father to the Colonel of the Life Guards had been forwarded to him saying that I was too much of a Bohemian in my ways; untidy in my appearance and all that kind of thing. Apparently Henry had gone on to suggest that the Brigade of Guards would be doing him a favour if they could knock a little discipline into me. While hinting at a degree of sympathy with me for possessing a father who made such requests, Captain Gow indicated that it was a policy that would naturally be implemented.

The first fortnight at Caterham was by far and away the worst. After that period, we were permitted a forty-eight hour pass to return home for the weekend – if we were fortunate enough to be living in the southern counties of the British Isles. Sturford Mead was within the prescribed range. So home I went – fervently relishing the renewed contact with home. And in a funny way I just wanted to share with them the horror of my recent experiences and to exhibit my shorn head as the most visible feature of what military training had reduced me to.

But there was one advantage in particular from being allowed to go back home, which was that I obtained a chance to ask Donald, who had after all been Henry's batman during the earlier part of the war, to put a good shine on my boots. For that reason, I had brought them back home with me – slung around my neck as I rode upon my Velocette motorcycle. In fact he put such a brilliant shine upon them, it was to last throughout the week – after which time I would be getting another weekend pass and another shine on my boots.

Jokes about the *Vy-cunt's* fuckin' butler were rife within the barrack room. But at this stage the severity of our training was easing up… very slightly. According to the textbook theory, we were now drained of our individualism and already shoehorned into the prescribed platoon of foot-stamping robots. So they could now permit us to revive our sense of personal identity just a little.

With a glimmer of personality rekindling in my heart, I made so bold as to crack a joke to someone about the way the Trained Soldier's hair was standing on end when we were passing him in the street. So that evening I was called out in front of the rest of the squad. He wanted to know what had given rise to my merriment. So I told him. But he was in a nasty mood and declared that I ought to have the courage to say things to a man's face, instead of behind his back. "Because I can take it, you know. I'm not afraid of anyone, I'll have you know."

The bastard had a chip on his shoulder about people laughing at him – but then so did I about any insinuation that I was a coward. So I replied, "No, Trained Soldier, nor am I."

For a moment he stood there, looking incredulous. Then he said, "You think the hell of a lot of yourself, don't you Weymouth? Well I think you're a cheeky pup. I'll be seeing you later." And he stalked out of the room.

I thought I'd really put my foot in it this time. I just sat there with butterflies in my stomach, waiting for him to return. But to the general surprise, when he did so, he had nothing to say to anyone. He just went to bed. Next morning, however, when I committed some trivial misdemeanour on the parade-ground, Sergeant McMahon called me out in front of the squad.

"The trouble with you Weymouth, is that you're gutless. You can't drill because you haven't any guts!"

I looked daggers at him – standing rigidly to attention of course.

The sadistic gleam returned to his eye. "You wouldn't be going to strike me, would you? No, you're not the sort of person who would dare to strike a superior officer. Are you, Weymouth?"

I didn't reply. I just glared at him. And he glared back – without either of us moving. Then he told me to fall back in line. This episode had one good effect in that it marked a point where a transition began in my relationship with the rest of the squad. Both Sergeant McMahon and the Trained Soldier now became friendly in their disposition towards me. They seemed to regard me as a bit of a personality. And it coincided with the move from Caterham to Pirbright, where the character of our training softened all round. I was subjected to just as much ridicule as before and I was still the butt of all their practical jokes, but it was now done almost in a spirit of affectionate regard.

For example, I was called out to play some fatuous game with the Trained Soldier, in which I had to balance a sixpenny piece on my forehead and then toss it up into the air so that it landed in a petrol funnel, which had been shoved down the front of my trousers. Well it hardly needs to be stated that, as soon as my face was tilted up towards the ceiling, he produced a jug of water from behind his back and poured it down the funnel – giving rise to hilarity all round. "Fancy a *Vy-cunt* pissing himself in public!" More laughter. And I had to find the whole business so jolly funny too!

But they managed to get me quite worried on some occasions, for I was never quite sure if they were being serious or funny at my expense. The time when I was nearly put under close arrest for immoral practices, for example. It was after lights out and Sergeant McMahon and the Trained Soldier were out of the room. Someone came up with the bright theory that farts go off with a blue flame, if you hold a lighted candle to them. But there were sceptics in the squad. And, of course, it had to be me who volunteered to test the theory so that the public curiosity could be satisfied.

Unfortunately our guardian angels had to return at the very moment when I was bending over with my pants down and a candle in my hand. And this was the kind of situation which army humour could never resist. I was to be put in the guard-room under lock and key. Naturally, I didn't really believe it, but they certainly carried the pretence a long way. I was ordered to dress and was then marched off to the very door of the guard-room, before it was revealed to me that everyone was having a giggle at my expense. And that was certainly a relief. I didn't relish having to face my father with the news that I'd been discharged from military service for gross indecency.

But they seemed to like me, which was the important thing. The only person to suffer from this alteration in my status was poor [B]. He had instantly replaced me in all the more dolorous aspects of being the squad buffoon. But when he saw how I'd emerged from that status myself, by offering some well-timed insolence to the Trained Soldier, he evidently thought that he'd best do likewise. Therefore in response to the continual nagging that he was receiving to get a better shine on his boots, he stood up one day and told the Trained Soldier to mind his own flipping business. And there was hell to pay. His kit went flying all round the barrack-room, some of it through the open window into the puddles outside. The wretched [B] was now in tears, which didn't help matters.

By the time the rest of us were ready for the transfer from Caterham to Pirbright, he appeared to be suffering from a nervous breakdown. He didn't return from a weekend pass and we were to hear later that he'd been invalided out of the army – on medical grounds – which in his case were doubtless quite genuine.

Between Caterham and at Pirbright – where we underwent the two parts of our training – we were tested by the War Office Selection Board (WOSB) at Barton Stacey to decide whether or not we were made of the right stuff to be an officer. Did we warrant the further expense of training us to lead each other into battle? We'd all heard cautionary tales about those who had been expected to pass, but in the event had failed. The story that came closest to home being told by Tim Sainsbury about his brother Simon who, as the President of Pop, had been one of the most revered boys at Eton. He had been failed for what was described as an irresponsible attitude – he had answered their query as to why he wished to be an officer, by saying that he supposed it involved a much more comfortable life. But he was later to prove his metal not only by passing his WOSB but also going on to be awarded the Stick of Honour, after passing out at the very top in his training at Mons OCS.

There was always this terrible fear in my heart that I might not make the grade: after all the promise in life that I had shown as a schoolboy, what might now come to the surface would be the fundamental weaknesses in my personality. After all, the orderly arenas that had been my lot had spared me from the sheer rough and tumble of fending for myself. But the greatest portion of my fear was that, if I failed, I would inevitably be losing my father's esteem. I had never been his favourite son, but he still admired my potential in life. Up to now, it looked as if I was a winner. All that might change if I failed my WOSB.

But I got through it all right; in fact, I was later told that I did impressively by Nicholas Cobbold's mother, who happened to be the wife of the officer in charge of that board. So all I had to do now was to complete my initial training at Pirbright – which in comparison with Caterham was all so friendly – before going on to Mons. We were still at the mercy of Sergeant McMahon, but during this final phase we were actually growing to love him. He could bark at us in any manner that he pleased, but the squad spirit was there. The terror that he had inflicted into our hearts over the past two months now just served to enhance our love for him. And it was with real sorrow that we finally bade him farewell, after a party which we threw in his honour up in London, involving a visit to a saucy revue followed by a slap-up dinner at the *Ecu de France* in Jermyn Street.

Mons was the school where principally all Potential Officers for the Cavalry and the Artillery were trained. But the first half of this training was concerned with infantry matters. The whole intake was lumped into a single company of four platoons with recruits from the Household Cavalry spread out amongst them. What came as a pleasant surprise was the prestige which we appeared to hold – as the sole representatives of the Brigade of Guards – in the eyes of all the others POs. We were able to lob it up, as the saying went, for the training that we were now receiving was cushy stuff when compared to the horrors we had experienced at Caterham. We were able to treat the complaints of all the others as derisible.

The prestige was ill-founded, if the truth needs to be told. They seemed to imagine that we must be very special people to have been selected for training as POs within the elite Brigade of Guards. But I'd seen for myself how the whole process for such selection was dubious, to say the least. It was true that we had experienced the same initial training as the Foot Guards who had now gone on to Eaton Hall instead of Mons. We had suffered as much as any of them and, I daresay, were equal in disciplinary excellence. But there was one hell of a difference between the ethos of the Foot Guards and that of the Household Cavalry. They regarded us in the light of being bumbling members of the same intimate family as themselves: more cavalry than guardsmen in spirit. But here at Mons, the savour of our elitist reputation might be savoured – for what it was worth.

Coupled to all this, however, was a hovering fear that I might fail to make the grade: that I might be Returned To Unit, as unfit for further training as a Potential Officer. Deep down inside, I was very much aware of the gaping holes within my personality; that there was far more anxiety than self-confidence in my current attitude. And I compensated for this by striving to develop in the direction of a parade-ground military shit – such as Donald had once told me that Henry had been.

This meant striving at all times to present in public what I imagined the concept of officer-like qualities truly entailed. And I got plenty of opportunity to display these when I was elevated to the rank of Cadet-Sergeant with responsibilities to see that others within the platoon were performing the various duties that had been allotted to them. The upshot of that was that my popularity began slipping away from me. Yet I remained on good terms with the batch from the Household Cavalry, who humorously played up our belief in our innate superiority over all other recruits, but I could feel even that notion begin to wobble inside me. I wasn't happy about such a pretence – it was at odds with the importance and need to excel.

Indeed, it might be said that I cultivated this sense of crisis. I didn't distance myself from it, develop a lighter frame of mind, detach myself from these inner doubts. I was there in the middle of it all and I could feel the urgency to deal with it piling up on my shoulders. So I was becoming too earnest – too serious about the whole requirement to appear officer-like – and I was losing the sympathy of the other cadets. I was being military according to the rules of the book, barking orders and giving sharp rebukes to anyone who didn't carry them out. It was noticeable that I wasn't making any new friends and there were many who regarded me with distrust.

I can remember acting with quite unnecessary officiousness when – in my capacity as the cadet-sergeant – I ordered someone in my platoon to open up the window beside his bed, overriding his protests that he would prefer to keep it shut. I was acting in strict accordance with the company regulations It suddenly became an issue of immense importance to me: the authority of my command required obedience. And for a moment there was real tension in the barrack-room with everyone waiting to see whose will would prevail. I picked up a piece of the equipment that he would require next morning on parade and told him that it would only be returned to him after he had done my bidding. There was a terrible pause, but he did finally comply. I had won the day.

But there were other instances which did not go quite so well for me – like the time I was marching at the head of the platoon, when they ganged up against me by gradually increasing the pace of the step at which they were marching, until it had reached something absurd. Nor were they responding to my orders to slow it down. A spirit of mutiny was humorously in the air and, in hindsight, I can probably say that the best retort on my side would have been to give a humorous display of being an outraged drill instructor. In such situations, humour is nearly always the safest remedy and my inability to call on it left me precariously vulnerable. But this looming breakdown in my authority was far too threatening for me to treat it lightly. I halted them and, thankfully, when I marched them off again all was well, but the warning lights about not distancing myself too far in spirit from the rest of the group were on.

> As spikey brittle as a sea urchin, I search
> to see a safe enclave for my cloven foot,
> rooting twenty fathoms deep in the rolling
> swell of the ocean's ferocious belly button.
> Fluttering with buttered feet on the shrinking brink
> of collapsed thinking, my piston fist must strike
> at the streaking faces, howling for domination
> in the rumbustious anarchy of grim survival.
> Driving the schizoid team of inner horses
> that I force onwards to the precipice edge, I pledge
> my humourless dedication to the nasty task
> of coming out from the treacle bin – on top.
>> And when you hear the snap of my command,
>> jump sprightly to avoid my reprimand.

But the crisis did not drag me under. There were the Company boxing competitions, for example, where I won my weight class – as indeed I was expected to do after all the prestige I had acquired in that field when at Eton. And on the surface at least, things might appear to be going well for me. I had already been appointed to be the Platoon Commander, then I was promoted to be the Half-Company Commander, which meant I was required to march at the head of two platoons at the passing-out parade. And I was given a grading of +22 for my officer-like qualities. There were only two who obtained a higher grading, and not by much. This was only the halfway point within our training at Mons, but my prospects for the final grading looked most encouraging at this stage.

To be awarded the Stick of Honour at the final passing-out parade was the ambition lurking somewhere at the back of my mind, but to achieve this I needed to push up my grading to somewhere only just short of +30. Much as I tried to persuade myself that I really had the capacity to get there, I was losing confidence all the time. Things might seem to be going right, but I knew inside me that they were not. The unpopularity I had acquired during the earlier part of the training now began to tell against me. The second half of our training was in G Squadron and was focused more on our duties as future cavalry officers but, as we started to work under a new set of instructors, I found I had few real allies.

In some respects, this was a more relaxed life all round and, now that we were moving into the summer, there were social events connected to the London debutante season to distract us from too great an absorption in our training. It was a problem to keep alert during the lectures, or even awake on some occasions – especially after returning on my motorbike from a London ball in the early hours of the morning. It was all very well trying to appear officer-like at all moments of the day, but there was now the additional requirement of absorbing the notes that we took. And my performance began to lapse in these matters – to an extent that my self-confidence was suddenly quite badly shaken. It became a real fear that I actually might fail the next test and get Returned To Unit. A panic set in and my whole attitude fell to pieces.

Unless I could feel that I was liked, there was no hope for me to emerge triumphant. So much of my functional efficiency depended upon a spirit of concord between myself and the people with whom I was working. And there was no chance that it could now be kindled. I had to display officer-like qualities by complete rule of the thumb. But it was just a façade, a big game of bluff, in the hope that I could persuade the instructors that I really felt like that inside. And my grading was slipping. It was down to +12, with the final days of testing still to come. But it was bound to work out all right... in the end. That was the way I thought about my life up to that date. The same pattern, as at Ludgrove and at Eton, must get repeated here at Mons. All I had to do was to bide my time and I'd suddenly see how I was sliding through to the head of the field.

But what if this didn't happen? What if they uncovered the façade and perceived how I was really feeling inside? There was nothing officer-like about that. I had an awful presentiment that this was bound to happen. And what would follow? Relegation? Returned to Unit? And how would my father then regard me? This last question was always close to the epicentre of the quakes that I felt within. I might try to stop myself from worrying about such matters. Stop thinking: just work. More and more officer-like qualities. I lay there counting them, like sheep jumping over a stile.

It didn't work out all right, although it could have been a lot worse. I prepared myself for the final piece of bluff when we were all taken out on trek. But during the course of it, I became involved in a most unfortunate episode. I had a vicious altercation over the wireless, with a cadet in an armoured car that I believed to be situated in a faulty position. Well it turned out that he was in the right position, whereas mine was wrong and, worse than that, his map-reader – at the moment of the dispute – happened to be Captain Morrison, the officer who was responsible for giving us our final gradings. My own promptly sank to -4 – all too close to a relegation score – which was indeed the fate experienced by my good friend [C] who was now required to toil on at Mons for an additional few weeks before he caught up with the rest of us. But it would have needed a total of around -10 to have involved the ultimate degradation of being Returned to Unit – without a commission.

As far as I myself was concerned, it meant that I had finally passed out, and that was something. But I didn't feel that there was any cause for celebration. I felt utterly dejected. This was almost the first occasion in my life when I had failed to emerge with the stamp of quality upon my performance. It was a major setback and I was uncertain what to make of it. I didn't deserve to have done much better. I accepted that, for I knew in my heart that I wasn't really made of the right stuff to become an efficient officer – or not until I had matured greatly as an adult human being. Captain Morrison had in fact told me as much when I went to discuss my grading with him. (He had said, "I think you will make a good officer – but not yet.") In the meantime, I had to carry on living with myself – when all I wanted to do was to shut myself away from the world, and hide.

> Impaled on a stage, and weighed on scales, with bits
> of litmus paper thrust distrustfully in odd
> body crevices, I'm shown the statistical proof
> of stunted growth and blundered opportunities.
> Wounded in self-esteem, I study my dented
> identity, feeling loathing and disgust for the sham
> ham actor, who practised his insufficient
> skills within that person that I strove to be.

Ceilings to ambition, once so lofty in height,
slide downwards to cramp my impeded vision,
while derision goads me to wriggle free from the grim
limits, newly imposed on walking tall.
> From deep within, I'll somehow bring to birth
> a structured character of human worth.

Chapter 1.2

Parents and siblings:
the background situation

Now that I was no longer a schoolboy, I was anticipating that a new manner of relationship might be established between my father and myself: something more adult and fraternal perhaps. But that wasn't to be. As the relationship between Henry and Daphne became increasingly unstable, he was probably reluctant to permit anyone else within his family to harbour ideas about stepping out of line. But I wasn't happy with the thought that the situation between ourselves should continue unchanged. I needed my adult status to be fully recognised.

It is also true to say that my respect for Henry had never really recovered from his decision to beat me, some three years previously – for no greater an offence than making a mess of spilt water on the bathroom's linoleum floor, when washing my dog. And now that I was this much older, his authoritarian parental attitude irked me with increasing vehemence. And the very idea of him writing to my Colonel in the Life Guards – to suggest that I needed some discipline drummed into me – was somehow typical of how intrusive this attitude might be, even though I was now an adult male, earning my own living away from home.

Henry's whole personality was too brittle – like sharp crystals glued together with precision, yet without any comprehensive design. Fundamentally he distrusted everyone and suspected them of deceiving him about their motivations. In the back of his mind he hid unfavourable images of their identities: to allow himself to view them with favour he had to make a positive effort to suspend his innate distrust. But if anything went wrong, he reverted to type. He saw them as betraying his trust, as deliberately hoodwinking him into suspending his original distrust. And I was living in a perpetual state of fear that this was just about to happen to myself. What would happen if I failed to pass out with my commission as an officer? How would Henry regard me if I failed?

Henry's judgement upon my performance in life was still the crucial criterion by which I measured my successes. On a deeper psychological level, I was still attempting to become the sort of person that he aspired me to be. Without him feeling that I had excelled, there would be no sense of achievement in my heart; so his opinion on how I was faring was all important to me. But the strain of the whole business was quite unbearable at times, especially as the doubts about whether I had the right stuff to be an officer began to take root in my heart. Behaving as if I had it was just a charade, which might collapse at any of the successive gradings.

My relationship with Daphne was something different. She had always held me in high regard and there was no way that this regard might suddenly be withdrawn. I felt as if there was a solid permanence in our relationship, which furnished me with an inner strength of a kind. She wasn't always at home nowadays, for she was often up in London, or taking trips abroad with Xan Fielding – accompanying him officially as his photographer in his research for books that he was writing. That had been taking them out to Crete, where during the war Xan had been responsible for organising the resistance of half of the island against the Germans. The subject of his current concern was the pirates of the Barbary Coast in North Africa. I knew with half my mind that they were close enough to be called lovers – but I never really thought about the matter with much concern.

The sense of a bond between Daphne and myself was a constant in my mind, even when we were absent from one another. I had been criticised at Caterham for awakening the rest of the squad at night, with cries of "Hellooo, Hellooo, HELLOOO!" This had become a traditional way for Daphne to greet us over the phone. So even though I was too exhausted to remember what I'd been dreaming, I knew that it must have been on an idea that I was communicating with her by phone – and probably telling her about all the terrible things that were happening to me.

Something to note is that, dating from the time when I left Eton, I took the decision to reverse the order in which I wrote their names at the beginning of each letter home. Now it was always "Darling Mummy and

Daddy...." rather than, as before, the other way round. Without remembering at this point precisely what thought prompted this decision, it was consciously made and must surely be indicative of the way I now regarded them.

Beforehand, the foremost position had been given to Henry because it was clear in everyone's mind that he was the head of the family and, with some element of male chauvinist values in sway, it had always been the order of precedence in which I held them to be. But the conscious decision to think of them the other way round may have been connected with my recognition that I was never liable to do well enough in his regard and so it was psychologically healthier to give greater weight to her judgement. Certainly, my sense of personal identity would in future be more wrapped up with Daphne than with Henry.

Weekend passes back home were by no means a rarity during these months of training, so I'd been getting back home to Sturford quite frequently. But as I've said before, it was often to find that Daphne was away and, while remaining friendly with Henry, as I did not feel close to him I was apt to avoid his company. Christopher and Valentine were also only at home during the school holidays and they were more concerned with keeping each other company than with developing any relationship with myself. Life at Sturford was very much an egocentric concern. I might drop in to see how old Nan was faring in the cottage where she lived in her retirement, just over the other side of the main road, or potter around the garden, even venture out for a stroll in the woods. But we all did our own things, unimportant though these might have been.

Over this particular period, Henry was probably feeling irritable with all of his three sons but possibly just marginally less so with myself than with the others. He was lumbered with our upbringing at a juncture in his life when he was beginning to regard the family he had acquired as a liability more than an asset. He was probably seeing a great deal of Virginia Tennant over this period, although not when any of us were at home. We were the complication in his life, so to speak, and it irked him when we did not fit readily within his plans. But as he saw it, the army was now grooming me into shape. There was greater cause for concern about Christopher and Valentine – particularly the former. For Christopher was always having a problem in satisfying his teachers that he was putting sufficient effort into his work. In trials, his place was invariably near the bottom of his Remove. And the particular subject that had currently given

This is the sort of 'slave labour', as I called it, that Henry made his sons
do on the Longleat estate. Christoper (above) is to my left.

rise to Henry's wrath, was the fact that Christopher had omitted to put his name down for the school boxing competitions.

I say this with feelings of criticism for Henry's attitude in these matters. Chris had never been of any use in the boxing ring and had only ever felt obliged to box because of my own prowess in that field. But it was a mere ten per cent of Etonians who entered these competitions. So why should Chris feel that he was under expectation to submit himself to such battering, when it was invariably the losers who suffered the most? The point which irked Henry was that Chris had sought to excuse himself by saying that he had merely "forgotten" to put down his name – this was construed as a case of deliberate deceit. Scorn was heaped on his head, on the grounds that he had just "funked" it. But it was a harsh verdict from one who had never seen fit to box when he himself was at school.

Caroline was out of my orbit nowadays, although I still loved her dearly. But we were both very much aware of the age gap. She appeared well established in her London social life, from the house at 90 Eaton Terrace where she and David Somerset had set up home – with almost two years of marriage to their credit. David had been taken into partnership by the Marlborough Gallery in Bond Street and this was working out very well for all parties concerned. It wasn't so much that David was supposed to be greatly knowledgeable about art. But he moved in the circles where such purchases are made. Their living rooms were adorned with samples of what the gallery had to offer, with paintings largely from the Impressionist, the Post-Impressionist or the Expressionist eras. It worked out that there was a brisk sales turnover – arising from their entertainment of potential clients back at home.

I did drop in to see Caroline whenever I was in London, although I never felt greatly at home in David's presence. There was an aloof bonhomie about his attitude towards Caroline's younger siblings, with more than just a savour of arrogance and disdain about it too. If he was there, I didn't feel truly at ease. But I imagined how these matters would improve as we got to know one another better.

In fact, I called in to see Caroline the day after I had finally received my commission as an officer. She was sitting there alone in her drawing-room when I arrived. With my heart still heavy from the low grading, I tried to conceal my feelings with a breezy smile.

I said, "I thought you'd like to hear that I've passed out!"

But Caroline was far better acquainted with the whisky-and-soda culture, than with any talk about officer-like qualities. Putting on the censorious tones of an elder sister, she replied, "How utterly disgusting of you!"

My sister, Caroline, and David at their wedding in 1950

Chapter 1.3

Sex: looking for the first nibble

At the time of my enlistment I was still a virgin and, apart from a few bold efforts to appear flirtatious in the company of the opposite sex, I had but scant notion of how to stimulate any erotic interest on their side. I felt confident that I was heterosexually oriented, but it was not a subject where I felt in the slightest safe. There had been that crisis half way through my time at Eton, when I had been wrongly accused of having a homosexual affair. I hadn't – the slur was unfair. At the same time I knew in my heart that there had been experiences, trivial enough in themselves, where I had enjoyed erotic games with boys of my own age. So I couldn't be one hundred per cent sure about these matters. There was always a sneaking dread inside me that I might yet surprise myself with such unwelcome psychological development.

As a result of this, I was hypersensitive over this period to any suggestion that I might be homosexual. The slightest hint of such a thought in anyone's mind would be sufficient to set me off blushing – which, of course I saw as offering prima facie proof of my guilt in such matters. And there was an instance of this very early in my army life.

We had just arrived at Combermere Barracks in Windsor, where among those who came from other public schools there was a natural tendency to enquire about the recent progress of boys who went there from Ludgrove. I was having such a conversation with an old Harrovian and learned how [E] had departed from the school with a nervous breakdown; then I went on to ask about another school friend and was surprised when the Harrovian grimaced. It immediately occurred to me he was insinuating homosexuality just because we had been friends.

Instantly, I knew that I was beginning to blush. I felt as if my guilt was there for all to read. In fact, I knew how they were all taking note of my blushes – causing him to give an embarrassed laugh. And I knew how the Old Etonians amongst us might now inform him about the scandal in which I had been involved at Eton. I was at a loss to know what I could possibly say and just mumbled something about not having guessed that my old friend might develop that way. But my blushing on this occasion served to render more acute than ever my fear that the subject of homosexuality might pop up in all sorts of unpredictable forms.

When at Caterham, I did my utmost from the very start to give a more accurate impression that I was as randy as the next man to seduce women. I hoped that this thought was conveyed to others by the display of pin-up bathing beauties, which I kept in the locker beside my bed. Indeed, there were a variety of crude jokes on the subject from some of our instructors.

Even Sergeant McMahon, who would never himself have stooped to crudities of that kind, joined in conspiracy with the Trained Soldier at the one dance, which we all attended in the NAAFI, to make a bet with some attractive girl to walk over and pinch my arse – just for the fun of seeing how I might react. I actually saw her approaching – on the arm of some other soldier – when as she passed she delivered her tweak deftly but utterly unexpectedly. I just stood there feeling astonishment that a total stranger should have seen fit to do such a thing to me, while regarding it as safest to say nothing whatsoever to the others about the experience. But Sergeant McMahon and the Trained Soldier more or less gave themselves away by their ribbing comments, hinting that they'd been watching from the bar, which was way up at the far end of the hall.

There was one particular weekend pass when, instead of returning home to Sturford, I remained up in London instead, hoping that I might get a chance to lose my virginity – with a prostitute if necessary. But I didn't have any such luck. I was dressed in my trooper's uniform, which I like to think might account for my rejection. But it was a prostitute standing in a doorway near Bond Street, who humiliated me by actually turning her back on me, when I approached her to enquire how much it would cost me. And after that, I didn't have the self-confidence to approach any others. I just went prowling round Piccadilly, taking in the sights without committing myself by accosting anyone.

Then, quite unexpectedly, there was a touch on my arm and I found myself being addressed by someone of roughly the same age as myself, who was in civilian clothes. He had come up because of my uniform, with its

Life Guards insignia, for he said that he too was a trooper in the Life Guards – in his case stationed at the Knightsbridge Barracks. The less information that I gave him about myself the better, for I knew how Potential Officers were a breed disliked by the other ranks.

We quickly got conversing on the subject of picking up girls around this area, which he insisted could be done with the greatest of ease. So I spent an hour or so with him, wandering into bars and looking to see if there were any who looked eager to be taken to bed. We did pick up a couple at one stage, but at the same time I felt that the whole situation was absurd. He was the one who was boasting that he knew the ropes – as indeed he did. All the chatting up was on his side. I remained silent for most of the time. And the girl who was supposedly my date, quickly intimated to me that she had a husband waiting back at home for her. I made my excuses to slip away very soon after that, feeling that I must don something better than a trooper's uniform if I were to make any progress in courtship.

> The magic mirror pulls a tragic face,
> grimacing at the sight it sees, representing
> the spent germinescent bud, freshly
> faded, and now but fodder for the rubbish bin.
> Princely treasures stacked in a heaped pile,
> those silent millions in the bank's echoing vault,
> halt my hunger not one jot when the cheques
> I sign are maligned as products of a forger's art.
> Starting to croon the tune of a song not sung,
> long since, I now wince at the coarse
> hoarseness of my cracked voice, which currently lacks
> a fine accent or melodious presentation.
> A peacock plucked `s a sorry bird indeed,
> whom none can find it worth their while to heed.

The inadequacy of my sex appeal, as displayed within these Piccadilly experiences, was in sharp contrast to the manner that I was encouraged to assess myself within other environments. There had been my fairly successful evening with Venetia Murray at the Rothermeres' dance, shortly before I began my National Service. And there seemed good possibilities that this relationship might develop further. She had written to invite me to come and stay for a weekend with her parents at their Wiltshire home in Manningford Abbas – quite near Sturford in fact. This was fixed up during the first real break in my training, which took the form of a spell of leave over Easter, just before I went to Mons.

Venetia Murray's grandfather had been the famous Gilbert Murray – philosopher and President of the League of Nations – while her father Basil had died shortly before she was born. The rest of her family consisted of her mother Pauline who was the sister of Robert Newton the actor, her step-father Sylvester Gates, a leading banker, and her half-brother Oliver, several years younger than herself: an equivalent situation to the relationship between Caroline and myself perhaps. Although I was a mere two months younger than her, I think she saw me in the younger brother role and I daresay that I found it difficult to wriggle free from her conception of our relationship.

Although I knew that I was regarded by her family as the sort of match that would be good for Venetia to make, nothing felt quite right about the situation from my own point of view. I wanted to feel that I was the big seducer of women – not just a comradely younger brother. It was Venetia who was playing the dominant role, vamping me while keeping me at an appropriate sexual distance. It was evident that she had no intention of becoming too easy a conquest. And once I appreciated this, my enthusiasm began to wilt. Moreover, I could sense that the parents viewed me as being a little too naïve for their daughter.

They were also amused by my own uncertainty concerning how to deal with Augustus' daughter, Poppet John, who was also a guest. She was notorious – I had been told – for her seduction of younger men. I found her attractive, but her soft glances merely served to terrify me into withdrawal. I could not possibly tell myself that I was the brave libertine whom I aspired to be. But it was still good to know that my sex appeal had not entirely departed.

The misconception that I was homosexual still haunted me, however. There was another instance of this shortly after I had arrived at Mons. When on a weekend pass, I was experimenting with the idea of driving on my Velocette as far as the station at Basingstoke, and then continuing the rest of the journey by rail. I persuaded the local publican to let me park the motorbike in his yard and I left the keys in his safekeeping. When I returned on the Sunday evening however, I had an unpleasant experience – as I describe in a letter that I sent home.

When I appeared in the doorway, I heard someone remark, "Here comes another one!" Well I stood waiting at the bar to ask for the keys of my motorbike. I heard some sniggers, and then someone was clapping out the time, and a small chorus began singing that song called The Roving Kind, stressing that particular phrase, and also the line, "his hair hung down in ring-a-lets." (His, and not her, you'll note.) Considering the fact that I am still suffering from the remnants of a Caterham haircut, I think this was a little unfair of them! Anyway the net result of it all was that I retired as quickly as possible. And for once the Velocette didn't let me down by failing to start at the crucial moment of escape. The other result is that I shall henceforward squirm in my shoes whenever I hear that song being played!

While I was at Mons however, I was obtaining my first taste of the London Season for debutante dances. There were quite a number of these invitations; some of them originating from the friendships I had previously established. There were Sarah Crawley and Jane Howell, for example, who used to descend upon Eton to take me out to tea. Well, I was now invited to join the dinner parties that they were giving for such dances. Not that I was always quite happy about my standing nowadays. Sarah, in particular, showed me that I had slipped down her flirting list – she made it plain that she had other fish to fry, most of them already commissioned officers in the Life Guards.

There was also the odd royal occasion to attend. One of these involved a dance at Syon House, where all the guests on arrival were strictly vetted. When I turned up on my motorbike, appropriately accoutred, I caused a frisson of concern. Security officials got in a flap and stopped me entering the gates, whereupon after producing from the breast pocket of the evening tails under my biking garb a genuine invitation card they ingratiatingly and egregiously ushered me through. On that occasion, I think I was going as Rosie Cotterell's partner – she was the daughter of one of my mother's childhood friends – and with whom I was having a very mild flirtation.

Then there was another occasion when I met up with Venetia at a dance being held in Buckingham Palace itself. All that I can really recollect about this one is that we discovered, as we were leaving, that you can't summon a taxi from the door of the Palace. We were told stiffly by a flunkey that chauffeur-driven cars alone were permissible. It required some degree of nerve, which we did in fact muster, to depart on foot to a point beyond the railings where the traditional taxi cabs could be hailed.

My greatest interest of all was aroused by the daughter of a retired Colonel in the Brigade of Guards, whom I shall call Xenia. I was invited by her mother to join the dinner parties that she was giving for two dances that Summer. From the first time that I saw her I fancied her... the more so after making her acquaintance. Although I felt my interest might be reciprocated, it was apparent that there were many others who fancied her as much as myself. It also transpired that to really capture her attention would take time.

PART TWO

COMBERMERE BARRACKS

Chapter 2.1

Authority: my failures as a subaltern

It might have been better for me if I had gone straight to Combermere Barracks, immediately on receiving my commission, without having a spell of leave beforehand. For the leave which I spent (at Sturford and at Cowrie) furnished me with a chance to brood upon my doubts about being a fit person to command others. I might think that I was happy at the prospect of going to Windsor, but there must have been a real dread in my heart in that my body managed to cook up a high temperature: it was psychosomatic – certainly not faked – and it disappeared almost miraculously every few minutes. My local G.P. was summoned on the eve of my departure, but could find nothing wrong with me. So I was left with no excuse not to present myself for duty at Combermere Barracks. This was in August 1951.

I encountered an instant warmth of acceptance within the officers' mess at Combermere. The percentage of Old Etonians was high, so I was already on friendly terms with a large number of them. Within recent intakes were James and Charlie Morrison, Michael Grimstone, Garry Patterson, Terence Goulder, Reid Wilson, David Stapleton-Cotton and Miles Burkitt – all of whom had been friends at Eton. And there were a whole lot of others – formerly unknown to me – who had now signed on but due to their vague acquaintance with Caroline – if not to reports about me being a bit of a character – were distinctly well disposed towards me. There was Michael Naylor-Leyland for example, the brother of Vyvian, who was once dating Caroline. And the list went on with names like Henry Montgomery-Charrington, Simon Galway, Victor Hoare and Christopher Phillipson. It was really not far from being an Etonian Old Boys' club – even if the other famous public schools had their representatives there too.

The tone was definitely one of general friendliness, which was mirrored in the welcoming manner of our colonel, Jackie Ward. But somehow this didn't put me at my ease. His predecessor, Colonel Ferris, had been promoted to a Brigadier. Jackie Ward had a relaxed, gentle approach to everything, which I found calming in my current crisis. And it relieved me greatly to note that he was studying the report on my +22 grading over the course of this interview, rather than moving on to my ultimate -4 grading. I took a warm liking to him from the start, which I never had cause to change.

Colonel Jackie told me to report to D Squadron, along with Angus McNeill, where we would be under the command of Major "Nipper" Wordsworth, whose second-in-command was Captain Duncan Llewellyn. The other officers were Christopher Phillipson, Derek Bartlett and Garry Patterson. My initial impression of Nipper Wordsworth was not that favourable. He was by no means at ease with his subalterns, partly no doubt because of his diminutive size and youthful – almost gnome-like – appearance. He probably felt that for his authority to be respected he needed to hold himself aloof and to deal brusquely with us. But I could feel he was just as highly strung as myself – from the start we had the ingredients of a dangerous relationship.

Garry, Angus and myself were put in command of three of the sabre troops, with each of them consisting of two armoured cars and two scout cars. I was to be in command of 4 Troop, to whom I was introduced. But Corporal of Horse [CoH] Dodson – with three stripes that is to say – was away on a prolonged course. And this was disastrous from the viewpoint of any young subaltern when taking up his duties with the Regiment, in that I should have expected him to show me the ropes, initiating me into all my new duties. Much of the tale of woe that follows can be attributed directly to the absence of any such guiding voice in my ear. And it was even more unfortunate for me, in that CoH Dodson's absence from the scene became extended long beyond what had been anticipated.

The man I had to rely upon to perform these duties was Corporal Alexander, who proved to have none of the attributes needed to smooth my path to taking over leadership of the troop. This was principally because his loyalties were entirely with the men, rather than with his officer. He shielded them from me, rather than the other way round, and over the

The bolshie shower – 4th Troop, D squadron –
supposedly under my command! I felt how I look... out of it

following months many of my misfortunes were a consequence of this state
of affairs. Then there was Corporal Guilliland, who couldn't even read a
map correctly – the basic skill required of any scout car commander. And
the rest of the troop struck me as being a pretty surly crowd – with the
exception of Rose, who like myself was a newcomer and appeared quite
happy to accept me as he found me, without giving the impression that I
was about to destroy whatever sense of camaraderie the troop had
previously enjoyed.

My real trouble was that I felt so utterly superfluous. This was a period
during which we simply had to ensure that all the vehicles in our troop
were in good functioning order. I was supposed to oversee the servicing and
maintenance of the vehicles, to ensure that everything was being done
correctly and according to the book. Yet, despite my training as a cavalry
officer, I had never even begun to comprehend anything about the
mechanics of a car. Instead of staying aloof from the men's work, I tried to
bluff my way through inspecting whatever it was they were doing. It didn't
work. Their faces showed the contempt and resentment they felt at my
being in charge of a job I knew nothing about. The headaches began to

return and the bouts of high temperature too. I took to my bed. The Medical Officer was eventually summoned, whereupon he took the decision to send me to the local military hospital for observation.

Sometimes the body works towards what it wants without reference to the resident mind. I was obviously generating these headaches and high temperatures psychosomatically – part of me must have been hoping to be excused from all duties. But there was another part of me which was genuinely horrified to discover that I was being hospitalised. I think I realised how my body was teetering on the brink of a nervous breakdown, in full knowledge that as far as my army record was concerned this would be judged as a failure. I was aware that I needed to recover to pre-empt that judgement being made.

I underwent a whole series of tests and, while I lay waiting for the medical verdict on my health, someone came into my ward wearing pyjamas but with a battle-dress top with Life Guards' insignia and a Corporal's stripes. He said he'd heard from the Colonel – who had apparently been visiting the hospital that morning – how a young officer from his Regiment had been admitted to this ward, so he'd been asked by the Colonel to look me up. He himself had a gammy leg, he confided, tapping it with his hand. So what was wrong with me?

Tapping one's head is not the same as tapping one's leg. I desisted but I sensed that I was undergoing some kind of psychological examination. Corporals don't make social calls upon young subalterns, whom they haven't actually met. I also doubted his story of the Colonel visiting the hospital – such an event usually required some kind of emergency. I suspected that I was being given an informal opportunity to spin some yarn about suffering from a serious malady, which might shed some light on whether my symptoms where of a psychological nature. This would have been something that the Colonel would raise with the doctors. And at the same time, this Corporal – who was probably a psychologist in disguise – was testing how I would cope with the intrusive attentions of an avuncular NCO. Could I handle the situation as an officer should? This would be pertinent to my fitness to command.

Anyway, I kept my psychological distance from him, telling him that there was nothing wrong with me whatsoever, which from the results of their tests the doctors would soon discover for themselves. He looked at me long and hard, inviting me to elaborate. But I didn't add anything and he withdrew from the ward. It seems that I passed. And I was soon informed that I was to return to barracks.

My absence from the scene hadn't really been noticed by anyone at all – which came as a relief to me. Once again I threw myself into the task of trying to play the part of the perfect commissioned officer. I can remember the rigidity with which I marched across from the mess to the parade ground when performing for the first time as the Duty Officer, almost as if I imagined that I was being filmed for some instructional course on the subject.

One of the Corporal Majors, who incidentally had refereed some of the bouts I had fought at Eton, commented dryly that it was clear for all to see just who was going to be the dominant figure in the Officers' Mess. But the charade was seen through by no less than Victor Hoare who had witnessed my act from the mess windows. I don't know exactly what he said, but from the ribbing I later got on the matter by some of my own friends, I wasn't kept in blissful ignorance. Conscious that I was now in danger of making an utter fool of myself, I hastily reverted to a more casual step when marching to take up my duties on parade.

I also returned to the task of endeavouring to establish a workable relationship with my troop. My efforts on this, though, quickly convinced me that the only way of reducing their subtly conveyed intolerance of me was to keep my appearances to a minimum. To conceal myself from everyone's view, I took to the privacy of my own room whenever the opportunity presented itself. This worked when we were in barracks but, as we were in preparation for the Brigade manoeuvres that were scheduled for October, quite frequently we were out and about on tactical exercises.

Each troop, for example, had to practise "snake patrolling" and wireless communications before the squadron could regroup for larger scale training. Snake patrolling is a procedure used by armoured and scout cars whereby any moving vehicle is covered by the one behind it. Nipper was so precise in his instructions that everything had to be done according to the book and I did my utmost to see that we did things in textbook style. But this was so time-consuming, it created more problems than it solved. Before setting off on patrol, for instance, we had to camouflage our cars with foliage or whatever. Now this was something that you could do quickly or with care. I made the error of insisting that we do everything with too much care. As a consequence, we were perpetually behind on the schedule that had been set for us. The only way this could be corrected was by cutting back on the troop's free time – skimping on the brewing-up and lunch breaks. This was not a recipe for happy troopers. I soon had a bunch of thoroughly bolshie malcontents under my command, who spent a lot of time comparing their lot with other troops in the squadron, where the tasks such as camouflaging were viewed as far less important than such army sanctities as brew-ups.

As my troop was always lagging behind the others in the completion of the day's work, Nipper became exasperated with me. Nor was it only because of my attention to detail – there was also the problem of it being our vehicles, more frequently than those of other troops, being the ones to break down. Or it seemed to be our wirelesses that went off the air at crucial junctures in an exercise. It would have been a lame excuse to put it all down to faulty equipment. The poor maintenance of that equipment must also have had something to do with it. So Nipper was forever coming up on the air to chide me for my negligence and to tell me to get a move on. But the more I got a move on, the more confusion I seemed to sow. The air in our troop was thick with mutinous mutterings: we were all detesting one another all round.

I did gather my troop together, after a squadron exercise, to try and analyse what was going wrong for us. And I did take the responsibility upon my own shoulders, urging them all to bear with me while I found my feet in these matters. I promised them that it wouldn't always be like this, but that it might take a little while before I got the knack of things. One trooper – a hardened malcontent – came up with the bright idea that I ought to sit back and watch how Corporal Alexander handled the troop on my behalf until I had acquired more experience. I could not brook such challenges to both my authority and dignity and I made it clear that I wasn't having any of it. We were back where we started, however, without any of us feeling that there was a solution in sight.

Cpl. Alexander approached me at one point when we were back at the barracks to warn me that I had best keep away from one particular trooper – who boxed for the Regiment incidentally – in that I was getting so much on his nerves that he was liable to bop me one. I let the warning pass when, perhaps, I should have hauled this particular bolshie squaddie over the coals. But the fact that Cpl. Alexander had warned me rather than cautioned the trooper for his insubordination was indicative of the morale of the troop. It was very much Me against the rest in those days.

It occurred to Nipper that my problems might stem from the fact that I didn't have a Corporal of Horse in the troop, so he supplied me with one on a temporary basis for the Brigade manoeuvres, which were now due to take place. This was CoH Bobbit. But Bobbit didn't resolve my difficulties. The armoured car which I had allotted to him broke down even more frequently than my own: once he was left for hours on end, waiting in the bitter cold and pouring rain for the recovery vehicle to arrive. I had promised to get it sent to him but an exasperated Nipper was pointedly unresponsive to my pleas to rescue Bobbit. When there was a repetition of this neglect on the second day of the manoeuvres, CoH Bobbit's morale also cracked and he began voicing the same criticisms that were already current among the rest of the troop.

I was experiencing my own problems too, of course. We had umpires from a different regiment attached to each Squadron and my own troop was accompanied by a young lieutenant in the Hussars. He was friendly and well-disposed and towards me... at the start. But there came a moment, after having taken up a defensive position next to a telegraph post to one side of the road, when I received an abrupt order to advance – "and quickly too!" Our umpire was perched on the rear end of my car, which he had chosen to better observe my antics.

On receipt of the order, I immediately unhinged the locking device on the turret's two-pounder gun, which I had been aiming at an angle down the road from just behind the telegraph post. In my eagerness to advance quickly, though, the now released gun barrel struck the telegraph post with some force and spun swiftly round, unfortunately on a trajectory that took in the young umpire's head. The barrel crashed into his temple. I caught a glimpse of him upside down in mid-air, before he fell onto the road behind me.

I scrambled down from the car's turret to investigate whether he was alive or dead and was greatly relieved to see him climbing shakily to his feet... but sadly in a state of outrage against myself. In fact he swung a couple of punches at my head but was so unsteady on his feet that they were wide of the mark. I did not retaliate, merely apologised for the unfortunate accident. Despite this apology, he declined to have anything more to do with my troop and was hastily dispatched elsewhere.

When it came to the time for post-mortem analyses upon the manoeuvres, CoH Bobitt made it clear to the Squadron's Corporal Major that he would mutiny rather than serve any additional spell under my command. In fact he went further than this – as I was to learn some while later – in saying that I was not only useless as a sabre-troop leader but also that I always would be just useless. One of the two of us must be replaced. And fortunately for my own sense of dignity, it was decided that he was the one to be transferred to the HQ troop.

I did take the opportunity at the post-mortem to get the aforementioned bolshie squaddie replaced. Quite apart from his

Squadron Leader Major 'Nipper' Wordsworth
relaxing on his shooting stick

ubiquitous surly attitude, he had managed to overturn his scout car during this scheme. And I also got one relatively harmless trooper replaced, on the grounds that the others disliked him. But I had my doubts that I was really getting to the heart of my problems in these changes. Nothing could really go right until I got myself sorted out. And there was little sign that such a state had yet been achieved.

It also seems evident that Nipper had requested the Colonel for a replacement for myself. If that had been agreed upon, I would have been given some desk job in Headquarters' Squadron. But Col. Jackie must have replied that he would like to see for himself if I was really that useless as a sabre troop leader: so Nipper told me to prepare my troop for a day's exercise, when he came along himself – with the Colonel and the Adjutant accompanying us.

I knew that I was being tested, but this didn't throw me into a panic. In fact I rose well to the occasion, eager to let the Colonel see for himself just how difficult it was to serve under Nipper when anxieties began to afflict him. And he gave ample example of this, snapping orders at me over the wireless, which he then repeated with modifications that were obsessively precise. Anyone could tell that he was a control freak, a pain in the neck to his subalterns, and that I was coping as well as could be expected under the circumstances.

But Nipper wasn't the only one to want to get rid of me from D Squadron. The men in my troop knew, as well as I did, that this outing was a crucial test of my leadership and that, if things went wrong, they might well expect to be furnished with a new subaltern. They did their utmost to try and make sure that things did go wrong. I shall never know for certain if the leading scout car commander really did fail to see the armoured car that was waiting in ambush for us beside the road up ahead. In any case he gave me no warning about it and, snake patrolling though I was, all the vehicles in my troop were out in the open when the enemy opened fire. To make matters worse, each individual driver then made it his business to endeavour to reverse his car into the nearest ditch.

Under the circumstances, I coped quite admirably with the situation. I remained calm in the delivery of my commands, despite Nipper coming up on the air with his superfluous criticisms – all in a shrill, high-pitched tone that he employed in moments of agitation or excitement. It may have taken a little time to sort things out, but sort them out I did. Thankfully Col. Jackie's comment to Nipper – delivered in my presence – was that I'd handled the situation correctly and that when snake patrolling my error was in not sending my leading scout car well up in advance of myself to avoid the danger of ambush – despite this putting the scout car under a greater risk. I was very happy to take this piece of advice, which meant that Nipper was obliged to accept that he would now be lumbered with me, perhaps for the duration of my National Service.

For my own part, it might be said that I was still in troubled waters, for things were to get worse. I was becoming unpunctual in my appointment… Nipper had already disciplined me, along with three extra Duty Officer parades. But I now had the humiliation, when I went to inspect the Guard, of being reported late on parade by Cpl. Maj. Radcliffe. He did it because it was by no means the first time that I had kept the

Guard waiting for inspection. There was probably an agreement between the Corporal Majors to report the matter to the Adjutant the next time it happened. Anyway, on this occasion, he agreed with them and added one extra Duty Officer parade to my score.

Another indication of my loss of respect from the Warrant Officers came when Corporal Major Roberts of D Squadron failed me on a driving test. But this needs a word or two of explanation. It was forbidden for any Life Guards officer to be seen riding a motorbike, so a car it had to be. I made plans for buying a second-hand London taxi – which in those days would have cost a mere £40 – but I eventually persuaded Henry to let me have an old Land-Rover, that the estate was about to consign to the knacker's yard. The residents of the officers' mess dubbed it *Roger the Rover*. The passing of my driving test for a car then became a matter of some urgency. I had been driving virtually since childhood, but whether to the standard required for the test was something that remained to be seen.

It was Angus McNeil who discovered that Corporal Major Roberts was entitled to pass anyone for a driving licence... of course, only after "stringent examination". As soon as Angus told me that this was how he had acquired a licence, I made my own approach to the Corporal Major. The result, however, was quite different. Roberts took me out and, on a trivial technicality, failed me. I knew damn well why he did. He didn't like – as he saw it – being used: he had suggested the idea to Angus, whereas I had approached him myself. Additionally, my general standing in the squadron was such that he was obliged not to do me any favours.

Yet, due to the complexity of the way army relationships work, the officers' mess was disconcerted at the way a mere Corporal-Major had taken it upon himself to fail a fellow officer on a driving test. So Tony Cheeseman, the Technical Adjutant, came and told me that I'd better let him take a look at my driving ability for himself. He took me out in an army truck, which I handled with all due competence and he passed me. I was promptly issued with a driving licence, virtually as a rebuke to Corporal Major Roberts.

Disrespect for me was taking deep root, however. An incident that springs to mind was the occasion when I went to the bar in the officers' mess to get myself a gin and tonic. No other officers were present. But while I was sipping it, I observed how the barman was standing there with an insolent expression, sucking the top of an unopened bottle of tonic water. It was his way of telling me that I might be an officer but, as the price for the imposed servitude he had to offer to the likes of me, I'd get served up with troopers' spittle. I daresay if I had reacted, he would have found it easy enough to sidestep my criticisms… saying that it was a bottle he had already paid for, or whatever.

I knew in my heart that my brother officers would have spoken sharply, if not a lot worse, to the man. But under the present circumstances of my general standing in the Regiment, I preferred to pretend that I had not observed what he was doing.

Within my own troop, I had lost the feeling that I had any true authority over them. I was unable to count upon Corporal Alexander for support and I was having difficulties enough with the driver and gunner of my own armoured car. They were becoming increasingly insolent in their attitude towards me. They still had this idea that, if things went just a bit more wrong with the collective performance of the troop, then I would be removed from their command.

I am sure that this was behind what happened when they presented my car for two-pounder firing practice on the range at Lulworth – the mechanism was rusted together so firmly that we could not even open the breach to insert a shell!

Of course, as the officer in charge, this was my fault. I should have inspected the unit beforehand to establish that the gun was in good working order. But, when checking that all the tasks required of them had been carried out efficiently, I had relied upon their word. The discovery that the mechanism had actually rusted into an immovable unit smacked of deliberate sabotage. They may even have pissed on it in their contempt for me.

But they were miscalculating if they thought that Nemesis would fall on my own head and upon no other. All right, I was lumbered with ten additional Duty Officer parades to attend. And Duncan Llewellyn who, while Nipper was on leave had temporarily taken over the command of D Squadron, warned me that the final indignity of replacement would indeed be inflicted upon me if such dereliction of duty were to recur. But my gunner and driver may have been surprised to discover that they received even greater penalties, in the form of punishment parades, than myself.

> Shiftily glancing to left and to right, I hobble
> the cobbled street, noting the sight of grimacing
> faces, peering from upper windows, with sills
> filled with rotten fruit – ready to fling.
> Clinging to final shreds of clothing, I climb

sublimely on a **public stage**, to **wage war**
with my **own toes, stubbed** in demeaning **dance,**
as I **prance** with **parrot-footed disability.**
Shrill piping **calls** for rescue **all**
unheard, I **gird** my **loins** for the **desert trek,**
checking the **chart** for a **non**-existent oasis,
and **placing dwindl**ed **faith** in **sheer grit.**
　　Of all the vessels that were ever made,
　　am I to be this ship for life's crusade?

The Regiment was due to move to Germany early in March next year and this final month of 1951 was given over to some inter-squadron schemes. Nipper had obtained permission to take his own Squadron down into the vicinity of Midhurst in Surrey, where his lady-friend Maureen resided. It was to be his ultimate act of courtship – arriving on her doorstep, at the head of this contingent from the Household Cavalry, to sweep her into matrimony and off to Germany with him.

We were all invited over to her house for drinks one evening. It was quite an eye-opener for me to see Nipper in the presence of the woman he loved – all giggly and uncertain of himself: far too busy with the task of trying to please Maureen, than to worry about retaining any dignity in the eyes of his subalterns.

But the tale of my misfortunes was still in the making. There was a particular scheme when D Squadron was doing a defensive withdrawal against C Squadron's advance. And it so happened that Reid-Wilson was the officer in charge of the troop that was advancing upon the same axis as my own. After firing on him, we spent a minute or two viewing one another through our binoculars and, with my general standing in the Life Guards being so low over this period, I expect that he rejoiced in recognising myself as his opposite number. He probably imagined that he could get away with some hassling tactics.

Anticipating this I feigned a withdrawal, just pausing for a few seconds before re-emerging in my former position. I caught him out there in the open, with his troops belting after me without any cover. If an umpire had been monitoring the action, his leading two cars would inevitably have been declared to be out of action. But in the absence of any umpire, they merely withdrew in confusion.

I was sitting pretty in this position, with open fields on either side of the road down which he would have to advance. My rear, too, was defended by a scout car keeping watch a couple of bends further down the road. So I remained where I was, waiting for my Squadron Leader's order to pull back. But there were dirty tricks afoot: Reid-Wilson stopped a civilian lorry and requested the driver to transport the members of his infantry support section, then he unloaded them at the bend in the road just behind my own armoured car. They ensured that they were not within sight of my scout car. Next, to my utter amazement, I was being captured by a handful of infantry who materialised from I knew not where. Reid-Wilson then came thundering down the road in his own armoured car, chortling with glee at the coup he'd staged.

There was nothing left for me to do but to capitulate with good grace, which is what I did. However, the truth then emerged as to how he had managed to infiltrate troops behind my position. I erupted in furious indignation at the prospect of him expecting to get away with such underhand tactics. So I announced quite simply that I hadn't after all been captured and that I would now withdraw to my next defensive position. This in turn infuriated Reid-Wilson, who deemed that in repealing the *fait accompli* of my capture I was cheating. When I started to transmit the glad tidings to Nipper that I was still alive and well, Reid-Wilson jumped onto the back of my car and tried to wrench out the aerial fittings. My response to this was to order my driver to move off with the enraged Reid-Wilson still clinging to one side of the turret.

As we entered the outskirts of Midhurst, with the tables turned and the erstwhile captor now suddenly captive, Reid-Wilson drew a Very pistol that was in his holster and, thrusting it through the driver's hatch, threatened to fire. Aside from this not being the action of an officer and gentleman, it was blatantly dangerous. My instinctive response was to shove him sideways from the moving vehicle, depositing him on the road. Jumping to his feet, he took a pot shot at me with his Very pistol. I watched the trajectory of the flare curl downwards across the line of my face and then ricochet from the engine cover towards a house that we were passing. Nobody paid much attention to this at the time, but our upstaged opponent was left standing there whilst we made good our triumphant escape.

When I got back on the air, though, it was to discover that both Nipper and Duncan Llewellyn, who had just been promoted in rank to lead C Squadron, were furious with me. Nobody supposed for one instance that it could be anyone's fault other than my own. I was responsible for throwing the manoeuvres scheme into chaos, as no one now knew where the exact lines of battle were to be drawn.

I was ordered to report back to base and, on the way there, my troop was halted by a civilian policeman who wanted to show me the damage caused by that shot from the Very pistol. He took me into a house, informing me how the shot had entered a bedroom window and burnt itself out beside a baby's cot. The parents were politely outraged at what could so easily have turned into a fatal accident; incautiously, perhaps, I apologised on behalf of the Regiment.

That wasn't the end of the matter, of course. There were official complaints and a military enquiry as to what exactly had occurred. Curiously, I was never called to submit my evidence to this. But I was given to understand that Reid-Wilson's own evidence set him clearly in the wrong, so that he received a reprimand of some kind, without it being necessary for me to say anything at all. But there remained a feeling in the air that disasters were liable to strike whenever I was on the loose.

Early in the New Year came the death of King George VI and his funeral ceremony, which culminated in St George's Chapel at Windsor Castle. We all had to participate to some degree, although my own duties were limited to lining the steps that led up into the chapel. I had arrived back in barracks in the early hours of that morning, then, because of a dreadful hangover, missed out on having any breakfast. I then rose to the misfortune of having to wear riding boots that had formerly belonged to and been made for Henry. His calf measurements, I was to discover, were distinctly more slender than my own. The net result of having what in effect was a tourniquet on both lower legs was that my blood could not circulate properly and my brain was starved of oxygen. This was on top of the hangover and an empty stomach. When I could move I was all right, but having to stand there to attention as the coffin was carried up the steps was courting disaster. What with live television coverage of the scene, I knew that I was within a whisker of committing the ultimate misdemeanour of my military career. How I did not keel over I will never know but, as it was, nobody but myself knew just how close I had come to such public disgrace.

After this, we remained in barracks for most of the time, getting our vehicles into readiness for our transfer to Germany and the British Army of the Rhine. I was maliciously informed how CoH Dodson had been applying to take even more courses, so as to delay for as long as possible the moment of taking up his duties with my troop. In fact, not one trooper displayed the slightest enthusiasm for serving under me. Personally, I felt that part of the blame for this sorry state of affairs was the spirit of non-co-operation that I was encountering generally.

There was a post-mortem on how we had performed in the manoeuvre schemes and I decided this was the moment to root out from my command some other bolshie elements in my troop. I took the opportunity to request the replacement of both the gunner and driver in my crew. Since others were also due for their demobilisation before we transferred to Germany, it meant that I was furnished with a new deal in the personnel of 4 Troop during these final weeks at Combermere. How these new relationships evolved I will come to in due course.

Chapter 2.2

Sex: an urgency to lose my virginity

The period immediately after I had been commissioned was spent at Warminster, where Angus McNeill and myself – along with Alan Morris and David Prebble, who were also fresh from Mons OCS – were required to assist in the running of a Junior Training Corps school camp. Much of our time was spent at Sturford, in the local pubs with which they supposed I must be well acquainted. I knew the Bath Arms in Horningsham, of course, which was currently run by Ernie Trollope; his attractive young daughter Vera being one of its principal attractions. She knew me just slightly from before, but now that I was a serving officer I saw our relationship in a totally different light. It wasn't merely a question of wanting to shine in her eyes, there was also the wish to be seen by my fellow officers as being skilled in the arts of flirtation.

Of course, given that I was the son of the man who owned their pub and, for that matter, the rest of the estate, my person was probably imbued with some unmerited glamour. Thus, I did have an advantage in attracting her interest and, not surprisingly, Vera did show a preference for me over my companions. They did find this rather curious, in that when we were at Mons I had not exactly excelled in my faltering display of being a dashing young officer. But the flirtation did not develop into anything of a profound or romantic nature. I think our greatest intimacy was a teatime date in Frome.

During the spell of leave before I actually had to take up my duties at Windsor, Daphne organized a weekend party at Sturford for me. Some of our house guests were down for a big party that was being thrown for the Morrison children at Fonthill. My own special partner was Venetia Murray, with whom I was hoping there might be romantic developments. And my cousin Sally-Anne was there, with Tony Armstrong-Jones invited to balance the numbers. He had been an acquaintance at Eton, where he had been a member of the boxing team – until he contracted polio. He took a whole lot of photographs over the course of this weekend, which found their way into *The Tatler*. But I made no special progress with Venetia, so my sexual aspirations remained just that.

Some words might be appropriate upon my sexual values at this time. Like most other people, I daresay, my attitude in such matters was a reflection of what I had absorbed from my parents. There was much in their attitudes that had been sparked off by the breaks with tradition that were common towards the end of the twenties. While their decade of togetherness had been the thirties, and they fully acknowledged the existence of marital scandals taking place all round them, they were really quite conventional and proper in their concept of marital accord. And within that concept, there was this in-written (if male chauvinist) idea that men were expected to have sown a few wild oats before getting married, whilst the women were expected not to have been the soil in which they were planted.

If Henry had known that I was growing fond of some girl who had indulged in previous affairs, he would have done his utmost to discourage me. Daphne would have been more tolerant – if she liked the girl. But she, too, regarded monogamy as the natural state of grace, while hoping that even flighty ladies might attain it.

As far as any of this affected my own attitude, I was indeed hoping to persuade a whole succession of girls to make love with me. But I remained quite unsure as to how I should judge them if they did. If they permitted me to make love to them but no-one else, then I would have felt truly flattered. It would have promoted my self-confidence and self-esteem to have seen myself as the kind of man for whom women finally abandon their restraint – while keeping the barriers in place for others. But I was instantly filled with caution whenever I sensed that a girl was trying to sweep me off my feet from a vantage point of being sexually aware. It was important to me that I should feel that I was the formulator and pace-setter within such relationships.

In any case, I kept hoping to make some sexual headway with Venetia who may possibly have still been a virgin at this time. But her idea was that I should fall head-over-heels in love with her and that she would then be able to develop the relationship upon the lines of an elder sister to her younger brother. However, this would have done little to promote my own self-imagery as the pace-setter. There were occasions on that weekend party at Sturford when I watched Venetia reclining back and looking at me with a melting romantic gaze. We may even have kissed, although tepidly. But it wasn't taken any further than that.

There was also an occasion when I went over for the day to Manningford Abbas, where she lived. Her friends Doone Plunkett and Tania Craig were also present and we all went to the fair at Marlborough. Venetia insisted that we consult the fortune-teller, who was the traditional gypsy woman. When she told me that I would marry but not to any girls I knew at present, Venetia looked peeved.

There was another occasion shortly after my arrival at Combermere, when I travelled up to London to take her out to dinner. Angus had promised to give me a lift back to Windsor if I could be at his mother's flat by midnight. We were ten minutes late and found that Angus had already departed, but the caretaker permitted us to come and wait inside – on the supposition that Angus might be returning for me. And once we were left alone, we soon found our way to a huge double-bed upstairs where we lay contemplating sexual congress, which never really occurred. But I daresay we made some advance upon our previous position. Venetia was amused by the whole situation, declining to believe that it had arisen unplanned. But in point of fact I was more naïvely innocent in these matters than she supposed possible. I eventually had to rush off to catch the milk train back to Windsor, while she took the taxi on to a girlfriend's flat.

> Inflating our chests like pouter pigeons on a ledge,
> we graduate in courtship from examining our badges,
> to matching favoured flavours of iced cream,
> or dreaming the scenes in lavish travel brochures.
> Gauche, but still brash, I stand fumbling
> with dumb buttons, in a cramped bunker where clanking
> mechanical gadgets – which I do not comprehend -
> send me fizzing in a tizzy of futile response.
> Fronds of glowing lava, treacle-thick,
> trickle in imagined pageant of love from the mountain's
> fountain, when in truth the dormant crater waits
> with bated breath, but no fire in its belly.
> So as I hover round to plant my kiss,
> I see too well that Cupid's arrows missed.

What came as a most unwelcome development at this juncture was the discovery that the trooper whom I had once met when wandering around Piccadilly (when I was up in London on a weekend pass from Caterham) was now stationed at Windsor and in the same squadron as myself. I made this discovery on the first occasion when acting as Duty Officer I was required to inspect those under close arrest in the guard-room. There was only one detainee and, when the Corporal Major opened the door of the cell, I found myself confronting Trooper *Piccadilly* – as I shall call him. He came to attention, looking straight to his front and stamping his feet while saluting. Returning his salute, I half smiled but his face never registered a flicker of recognition. Under the circumstances, it would have been inappropriate if there had been any. When enquiring later from the Corporal Major what his offence had been, I was given to understand that it related to homosexual matters.

A few days later, after Trp. *Piccadilly* had been released from custody, I saw him approaching in the Squadron Yard. Once again, as I returned his salute, I gave him the faintest of smiles. After all, I didn't wish to appear too snooty now that I had acquired my commission. But my smile must have been misunderstood since, on the next occasion we passed one another in the Squadron Yard, I was horrified to perceive that he was returning my slight smile with what can only be described as a lascivious leer. I didn't really know what to do about it.

All right, I was careful not to smile at his salutes any more, but I hadn't a clue how to deal with someone who was convinced that I was a closet queen who was leching after parts of his body – something he deemed ripe for exploitation. And he must have talked about it to others, since Derek Bartlett – who was in command of 7 Troop, to which Trp. *Piccadilly* had been transferred – passed on a word of caution from one of his men that *Piccadilly* might have designs on me. I expect the real question had been as to whether I was myself that way inclined. But despite my low standing in all other matters, this wasn't part of my reputation in the officers' mess.

I think there were some other Corporals of Horse who may have been enquiring if I was queer. Anyway, I suspect Angus of passing on that story about how the clientèle of a pub at Basingstoke had reacted to my appearance by singing *One of the Roving Kind*. For that is what one of the Corporals of Horse – a man named Woods – now began doing. Whenever he was standing in the company of others and just on the fringe of my hearing, he would burst into song. I never did manage to acquire a liking for CoH Woods.

But it was *Piccadilly* whom I really needed to convince – or disabuse, if that is a more appropriate word. And this finally occurred when he went to a great deal of trouble to bring a form for me to sign for him – he engineered his way up to my bedroom where I was relaxing while also keeping out of harm's way. I suppose he had been intending to suggest that I get him transferred to my troop or, perhaps, even to work as my batman. But in any case there was no justification for him coming up to my bedroom on the pretext of having something that any passing officer could have handled.

I took the bull by the horns: I asked him directly if he wasn't the man I had met at Piccadilly Circus, a few months back, when we had taken a drink or two together. My conveyed uncertainty destroyed his assumptions about me – the astonishment on his face was quite delightful. Neither of us took the liberty of smiling at one another again. But I think he must have been demobilised shortly after this as I saw no more of him.

The acquisition of a car was of course something utterly essential in the pursuit of a healthy sex life in the Life Guards. Not all of the subalterns had cars, so I did perceive that the ownership of *Roger the Rover* was a considerable advantage in that it enabled me to drive where I pleased in acceptance of any invitations that came my way.

Desperate though it was becoming that I should establish my successful heterosexual identity more firmly in everyone's eyes, I was not having much luck in these matters upon the social scene. The Crawleys gave a house-warming party after moving into a new house in Sussex and a great many of the Life Guards officers were invited. But it was notable how Sarah no longer saw fit to include me within her most intimate group of guests. I was housed elsewhere in the neighbourhood.

I remember, in particular, on this occasion how I upset people at the party by drinking too much. It wasn't that I was doing anything too reprehensible; I was merely trying to drown my feelings of inadequacy and incompetence, in the hopes that some bolder and more impressive line of behaviour might surface. Yet, I was stepping back into a private fantasy world where, because my actions were inebriate and blundering, it made it even easier for things to go wrong.

I know that I gave offence to Liz Hoyer-Miller at the Crawley dance. I clung too tightly to her (and perhaps too lasciviously also) as we swayed to the music. She dumped me as rapidly as she could, transferring her attentions to Simon Galway – he who made some fierce comment, when we were both back at Combermere, about my drunken behaviour being absolutely disgusting. Such an aggressive rebuke from someone of slightly senior rank to myself was something else that I didn't really know how to handle.

There were other incidents. One was when John Slessinger had his 21st birthday ball up in London. He had completed his National Service in the Life Guards just shortly after the time when my own batch took up their commissions. While I was still comparatively sober, I danced with Xenia, the debutante I had most fancied during the summer months. In response, she invited me to join a weekend party at her home near Chippenham in Wiltshire. I accepted with alacrity. I think it was at this moment that I became convinced that Xenia must surely be the real girlfriend who had hitherto been lacking from my life.

Towards the end of the evening, I got very drunk and, once again, started behaving a bit lecherously. When I danced with Xenia a second time, I tried to persuade her to go off with me to a nightclub – *The Carousel* – which was then the place most in vogue with young officers from the Brigade of Guards. By now, though, she was merely alarmed at the drunkenness of my behaviour, so she quickly and adroitly left me stranded at the bar.

Next morning – back at Windsor – I was squirming with embarrassment at the memory of the previous evening. It wasn't just the memory of my inebriated behaviour towards Xenia, my greatest embarrassment was suspecting that my invitation for the weekend at Chippenham was now withdrawn. However, my mind was soon put at rest on this point when I received a letter from Xenia attempting to smooth any ruffled feelings that I might carry for the way she had ditched me.

The next event was a surprise invitation from Ronnie Fergusson – who was later to father Sarah Fergusson – to come and have dinner with him at Sandhurst. He was himself in the Life Guards and had been at Eton with me, although I had known him rather better when we were at Ludgrove. Unbeknown to me at this time, Ronnie regarded Xenia as being his own girlfriend, comparatively innocent though the relationship may have been. But it would seem that she must have mentioned my name to him just once too often. When he learnt that I had been invited to this weekend at Chippenham he took it upon himself to discover whether I was liable to set myself up as a rival for Xenia's affections and, if so, how he should eliminate my challenge.

When I received his invitation, however, I supposed that it arose from a genuine desire on his part to be friendly. I drove over to Sandhurst without the slightest misgivings, believing that I was going to meet up with at least a couple of old friends – namely Mark Jeffreys and Michael Boyne – and an Old Harrovian called Trevor Dawson whom I was meeting for the first time. The conversation soon got round to the coming weekend at Chippenham to which Ronnie and Mark had also been invited; it was only then that it dawned upon me that Ronnie regarded Xenia in such a possessive light.

To this realisation, I exclaimed, "Oh, so you're soft on Xenia as well?" By saying this, I was of course coming out into the open as a potential rival. After this there was a noticeable hardening in his attitude towards me.

But as far as I was concerned, the subsequent weekend party at Chippenham was a huge success. The house itself, set in an open garden, was spacious and Georgian – much like Sturford in fact. As to the parents, Xenia's mother was a cultured, soft-spoken, good-looking lady, while her father, who was a retired Colonel from the Brigade of Guards, was elegantly reserved and distinguished in his appearance. But he had played a more distant role in his daughter's upbringing. Xenia herself had a free run of the house and with no siblings competing for space or attention her attitude within the household always struck me as being on the bossy side. I found myself welcomed with a quiet warmth – I think that my arrival on their domestic scene was, at that time, viewed with favour. I was also on my best behaviour in that I was very anxious to please and burning with the fresh realisation that I was almost in love. Ronnie and Mark, however, were strictly on the defensive as Xenia's mother showed her disapproval and they were tongue-tied by their suspicions about my own intentions as regard to Xenia.

At the time, it struck me that Xenia was giving me considerable encouragement, going out of her way to joke with me and to tease me generally upon my lack of sophistication in adult matters. When I finally knew her better, she denied this, declaring that she had liked me but found me far too childish to take seriously as a potential lover. But this denial contrasts with what Ronnie himself was to say after he had finally rejoined the Regiment. He had perceived how she was giving me too much encouragement and that he regarded this weekend as having been the beginning of the end of his (very chaste) affair with Xenia. Another point that I later gleaned from Xenia was that Ronnie attempted to diminish me in her eyes, by telling her how I'd enquired if he was "soft" on her. Such an expression, he maintained, was not upper class usage.

At the time of our commission only a minority of us subalterns had bedded a woman. Among our intake, it was just Angus who had passed this particular rite of passage. His appearance was more of a fully-fledged male than any of the rest of us. For one thing, he was six foot six inches tall, which all helps in the acquisition of female admiration. He was more mature in personality, too, and I knew that he was telling me the truth when he hinted at the occasional adventure that had come his way.

The next occasion to which I could look forward was an invitation from Henrietta Montagu-Douglas-Scott to attend the New Year's festivities at Bowhill, the Duke and Duchess of Buccleuch's stately home up in Scotland. She was not only a distant cousin of mine but also one of Xenia's most intimate friends. I imagined that I was being invited at the special request of Xenia, which turned out not to be so. Henrietta invited me for herself or, possibly, for Joanna Smith – whereas I didn't really regard either of them in a specially romantic light. But Xenia was more interested in developing her relationship with [M], upon whom she had vainly set her sights during the previous London season.

Poor Ronnie had been invited, but declined in that he was dissatisfied with the current situation between Xenia and himself. Mark, however, had accepted and we arranged to drive north together in *Roger the Rover*. This turned out to be quite a terrifying experience in itself, for Mark took turns at driving. After the third minor accident, I became thoroughly unnerved at being driven by him, then he admitted that he had yet to pass his driving test. This meant I had to take over the wheel for the remainder of the journey.

The visit to Scotland could not be rated a success. There was ample opportunity for me to woo Xenia and she was indeed flirtatious with me. But the fact remains that her real interest was in [M], rather than in myself. It was [M] who bestowed upon me the sobriquet of "Puppy" – on the basis that I went careering round the house, suddenly pausing to make a puddle on some priceless carpet, whereupon my habitual tail-wagging would stop as I perceived that people were angry at my incontinence; then, to pre-empt them smacking me I would lie on my back in the hope that they might indulgently pat my stomach in forgiveness. It seems that I gave them an impression of effervescent bewilderment concerning society's conventional behaviour, while being incapable of avoiding the next *faux pas*.

Xenia was delighted with this name for me – as if she herself was an elderly bitch who had long outgrown such adolescent behaviour. But it was uttered in a tone of affection, which permitted me to feel that I had her attention. In reality it was Xenia's effervescent immaturity that made her so attractive to me. We were a couple of puppies scampering round and making puddles on the carpets of society. The only difference was that Xenia used to tug at the ears of the elder dogs, supposing that if they could be induced to become puppyish, would signify that she herself was mature.

> I **stand** bemused, having **licked** my **wounded love**
> on a **lunar pinn**acle, **watching** you **spin giddi**ly
> in the **middle** distance, romping with sophisticates,
> and **stomp**ing as an **unprom**ising **pupil** in their **dance**.
> With **chances meagre** as a **drone's**, I **thrust** my artless
> **heart** as a **gift off**ering – proffered in fumbling
> **fingers** – **dangling dingy** and **unobserved**,
> absurdly neglected on the **fringe** of your **heaped toys**.
> The **noise** of your **silly suitors sinks** my **pride**,
> as they **ride** a **tide** which **floats** them **freely** to the **golden**
> **goal** of **your** regard – whilst **I**, **distinctive**
> in a **pink puppy**'s attire, **tire** of comparison.
>> But can't you see, (or is it that you're blind?)
>> that they are species of a different kind?

I found ample opportunities for more puppyish behaviour. This was a gathering of sophisticated aristocrats. Ian Gilmour, Dalkeith and Blandford were in the group just older than myself. But it seemed that they were all fully conversant with the traditions of such weekend parties. A whole system of rules and etiquette was in force and it was judged gauche to be out of step at any time. The paper games and the acting games were all part of this established order; this insight made me realise that we had missed out on something in our upbringing at Sturford. Perhaps it was because parties at Sturford had nearly always been an adult concern and not geared to the children participating within a family life.

Yet the Thynnes were quite closely related to the Buccleuchs. I was shown a portrait of their own Thynne ancestor who had been the daughter of the 2nd Marquess of Bath. Despite all my gaucherie, I was still accepted as being one of *them*… as I was, it was generally supposed that I would mature with age. This was in contrast, for example, to Mark Jeffreys whose standing was regarded as just not right for their circle and, despite his commission in the Brigade of Guards, he was kept at an arm's distance. But I too quickly noticed how he didn't really fit: there was an aggressiveness to his personality that made him quite unpleasant at times. It seemed so odd to think that formerly, towards the end of my time at Ludgrove, he was probably to be regarded as my best friend.

Henry's mother had, in fact, been Scottish; while Daphne, too, had plenty of Scots blood in her veins. But I hadn't been raised to think of myself as anything other than English and Cornish. And this was sharply in contrast to Xenia who, despite having dwelt for most of her life in the West Country, regarded herself as a Scots lassie. Like so many people who have any Celtic blood at all within their veins, she found it more romantic to identify herself as coming from over the border. It all made me feel that I didn't really belong within this scene – whereas Xenia was completely at home.

It was with a heavy heart that I finally set off on the return journey – alone, since Mark had opted to return by train. I hadn't even succeeded to extract from Xenia a promise that she would attend the Life Guards' farewell ball at Combermere as my partner. It could be that she was hoping to receive her invitation from Christopher "Christo" Phillipson, whom she regarded as a good friend, or it could be that the bad feeling that now existed between Ronnie and herself dissuaded her from wanting to attend with anyone at all. But it left me in a flurry of uncertainty as to whom I should invite. In the event, I got invitations accepted by both Venetia Murray and Rosie Cotterell – with me only managing to warn each of them at the very last moment of the slight confusion in numbers.

It was not a particularly successful evening for me. My two partners had never met one another before but, when I collected them, they both initially accepted, in a pleasantly jokey fashion, the oddity of my plans for the evening. On the drive from London to the dinner and ball at Windsor, though, the tension began to mount. As we neared our destination, Venetia began saying that she had pains – possibly period pains – and wanted to be driven back to London immediately. Under the circumstances, I did not feel that I could oblige. What I did manage was to get her a lift back with someone who was leaving early to go to a nightclub. It was an experience that might have warned me at an early age that monogamy has some advantages in its sheer simplicity.

But in any case, it was Xenia that I was really wanting to woo. And my hopes were given a fresh boost when I received an invitation from Idina Peacock, to attend a weekend party at their home in Nottinghamshire. As on this occasion neither [M] nor Ronnie were to be present, it did strike me that I might finally be paired, at her special request, with her. But it didn't work out like that.

Nicky Beaumont accompanied me from Combermere, but the big rival this time turned out to be Dommie Elliot whom I had also known at Eton. Being just slightly older than myself seemed to bestow upon him all the glamour that I seemed to lack in Xenia's sight. I spent much of the weekend glowering with jealousy, watching Dommie slip through the partition door that separated my own bedroom from that of the girls in order to chat them up with the full confidence of an adult male. In fact, his whole demeanour was of someone who knew the ropes of the sexual ring, whereas mine was surly and disgruntled, which constantly antagonised.

The truth of the matter is that I was getting nowhere in my efforts to find copulatory pairing with a female of the species. And all this while, there were those who wondered if I were of genuinely heterosexual disposition. It even occurred to me that I might be mistaken in my own heart about such orientation. I couldn't know that I'd enjoy copulation until I had some experience behind me. But if I was so inept at persuading some girl that I fancied to think in similar terms, then it might be sensible to lose my virginity as promptly as possible with a whore. There was very little to inhibit me from such behaviour within the aristocratic circles in which I had been raised. All members of my family had long been expecting such an event to happen to me. Even Xenia had expressed an eagerness to hear about any experience that I might have had with tarts. I'd say that about half the young officers from the Brigade of Guards lost their virginities in this fashion. It being the culture of the times. And it was at *The Bag of Nails,* where the most attractive hostesses were to be found.

Angus had for some while now been in the habit of driving up to London with such a purpose in mind and of late had always been dating the same girl – although he still had to pay for it nonetheless. Well there came the moment when I decided to get it over and done with. So Angus agreed to introduce myself, Garry Patterson and Nipper's younger brother – who had just taken up his duties with the Regiment – to the club's proprietor on his very next visit. And that way, we were promptly made members.

Before going along to *The Bag of Nails*, we all had a number of drinks in some bar. I was therefore quite mellow before the ordeal even began, but I hadn't yet drunk sufficient to dispel the anxiety from my mind. That was a matter to be rectified over the course of the evening.

In point of fact Christopher had accompanied Angus on a previous visit but, in the case of both Garry and myself, this was to be our first such experience. We were seated at the far end of the room, without there being many other clients present. As far as officers from the Brigade of Guards were concerned, we were all still officially in mourning over the royal death, so weren't supposed to be indulging in entertainment of any kind whatsoever. As soon as Linda arrived (the particular girl whom Angus was screwing), they went and sat at their own table. Christopher was the next to take the plunge, picking up an attractive girl called Denise. Then it occurred to me that the longer I waited, the less of a choice there would be. So I hurriedly stumbled over to Pat, the only pretty one remaining, who turned out to be from Ireland. And Garry finally had to be content with one that was left over.

I found conversation difficult, although that was no fault of hers. It was simply that I didn't know how to handle the situation. It was solemn talk – about regimental duties and Anglo-German relations; also about the King's funeral and how I wasn't really supposed to be doing things of this kind so recently after he had been buried. She thought that it might pass unnoticed, I remember. There were times when the conversation simply dried up. And the less we talked, the more I drank. The bottle of brandy was soon half empty. I suppose she had her instructions to get the customer on to his second bottle before there should be any talk of leaving the place. On several occasions she urged me to offer a glass to members of the band, on the grounds that they were beginning to look weary. I was too unsure of what social custom required of a man in my position that I felt unable to refuse her demands.

Meanwhile her friend Denise, whom Christopher had booked, signalled to Pat to follow her out to the ladies' room; when they returned, I noticed how she was regarding me with an increased interest. She had been informed, no doubt, that she was about to lay the son of the Marquess of Bath – a patrimony that gave me a certain curiosity value, I suppose. She had probably heard how it was to be my first copulation, too, since I can hardly suppose that my friends had deceived her into thinking otherwise.

As soon as Pat had persuaded me to buy that second bottle of brandy, the tactics changed. She knew that she'd never get me on to a third, so her concern now was to maintain me in a fit state of consciousness to drive her back home. By this time, however, I was enjoying myself: inspired by the idea that I was a brilliant dancer, I waltzed her round the floor until a stumble nearly put me down on the floor. She did then manage to prevail upon me to take her back to her flat... although as we went round Hyde Park Corner, we were stopped by a policeman, who sprang towards the car from out of the darkness, for I remember not what traffic misdemeanour.

I was definitely drunk, but I can only suppose that my speech was still relatively clear in that he let me drive on with a verbal warning.

The copulation itself was disappointing. The zest had departed from me during the drive home and I felt uncertain about formalities concerning who was supposed to undress first, when the cheque should be written and all that kind of thing. On top of all that, I was beginning to feel ill. In fact I never came to a satisfactory orgasm in our love-making, in that I had to scramble out of bed to be sick. Neither of us felt particularly amorous after that. In the early hours of the next morning I wrote out the cheque for £10 as requested, then surmounted my hangover sufficiently to drive back to Windsor in time to be on Squadron Parade. Despite the relative inadequacy of my performance, I still felt triumphant in that I had finally managed to shed my virginity – at the belated age of nineteen that is to say.

> My **nerves** a **jitter** in a **makeshift calm front**,
> the **stunt of rising** on **two stilted legs**
> to **beg** the **lady's presence** beside me, **dries**
> my **red blood**. But **now** the **die is cast!**
> Elastic in my **agitation**, I **play** the **braggart**
> and **swagger** stumbling in a **shackled waltz**, **courting**
> **thoughts of fondl**ing her **naked flesh**, enmeshed
> in a **net of sudden obligated** coition.
> **Fished freshly** from **separate oceans**, and **grossly**
> **foreign** – **one** to the **other** – the **deed** gets **done**,
> and the **mon**ey, on **sor**did de**mand**, is **hand**ed **over**
> to **fill bills spill**ing from her **treasure trove.**
>> But now the carnal taste is on my tongue,
>> I'll celebrate that life has just begun!

The girl with whom I came the nearest to developing a romantic relationship, during these last months before we all moved to Germany, was my childhood friend Lady Caroline Childe-Villiers. She was a distant cousin in that her deceased father was the Earl of Jersey and from the same stock as the 2nd Viscount Weymouth's mother had been. I hadn't greatly liked Caroline when we'd mixed during the war years – indeed she'd been far more my brother's friend than mine – but just prior to my National Service I'd had some success with her at the dinner before the Rothermeres' dance. So it was with some excitement that I joined up with Charlie

Morrison and Lawrence Kelly in a night out up in London, in the company of her, Sara Long and Annabelle Stewart. And this formula for an outing was repeated on two other occasions.

Nothing of any significance ever took place between Caroline and myself, although this was largely due to the circumstances of our always being in other people's company. I feel sure that we would both have appreciated it if the opportunity had presented itself. As it is, we had to make do with memories – which fell short even of a first kiss – merely of dancing close to one another at *The Carousel*. The move to Germany left us with insufficient time for significant amorous development.

Chapter 2.3

Identity and activities:
hesitant individualism

Doing my army National Service was something that, when it comes to discerning the formative influences upon my life and personality, I regard as being in a partition by itself. And to some extent it had an oppressive effect. When I was training at Caterham, they had stated quite openly how they were concerned to suppress all individualism in order that I emerged as someone who could more readily coalesce within a fighting unit such as they desired. The more they drummed the individualism out of me, the more I felt separated from those aspects of my identity that I cherished the most – the idea that I might develop as an artist, or author perhaps.

There had in fact been very little opportunity to paint since I left Eton. There had been one unsatisfactory painting: the statue at the end of the pond at Sturford, which I had painted during the weeks prior to going into the army and, then, nothing more until the spell of leave I was given after obtaining my commission. On that occasion, I set up my easel beside the small waterfall at the head of the Half Mile lake at Longleat. This was interpreted by Henry as me just "swanking", in wanting to get his tourists to come up and watch me paint.

But I also painted a fish vase while I was down at Cowrie during that same spell of leave and soon after I had worked on a whimsical still life – using a witch-doll that I had found up in the nursery. There was another still life – depicting an officer's warm coat and city umbrella – that I painted in my room at Combermere. Nevertheless, this certainly wasn't one of my more formative periods with regard to art.

Around this time, Christopher told me that my former art teacher, Wilfrid Blunt, had written to him requesting that I supply a painting for an exhibition they were going to hold in the drawing schools at Eton. It was to represent the works of Old Etonian artists – with names like Duncan Grant upon the list. It would have been better if Wilfrid had written directly to me or, perhaps, it was just a case of Christopher losing the note he was supposed to pass onto me. In any case, the upshot was I misunderstood the purpose of the exhibition – which was to display works painted since leaving Eton.

Accordingly, I handed Christopher a pile of the best paintings I had done while I was still at Eton. The only post-Eton one that I included was of the statue at the end of Sturford pond. This was distinctly sub-standard and has since been destroyed. But in the event it was all they had that qualified for the exhibition. It was heralded in the Eton Chronicle as being the worst painting on display. Thankfully I didn't hear about this until some while later, so my feelings were to that extent spared.

I surreptitiously took to painting that other still life within the privacy of my own room at Combermere. This was the period when – as I have already described – I'd been there several months and finally realised that my physical presence in the Squadron Yard – or in the officers' mess for that matter – was best kept to a minimum. My absence did not go unnoticed but, as I was keeping out of his hair, Nipper was prepared to turn a blind eye to whatever I might be getting up to.

There was one occasion, though, when I went to the drawing schools at Eton to show Wilfred Blunt the various paintings that I had been working on but found only Oliver Thomas present there at the time. He gave me some critical appraisal of my works, but it does need to be remembered that this was an uninspiring period within my artistic development. Yet it did lead to Wilfrid inviting me to a dinner at Baldwin's End, where he lived with Giles St Aubyn, Tom Barker and Tom Lyons. This was the first time, as an old boy, I was able to mingle with my former mentors on terms nearer to equality.

I also did some writing during that spell of leave down at Cowrie, beginning a story about a woman – rather like Miss Prokinar – seeking a husband through a matrimonial agency. It was an adequate attempt at comic composition, without the will for me to see it through to its completion. Life wasn't genuinely humorous for me these days, so I didn't feel like offering a more optimistic view about it in the fiction that I wrote.

Hassled as I found myself to be these days on the question of maturing from my adolescent ways, I was inclined to slink away from the communal throng on all occasions when there wasn't something happening in which I was specifically interested. I was anxious that, if I just sat in company, my immaturities would be put in relief to others. Far safer for me to be sitting within the retreat of my own room, biding my time for the next opportunity to scintillate with a display of extravagantly egocentric exhibitionism. My extroversion went hand in hand with my introversion: neither term would be sufficient to offer a clear description of me in those days.

But the extroverted side of me demanded that I should cultivate an idea of myself as someone of independent spirit and self-expression. And after drinking a gin and tonic or two at the social events I attended, I found it a lot easier to behave in this fashion. I livened up instantly, feeling a diminished inhibition concerning the limitations of permissible behaviour – small enough though the examples of such behaviour may have been. I can remember my hostess, at a dinner that was being held in the Berkeley rooms of the Hyde Park Hotel, getting the waiter to persuade me to put my dinner jacket back on because I had been embarrassing her by dancing in my shirt sleeves with my colourful braces on display.

The truth of the matter is that on every possible social occasion I was drinking more than was good for me. Not usually to the point of drunkenness, but often to the point when the extroverted side to me was released. This led to me acquiring a reputation of not being able to take my drink, although such scoffing came from fellow subalterns far less capable of consuming such a quantity while still remaining on their feet. My behaviour may have been excitable, but I seldom lost my balance or slurred my words.

There was even an occasion – after that evening already mentioned at the Hyde Park Hotel – when I returned to my car only to find two policemen about to impound it because I'd parked in a restricted area. Despite my inebriation, this was dealt with in an amicable manner. Such was their belief in my sobriety, when it was discovered that my battery had run flat – due to the headlights having been left on – they pushed the car down Knightsbridge until the engine fired. I say this not from any present pride at what one could get away with in those days but in evidence that in an emergency I could, despite an excessive intake of alcohol, be a model of sobriety.

There were also odd occasions when I drank more than my stomach in any case could tolerate. The one which comes the most vividly to mind took place at Pirbright, where D Squadron had gone for rifle and machine-gun practice. There was an evening when the officers were invited over to the tent which was serving as the NCO's mess and, of course, it was I who was challenged to play the game of Cardinal Puff – which, for the uninitiated, consists of performing a routine of increasing complexity, such as repeating words and gestures, before drinking to the health of Cardinal Puff for the first and eventually umpteenth time.

The complexity of the rules is intended to provide a pretext for them to be modified as the game proceeds in order that the victim is constantly making mistakes that are penalised by requiring him to take another drink. As always happens, I was soon swallowing more than I could hold down. Especially as, due to the skulduggery of my fellow officers, what was originally beer ended up nearer to neat whiskey. The moment arrived when I was pouring it down my throat and then rushing straight outside to throw it up again on the grass. But the fact that I kept returning for more, without chucking in the sponge, impressed them. And I was thankful for that small boost to my image. But it did little to compensate for the next morning's hangover, of course.

The excessive drinking might be put down to the suppression I was undergoing, which inhibited me from emerging in what I might suppose to be my true colours. But this repressed colourfulness displaced instead onto the surface of my Land-Rover, which I painted with my own hand in convergent tones of blue, green and crimson. In terms of the prevailing culture in the early fifties, this was indeed a most daring choice of paintwork for a car. The personality of *Roger the Rover* was, in that respect, an unsuppressed extension of my own identity. Jokes were made in the officers' mess about how tipplers were unable to determine whether their blurred vision was the result of the previous night's intake or the technicolour decor of the car.

Owning a car, however, rendered me vulnerable to exploitation by friends wanting to borrow it. I found it difficult to say no to such requests at this time. It was as if psychologically I felt that at birth I had been served with too many of the world's blessings upon my plate. When others demanded a share in them, I felt that it would have been mean of me to say no. But instead of gratitude, I found my generosity of spirit being taken increasingly for granted. NCO's as well as officers were borrowing it on trumped-up excuses that it was urgently required. It would come without any fuel but when it started to be returned with damage and without even an apology I finally realised how I was virtually being treated with contempt. So I lent it out no more.

But I rapidly became attached to *Roger* – it was as if he were an extension of my own identity. "To roger" was military slang for copulation, so in thus naming my car I was to some extent presenting an image of myself – in the person of my car – as someone of copulatory zeal. And I did have the feeling that I might be going places sexually just as much as geographically. At the same time nobody could say – except for the colouring – that *Roger* was particularly flash. There was far more of a rough and ready, tough, get-there-in-the-end durability about the image that I was thus imagining for myself.

> My window on a white world has suddenly widened,
> to feast my eye's vision on bright colour,
> a full-sighted perspective of the dizzy reels
> of movement that wheels furnish to the static man.
> My plans for living now encompass a new
> blueprint. Mobile in readiness to roll to adventure,
> and splendidly accoutred in a private armoured car,
> I charge boldly forward on chosen fields.
> Wielding my good looks to their best advantage,
> I can't complain if your sturdy solidity rids
> my image of excessively aristocratic elegance,
> spelling out a story that's different to mine.
> We're bonded now, as in a kindred breed,
> but I shall steer, whilst you're my trusted steed.

And despite all my highly strung excitability of disposition, I remained – as I always had been – doggedly determined in my general behaviour. I think this came into focus on the occasion when, after driving up to Bowhill in Scotland, I had to make the return journey. There was a sudden deterioration in the weather, the day before I was due to depart. My hosts and various guests advised me strongly to put my car on the train and ferry it back to London. And this was the point when Mark Jeffreys announced that he, in any case, was returning home by train. But in fairly typical fashion, I decided to continue with my previous plan – despite a warning that the passes were now closed by snow.

It was a memorable non-stop drive, from which various images come to mind. One was of the car gracefully waltzing round in slow circles as it descended a steep hill (The tyres were overdue for replacement, having had their tread worn smooth). And when I finally got up to the particular pass that I had chosen for the crossing – involving the most direct route south – I was driving across virgin snow, with only the telegraph poles to indicate to me where the road might lie. But once I had started upon something, it was not really in my nature to give up. And the fact that I did get back home safely to Sturford seemed to justify my, perhaps foolhardy, doggedness. An additional piece of good luck in avoiding disaster was that I arrived back home at about three in the morning with the engine spluttering its last gasps as I ran out of petrol. On the last three hours of my journey I had not found one petrol station open: to have run out even a mile from Sturford would have necessitated that I spent the rest of the night in the car to protect my luggage. I felt as if I had been given divine protection over the course of that journey!

The Bowhill experience brought home to me another important aspect of my identity: that Scotsmen felt a pride and unity in their nationhood that couldn't really be matched by Englishmen. Or not by Englishmen in the West Country, who were perhaps out of focus from the central national organization of our society. I cannot say that I was as yet even remotely conscious of my identity as a Wessexian, but I was becoming aware how Scotsmen held some manner of advantage over me. And a West Country girl like Xenia had no hesitation in regarding herself as a Scots lassie, whenever such issue really needed to be stated. To have watched her there, cavorting in her reels with clan kinsmen, left me in no doubt that I was somehow omitted from that side of her personality. So the questions were already stirring within me as to how I should compensate for this deficiency within my own sense of identity.

It was at Bowhill, too, that I participated, for what was perhaps the very last time, in a pheasant shoot. My interest in shooting had long been on the wane, with the glimmerings of a conscience on such matters formulating within my heart. Nonetheless, I was still quite happy to participate. But this particular occasion was far from being a glorious experience for me. I remember, as I walked with the beaters, snapping up a woodcock when it swerved overhead.

But I made a real fool of myself in the final drive. There was an eminent Polish photographer in attendance and the idea was that he should take a photograph of me with a downed bird somersaulting through the air towards me in a cloud of feathers. He placed me on the skyline – where, incidentally, everyone could watch my miserable performance – then dancing up and down in what are known, I believe, among those who do such things as bunny hops, he readied himself and camera for when I brought down a pheasant. I kept missing. And with the psychological pressure mounting, I kept on missing. The other guns stood waiting until eventually there were no birds left for them to shoot at. There was a cool absence of comment from anyone at all, when we all finally gathered at the end of the drive.

It would be wrong for me, however, to give the impression that the hunting instinct had yet departed from me. I can remember two occasions at least – one of them during that weekend party at Sturford with Venetia, Sally-Anne and Tony Armstrong-Jones – when we all went shooting rabbits at night on Imber firing range, perched upon the front of Henry's (far superior) Land-Rover. Imber by night furnishes a weird atmosphere and we were blazing away at anything that came within the beam of the headlights. And it was quite a slaughter, so the blood lust was far from tamed within my heart. Nonetheless, it was waning, or at least ready to wane once other interests had taken root.

But this wasn't really a time for augmenting my identity with new skills and activities. Although I did participate in a rushed horse-riding course for the recent intake of officers (after all, we were members of the Household Cavalry). Within a single fortnight, we were required to accomplish a variety of equestrian skills, like making our mounts change step while cantering. We were even taught to vault into the saddle of a cantering horse and to attempt jumps with arms folded and feet out of the stirrups. Needless to say, falls were frequent. And still wearing my father's old riding boots, as tight as ever around the calves, I suffered at least one blackout after the bump of falling. But in any case, these weren't skills that were to be of any use to me. I hadn't ridden since childhood and I certainly wasn't going to take it up again now.

Events like the general election at this time, which might have been expected to reveal how my inner values were evolving, were not as significant to me as others might anticipate. I think I am right in saying that at nineteen, I was still ineligible to vote. But I certainly joined in with the general spirit of rejoicing in the officers' mess, at the sight of Atlee and his Socialists being finally driven from office. Rejoicing too fervently actually, in that a party of us climbed into my car and went zooming past the Burning Bush at Eton, flinging thunder flashes into a group of beaks as they assembled for Chambers. I should have anticipated that the number of my car would get accurately noted: a complaint finally reached the

Colonel, who made arrangements for us all to go and deliver a personal apology to Mr Birley, the Headmaster. Quite like old times!

Despite all our spirited rejoicing, we probably did realise how Churchill might now be a bit too old to resume his leadership – to be as dynamic in peacetime as formerly he had been in war. But these were thoughts that we preferred to keep to ourselves. It was far more a question of thinking that we were all finally back on the road for re-establishing the social order much as it had been before the war. We might all be a lot poorer as a result of the war and the subsequent Labour government but now this trend was, at last, being reversed. Or so we thought!

On the other hand I didn't really believe that the upper classes deserved to get it all back again, to have it just as good as they'd had it before. I had for some time felt a political unease concerning the more unsympathetic comments that were voiced in my presence by those from the same background as myself. And I did feel that, as a class, we owed one hell of a lot to others in return for past blessings. And when it came to individuals, I saw that I owed even more than that, as the following tale about Nanny might indicate.

Nanny had been going through a rough patch in her life of late. Her existence had been centred around our welfare, to the exclusion of all other concerns, for more than twenty years now. She'd been housed in her own cottage in retirement, just opposite to Sturford, but this was sold and she was relocated in another one, as close to Sturford as the first one but more convenient as it was on the same side of the road. Although it was cosier, it was also different and she found it difficult to adjust to the change. It is also a fact that none of us visited her quite as frequently as we formerly had done. Whether or not this contributed psychosomatically to her illness I don't know, but she suffered something like an intestinal blockage. I learnt that she was in hospital in Bath and that no one from our family had been in to see her.

I was on a brief spell of leave before the Regiment crossed over to Germany. On learning where she was, I visited her and found her in a depressed state. When I first arrived, she appeared to think that she was dreaming and it took some while before she could even respond to me. But when she finally did, it was with a pitiful gratitude. It made me feel so terrible that none of us had seen fit even to enquire about her welfare.

I decided to do something about it and I wrote to a short list of people – in addition to the members of my own family – for whom she had worked as a nanny in the past, hinting that she might be dying and how much she would value a visit or even a letter from them. And I was to learn much later – after her recovery – that there was a tremendous response in terms of bunches of flowers and other gifts. Nan was to make it clear to me how much she appreciated that I had put the word around and make her feel that she was still wanted and loved by those who had once been dear to her. Without exactly looking at me, she said very softly to me, "I know who saved me." This was her own way of expressing the matter. Not that I was then able to think of a reply. Besides, I wouldn't have been able to say it, in that I had such a huge lump in my throat. But it was precisely the things we couldn't say that were all so excruciatingly eloquent.

Those **first** attentions that we **took** for **grant**ed as our **due**
filled the **blue wat**ers of our **nurs**ery la**goon,**
attuning **each** in **confid**ence and **self-respect**
for the **next phases** in **life's** crucial **strides.**
Widely **sca**ttered as we **find** our**selves** to **be,**
we **deal** you **visits** – as **if** to a **memory** location,
spatially impressed, and **treated spic**ily with affection
and re**spect,** with**out** the **bond**ing of **constant return.**
I **burn** with **shame** that your **plea** for un**stint**ing
integration on the **outer fringe** of our **grand**
family – **reward expect**ed for e**clipse** of **ego-**
trips more **personal** – **left** you be**reft** of **comp**any.

No matter what the coin, I am afraid
our debt to you will never be repaid.

Chapter 2.4

Parents: sparring skirmishes

Something we all realised to some extent was that our parents were no longer getting on very well together. Shouting could sometimes be heard when I was walking in the vicinity of the drawing-room. And I once caught Christopher with his head round the partition door which separated our side of the house from theirs, gleaning what he could from the exchanges of abuse that were coming his way. I think he was in the habit of such eavesdropping, so he probably knew a lot more than I did about the state of the marriage. It was also true that Daphne was spending more and more of her time away from Sturford, but I fell short of perceiving that they might actually be contemplating divorce as the solution to their incompatibility. Even if they did appear irritated with each other, I assumed that this was an acceptable part of marital life and that they were still quite well matched.

Inasmuch that Daphne was so frequently absent from the scene, it was becoming especially important that I should learn how to get on well with Henry. After my excellent showing at Eton, I know that he had been taking it for granted that I would do well in my army training. He saw me (in good fascist style) as someone fitted to rule; my final low grading he attributed to the humorous story of how I had disputed with my instructor his reading on the map of the position I was now occupying. Naturally it was flattering to me that Henry should regard the failure so, but it frightened me that he might wake up to the fact that there was something more radically immature about my whole development in life.

I had managed to get through the period of my officer training without any serious disputes arising between Henry and myself – probably because we had so little time to spend in each other's company. But the situation changed once I had received my commission and had moved back to the comparative proximity of Windsor. Something that I know got on his nerves was my continued interest in painting. He had always been so sure that it was a passing interest, which now that I had reached adult life would rapidly fade away – just as my interest in butterfly collecting had passed. And he'd been at pains to mock me when he'd observed how I would set up my easel where the tourists who came to Longleat might stop to watch what I was doing. According to him, I was just showing off to them: wanting to hear my praises on their lips. And he'd supposed that a slight touch of ridicule might nudge me away from such an undesirable occupation.

I came to see how he might find it intolerable if I finally decided to paint professionally. For one thing, my approach to art wasn't such as to incur his admiration. Not photographic enough might be another way of putting it. But even if he had liked my paintings, this would not have changed his view that art was not a serious profession. And he was convinced that I was cut out for better things.

It offended me, however, that he took my personal aspirations all too lightly. When I asked him to have the paintings I had done at Eton framed by one of the estate carpenters, he refused. So I was left with the task of framing them myself – which I did, even though the carpentry looked distinctly amateur. And it irked me considerably when, around this time, he granted his friend Robin Campbell the full use of his estate carpenters to frame his paintings for a pending exhibition of his latest works. These were matters that led to a few heated words, but not exactly to a quarrel. Having framed all my paintings, I arranged them round the walls of the Orangery in what should rank as my first personal exhibition. And there they remained until I moved to Germany, when Henry took them down for storage elsewhere. Not that this really offended me in that I had expected as much. Perhaps, then, I had doubts in my own heart that I would ever really take control of my life sufficiently to emerge as an artist. So I took such depreciation in my stride.

The intended occupation that I most frequently proclaimed was to join the Foreign Office and become a diplomat. Not that this idea carried Henry's approval either. There was no money in diplomacy. Who ever heard of an ambassador becoming a millionaire from his salary? No, all of these ambitions were really quite futile and he was confident that, eventually, I could be dissuaded from making such a fool of myself.

He probably regarded my whole relationship to adult life as being a bit tenuous these days. I wasn't someone who had firm ideas on what I might eventually do. And he had troubles enough of his own. With Daphne's frequent absences and with the family's integrity beginning to fall apart, I daresay he found my endeavours to establish my own position in life to be an unnecessary complication to his own sense of order. Around this time we had, in fact, been getting on each other's nerves and there was a particular weekend in October when the irritations spilled over into real anger.

This was during the period when I only had a provisional licence to drive the Land-Rover that had just been given to me. I was eager to drive it on all possible occasions, so I arranged to give a lift to the Morrison brothers whose home was at Fonthill, not far from Sturford. That way I was complying with the law in having someone who had passed his driving-test at my side – as far as Fonthill in any case. I then continued the journey illegally, in that I was unaccompanied; the additional mileage that I had incurred also made me very late for lunch at Sturford, where Henry had been waiting for me. I arrived at twenty past two. The atmosphere over lunch was frigid and I greatly missed Daphne not being there to smooth things over for me.

Tempers reached boiling point, though, when I asked him if I could have the use of Harold Mather, his chauffeur, to accompany me back to Windsor next morning. I daresay I offered once we got there to place him on a train back home, although it seems evident from the sequel that followed that this point was lost on Henry. He seemed to have formed the impression that I was just asking for a free lift. In any case he dismissed the subject with a curt "No". My own feeling was that I hadn't been given sufficient reasons for this refusal; just a verdict, which I regarded as irrational. But when Henry perceived that I was questioning the finality of his judgement, he suddenly exploded. I can't remember what he said, but some abuse flooded from his lips in general denigration of my personality. The meal was concluded in an atmosphere of complete hostility, whereupon, without even bidding him farewell, I just took off back to Windsor.

A few days later, I received a letter from Henry, making an admirable attempt to clear up the ill feeling. I want to quote parts of it as it throws considerable light upon our relationship at this time.

Dearest Alexander,

First of all I want to apologise for having lost my temper with you in such an absurd and childish way...

Secondly, I am writing this letter as I feel that you and I must do something on both sides in order to cease these endless annoyances which lead to quarrels, before it has all gone too far. The point is, old cock, that I am exceedingly fond of you and admire many of your estimable qualities, but the trouble is that you do things and say things which drive me to a point of frenzy and fury. I am sure that I have the same effect on you.

Today Donald told me that you had sent a telegram saying you would be here for lunch. One o'clock arrives and then Donald asks me whether to begin, or wait... One-thirty – two o'clock – and still no appearance, and no message. Then at two-twenty you roll up in your car, admitting you were late because you had given some friends a lift somewhere...

Now you know Alexander – you know only too well – or if you don't, you must be zany – that this sort of inconsiderate behaviour annoys me beyond words. It isn't necessarily the extra trouble which you give everybody, but it is the inconsiderate manner in which you behave towards other peoples' lives. You give the appearance as if everyone was at your service, and that they must put themselves out to suit your convenience. Bring your filthy washing back and expect Mrs Sims or someone to wash it. Expect Mather to go to London at a time which suits you best in order to help choose a taxi for you. There are many things like the above which you have done in the past, and which I can't now remember.

When I have made up my mind about something – such as Mather not driving you back to Windsor the other day – don't go harping and returning to the subject like you did. That again infuriates me.

And Alexander, one more thing. You actually came down today in the Land-Rover without an L-plate, and without having passed your test. You simply must

*remember that the row we had last time was about that
sort of thing. It so happens that you have now departed
without me knowing, so thank heavens for that.
Otherwise I should have insisted on Mather
accompanying you back – and what is more, you would
have had to pay for his train journey back home.
Do please come down again. But before you do – pass
your test – that is, if you come by car. Can you see what
I mean when I say how, in my opinion, you are so
thoughtless? Anyway I'll really try to make an effort to be
reasonable.*

*If you do happen to be down this way on your big
manoeuvres, try and stop your regiment parking their
bloody armoured cars on my rhododendrons.*

Love Dad.

It seems that I complied with Henry's suggestion of refraining from a reply.
Well-intentioned though his letter now strikes me as being, I think I'll offer
my comments here. I feel sure that I was indeed inconsiderate as a young
man, yet part of the fault was the way we had been left to our own devices
throughout our upbringing. We had never been trained to be especially co-
operative within the home environment; nor had we really been
encouraged to consider anyone's problems other than our own. So I was
indeed emerging as a product of that mould. Individualistic to the point of
egocentricity perhaps.

Even with this point aside, it doesn't strike me that Henry yet
appreciated the degree to which his own behaviour needed to change
before there could possibly be a lasting peace between the two of us. He
didn't identify me yet as an adult and it was difficult to listen to his
authoritarian rulings without feeling that my manhood was being
repressed. It didn't occur to him that he might have got better co-operation
from me if discussions were to take place where my own opinions and
judgements might sometimes win the day. I had literally obeyed him for
too long and a resentment of it was beginning to gnaw away at me inside.

There is but one other quarrel, which was over money, that led to an
exchange of letters. To coincide with my obtaining a commission, Henry
had raised my allowance to £500 per annum, paid quarterly. This was
probably more than some of the other subalterns received to supplement

Henry, the 6th Marquess of Bath
(Baron)

their army pay. But with all the social events of the London season to attend, life was notoriously expensive for young officers in the Brigade of Guards. The prospects, though, of a spell out in the British Army of the Rhine meant that soon my social expenses would be slashed, so my financial position was quite reassuring.

But at Henry's insistence I had equipped myself with a wardrobe: shirts from Turnbull and Asser to suit every possible occasion and all else that he deemed a young gentleman might require. It was an excessive wardrobe and much of it was soon stolen, although by whom I never discovered. But the sheer ostentation of such possessions had been an invitation to thefts of this kind. What Henry didn't seem to perceive is that he was setting me up in the eyes of others as an aspiring dandy, which wasn't much in character with how I was developing. I also felt all the awkward burden of an imposed image.

Due to these heavy initial expenditures as well as, around this period, my not infrequent visits up to London, I found myself just slightly overdrawn – by about £25. This would soon have been corrected as my impending transfer to Germany with the British Army of the Rhine meant I could easily meet my expenditures from army pay. But Henry's standing instructions with Drummonds, with whom we banked, were that any cheques that I might present after my credit was exhausted must be bounced. Moreover, I now learnt that he had written to the manager, demanding to know why, when his instructions had always been to the contrary, I had been permitted to go overdrawn. All that I required was that while we were still stationed at Combermere there should be some discretion in the management of my account. So I raised the subject with Henry one evening at dinner, when I was back at Sturford on a weekend pass.

Unfortunately I found myself coming up against the same inflexible outlook that I had experienced throughout my adolescence. There was no question of him concluding that I was now an adult and must be treated differently. He told me that he wouldn't permit me to go overdrawn. When I attempted to persuade him that my request was, in fact, quite reasonable, he curtly closed the conversation by criticising me sharply for having brought up the matter at the dinner table. I realised that he was on the verge of losing his temper with me, so I shut up. From my own point of view, his endeavours to retain strict control over my life were excessive and not found in any other father that I knew. Indeed, as an adult, it was really for the bank itself to make such decisions as to whether they would permit me any credit. So I took up the matter with him a second time, but on this occasion by letter.

Dearest Daddy,

I know that to reopen a subject irritates you, but owing to the fact that I wasn't given a chance to state my case, I am doing so now... Nevertheless I apologise for mentioning the subject at dinner yesterday... However the facts of the case are as follows. (a) My allowance is sufficient. Anything greater would involve superfluous generosity on your side. (b) I have been informed by Drummonds that I have gone overdrawn, and that you have instructed that any further cheques should get bounced.

So I am wondering what your motivation might be for refusing to let me go overdrawn. It seems easily, if somewhat sordidly explained. You feel that if I were allowed to go overdrawn, I would sooner or later take advantage of it, and go plunging into an overdraft – from which it would require a tractor to extract me. That tractor (you suppose) would be yourself.

If I am right in thinking that you take this view, then it can all be summed up in the word "mistrust". It is mistrust. You do not trust me to act sensibly when it comes to the question of credit. And even if you cannot furnish me with a fully flexible allowance, then perhaps I could be permitted to go overdrawn up to a given limit; perhaps up to a figure for which I myself could offer the bank some surety.

If all is impossible, I shall of course manage to get by. As you have often told me in the past, there is a way round everything. I could borrow on post-dated cheques, which would in practice amount to an overdraft. But I must stress that I'd far prefer to act on principles of mutual trust, than start scheming on how I can get round your rules.

Please give the matter your careful consideration, and tell me what you think best.

Love from Alexander.

Henry's reply to me was as follows:

> *Thank you so much for your very nice letter, but I do want to make it perfectly clear that the reason I will not let you overdraw is in no way because I do not trust you. In absolutely no way whatsoever. It is merely that one has to draw the line somewhere. The point is that, if one doesn't make a rule of this sort, every single person in the world would overdraw. In my own time I have done this to no small extent – when I was about your age – and my father had to pay up!*
>
> *I'm afraid I shall continue to stick to my rule, in spite of the fact that you say you have bought only the merest essentials for your trip to Germany. I have written to your bank today informing them to this effect. I do however want you to realise that I am in no way annoyed with you, but it is one of my rules which I propose to stick to with all of my sons – and no argument will persuade me to be different.*
>
> *I went to the dentist in London yesterday and discovered that you have not been to see him, or even made an appointment to do so. May I inform you that unless you do so before Christmas, you will in future pay for all your own dental treatment, as you promised me faithfully that you would go.*

The correspondence between my father and Drummonds led to the manager requesting a meeting with Henry, when it was tactfully pointed out to him just how detrimental it might be to my career, if my cheques started bouncing when I was serving as an officer in the Household Cavalry. The question of credit was thenceforward left as a matter for my bank manager to decide – and, incidentally, has never been abused. But it marks a moment of small triumph in my life in that my father now felt actually obliged to modify one of the rules that he had set up to govern our lives – if only because it concerned matters that were not strictly under his control.

But as I've said before, his home environment was experiencing the tremors such as precede an earthquake, even if the rest of his household seemed unaware of the shocks that were to come. The first occasion when someone saw fit to hint openly to me that the marriage might not last was when Iain Graham-Wigan came down to visit me from his regiment (He had joined the Rifle Brigade, with the intention of signing on as a regular army officer). We went out to lunch in Windsor somewhere and I heard all his latest history. But he had always been one to take a sadistic delight in the discomfiture of others and he did so on this occasion by tossing me a query about my mother's antics.

"So what's this I hear about the way she's carrying on up in London…? There's a private house, it's said… She gets up to all manner of things up in London, I'm told… People say that orgies take place… She's a thoroughly immoral woman, by all accounts…"

Perhaps I should have taken umbrage at the words he uttered, but it had suddenly struck me that I might be hearing the truth. And he'd been a good friend – for some of the time – so might be permitted an indiscreet comment or two. I did in fact know that Daphne often went to stay up in London. And what they might get up to was anyone's guess. At the same time, I knew how Iain had always been someone to get his facts wrong – especially when it came to sexual matters. I didn't quite know what to think, but I felt perturbed: much as Iain, I imagine, had been intending. It was all too close now to the date of my crossing to Germany to expect to find out what might truly be going on. So my unease on the subject remained unalleviated.

> Rooted in astonishment I stand, twitching
> the itch of incredulity, a fool for doubting
> the folly of belief, grieving, and yet admiring
> the dire audacity of whoring in one so dear.
> Near the ilk of my own former antics,
> romantic at heart, I blend in her glowing soul,
> identifying deep, through back streets
> of fleeting sub-conscious memories of guilt.
> My stilted morals wince and wilt at the farcical
> charges you level at her ruffled reputation,
> ungracious in pouring spunk on raw sores,
> and chortling gleeful at my own discomfiture.
>
> > The priceless treasure of my childhood's heart
> > should not lie open to such vulgar farts.

PART THREE

WOLFENBÜTTEL BARRACKS

Chapter 3.1

Authority: triumphing through adversity

It was March 1952 and the Life Guards had taken over from the Royal Horse Guards in Wolfenbüttel Barracks as part of the British Army of the Rhine. Life was very different for us in Germany. For one thing, we were now largely deprived of any extramural social activities. Personally, I never received a single invitation from any German family to enter their home during the entire period that I was out there. So this meant that we were all far more reliant upon each other's company than we had been at Combermere. There were more occasions when we were all just sitting there in the officers' mess, with a gin and tonic in hand and nothing in particular to do, but with an increased chance of getting on each other's nerves. Still, I had a very nice room of my own, as indeed had all the subalterns. Wolfenbüttel Barracks had been built to house one of Hitler's elite SS regiments, so we lacked no luxury – double-glazed windows and everything else. I sometimes wondered what the predecessors in that room may have been like. Not that it troubled me greatly!

The initial weeks were spent in getting our vehicles ready for action – taking them out to get a look at the local German countryside, which was splendidly open and scattered with small agricultural villages. The new replacements that I had in my troop were a pleasant crowd, so the relationship between us got off to a good start. Rose was the one remaining from the old batch, and he had now been joined by Macdonald, Ward, Winthrop, Callan, Hitchcock, Rich and Turner. An additional bonus was that Corporal Alexander had been posted to temporary duties elsewhere within the squadron, which removed from my presence what had perhaps been the main source of disrespect. I was still left with Corporal Guilliland; and Corporal of Horse Dodson was back at long last on duty with the troop, having finally completed his series of courses. Having a Corporal of Horse who was competent to take in his stride much of the troop's administrative organisation made an immense difference. A huge load of responsibilities was immediately lifted from my own shoulders – so much so, I marvelled how I had coped for so long without such assistance.

With the troop's administration now in competent hands, I was at far greater liberty to absent myself during days when we were in barracks. I had my own activities to preoccupy me within the privacy of my own room, as I will relate. But I was also discovering that the more I absented myself from the scene, the easier it became to maintain good relations with my troop while we were out on trek. It all felt like progress.

Nonetheless, I can't say I felt satisfied with the prospect of spending the final nine months of my National Service cooped up in Wolfenbüttel, deprived of any opportunity to make a real start in my courtship of Xenia – or of anyone else for that matter. I was also aware that I couldn't really be counted as a popular young subaltern among my peers in the Life Guards. (Not *unpopular*, I would say, but certainly not one of those who were fully at their ease when sitting in the mess.) We were all looking for our own individual pretexts for getting posted back in England for some part of the London season. The way it worked was that the applications of those who ranked higher than myself were the most liable to succeed. There was also the consideration that so many applicants who had put down their names for all the more traditional courses – such as radio communications or gunnery – I knew I wouldn't have a chance in those fields. But there were some alternatives that evidently appealed to no one at all, namely parachuting as well as boxing. So I put my name down for both of those and then waited to hear if I'd been accepted.

Back came the answer that they weren't interested in taking on any National Service officers for the parachute course; I'd have to sign on before they would consider me for that. But my application to attend the boxing course went through without any hitch. That meant that I could look forward to a brief spell at Aldershot – which was near enough to London – in October. And in the meantime I'd just have to take care of myself as best I could.

In the event, it turned out that things did begin to go better for me. It was largely a question of cutting corners, as far as I could see, and being less bogged down with matters of detail. And it was also a question of Nipper appearing less of an ogre in my eyes. The image of him as a newly married man, quite well under Maureen's thumb, made it seem curious not to be snapping to attention at his bark quite so alertly as I may formerly have done. There were a couple of days on a wireless exercise when Nipper was obliged to share a tent with Christopher "Christo" Phillipson and myself, who proceeded to drink rather too much. We rather upset Nipper, keeping him awake with our inebriated giggles, which arose from the series of schoolboy pranks that we were playing on him. The sight of him lying there complaining but virtually impotent, with his sleeping bag pulled up over his head, did rather take the edge off his authority. Or, he was becoming humanised, was the way I judged the matter.

This might be an appropriate moment to interject a story about Nipper that was told to me by Brigadier Ferris St George who was visiting the Regiment around this time. He was chatting with me at some cocktails that were being given in his honour and he must have sensed – or heard – that I was experiencing some problems with my squadron-leader. He told me the image of Nipper that he always recollected was from the days when he had first joined the Regiment, during the course of the campaign out in Normandy. He had initially felt dismayed by his decidedly youthful appearance. But his respect had quickly been earned when he saw how those boyish features remained unflinching in the turret of his armoured car when they suddenly came under fire. In other words, I was being advised that I should hold him in greater respect than I currently appeared to.

Part of the turn around in my own fortunes with the Life Guards must be attributed directly to my efforts to sort out the pecking order. When I had first arrived at Combermere the cards had admittedly been stacked in my favour, for the fact of there being so many Old Etonians in the mess worked greatly to my advantage. But I had let the opportunity slip and had watched my standing quickly erode to the point where I was troubled by an increasing level of disrespect. And now that we were all cooped up together at Wolfenbüttel, obliged to share each others' company far more than at Combermere, personal irritations were all the more noticeable.

My first clash was with Robin Keith – from both Ludgrove and Eton, of lighter build but older than myself – when he threw his drink over me, for a reason that goes unremembered. For the first time in a long while, I responded with an appropriate degree of counter-aggression, hauling him to the washroom where I held his head under a tap. It was passed off in a spirit of fun and games, but I accounted the episode as crediting me a plus.

A few weeks after this, there was a clash with Simon Galway. He was always inclined to be very aggressive verbally, so he had it coming to him. In response to some such incident, I commented: "So you think you're pretty tough, do you?" And he retorted: "Yes. Anyway I'm a fucking sight tougher than you, young man!" And he gave me a shove so that I tripped backwards over a low table that was behind me. Picking myself up, I said: "I'm not so sure about that. We'll have to see." We closed into a wrestling clinch, and I soon had him pinned down on the sofa. "Shall we call it equal?" I asked. And after a moment's hesitation, Galway agreed to this description of our relative strength. But once again, in my mind's account this was chalked up as a credit.

The next tussle was rather more in anger and this time it was with Ian Bailey, who was now serving as the Technical Adjutant. It was quite late at night, with Christo as the only independent witness. But for some reason, again unrecalled, Bailey threw his drink at me – more or less in fun. Still more or less in fun, I picked up a water jug and retaliated. Bailey then hurled a tonic bottle at me. I went out, refilled the jug and came back and emptied it over his head. Bailey was now angry, hurling a whole volley of tonic bottles at me. Fleeing from the mess, I refilled the jug and returned to pour it over him. But this time he flew at me as I approached and, taking hold of me by my shirt – which ripped, incidentally – he tried to pour a bottle of gin over my head. We were soon in a clinch when I wrestled him to the floor. But he tried to lash out at my face, so I shoved my thumb in his eye and gouged, scratching his face in the process. I asked him if he was going to desist and he said yes, but we separated on somewhat frigid terms.

Next morning I was in the mess when Galway remarked casually to Bailey – as if he hadn't already gleaned the full story from Christo: "Hello Ian, how did you get that scratch on your face?"

"I cut myself shaving," he replied huffily. Then, observing that I was present, he added, "Oh you mean this? I got that while pouring a bottle of gin over Alex's head."

"And who got the worst of it?" I muttered – to which there was no reply. Galway merely smirked. But I felt pleased it should be appreciated that I wouldn't take too much aggression lying down.

There was another episode to come that was even more spectacular. To supply some background information first: my own greatest antipathy in the Life Guards was perhaps for Livingstone – largely because he had tapped into those feelings of disrespect for me, without any awareness of the prestige I'd known in better days. Livingstone was one of the first boys to be admitted to the Household Cavalry as a Potential Officer from one of the lesser public schools – it might be commonplace today, but at the time it represented an effort to broaden (just slightly) the egalitarian basis for a commission in the Brigade. I certainly didn't take against him on that score but it riled me greatly when, from a position on the sidelines, he made gibes at my expense to secure his own sense of solidarity with the others.

The mutual antipathy had come to a head when we were sent to represent the Life Guards at a gunnery demonstration, even having to share a room together overnight. And there came a point when Livingstone spoke to me in private with the same contemptuous tone that he had offered me too frequently in public. So it was time that I let him know that I wasn't going to take it from him. Which I did – just verbally but aggressively, so that he at least knew that he must watch his tongue if we were alone together.

Back at Wolfenbüttel, I suspect that he must have said something about the exchange, for others seemed to pick up on the store of untapped ill-feeling between the two of us. I dare say also there was some confusion in people's minds at this juncture over my place within the communal pecking order. Anyway, it was Victor Hoare who (as a Captain) was probably the dominant figure over the current group of subalterns and he may have been wishing for some personal enlightenment on these matters. We were all sitting round in the mess when he came up with the suggestion that our boredom could be alleviated by a gladiatorial bout. Two of us should be pitched against each other in a debagging contest.

"We give them this choice. Either they try to debag each other – or otherwise all the rest of us will debag them. Now to choose the contestants…" And his eye crept unsubtly round the room while we waited to hear whom it would be. "I think we'll have Weymouth and Livingstone."

Under different circumstances, I might well have tried to turn the situation round against him, by suggesting that he was selecting others to debag me when he knew that it was a task he wouldn't be bold enough to tackle single-handed. But he had picked upon two officers who disliked each other – which I suspect he knew very well. I hold it to my credit that I did turn to Livingstone to say quietly: "Well, shall we take them all on together, John?" But he gave an embarrassed laugh and replied: "I somehow think it will be easier to fight one person, than twenty!" I couldn't have wished for a more pleasing answer. So we got up and fought.

In build, he may have looked sturdier and more athletic, but he turned out to be no match for me. I quickly had him thrown to the ground and partially debagged – although to complete the job single-handed was virtually impossible, as I soon discovered. But I was unanimously pronounced to be the victor and was able to resume my seat with my prestige enhanced. I was now feeling too exhausted to throw the challenge he deserved – in Victor Hoare's direction. Equally, perhaps there was no longer any need for it, for he had been suitably impressed.

"Do you know, I thought Livingstone was going to win that fight hands down?" he said. Bailey gave a chortle in the background. "I didn't, and I should know! I've had a fight with Alex myself." Victor looked at me with curiosity. "I wonder: it's possible I may have been underestimating you!" I left it at that.

> I sit without the wit to cover my lap,
> crapped on in cramped crevices with cretins' excreta,
> bleating my protest to a deaf world, enfurled
> in whirlwind problems of graver consequence.
> Menstruating more than monthly, I clutch
> my crutch in defensive gesture, instilling a will
> in others to fill my platter full of bullshit
> taunts. The dawn will reveal the man – or mouse!
> Aroused with dragon's breath at the tenth hour,
> I glower my warning glare from staring eyes,
> sizing up potential opponents, and flaunting
> a daunting garb – as macho as a Mexican bander'o.
> And those who cannot beat me to the draw
> shall stumble down the ladder one place more.

Above all, perhaps, the main element in the gradual turnaround in my fortunes was that things began to go right for me over the prolonged series of manoeuvres throughout the summer months. It suddenly transpired that I could do nothing wrong. On the first occasion that I got the troop lost, we blundered through a wood to discover a Squadron Headquarters on the open plain below us. It was a fifty-fifty chance whether it was ours or the enemy's. I attacked anyway – and this time it turned out that I had done the right thing, winning the day for our side.

Even in the divisional schemes I managed to excel myself: I got lost in a maze of woodland tracks, ending up (twice over) sitting on the bridge

Above: My early morning ablutions on the back of one of D Squadron's scout cars

Left: This is us waiting not for the enemy but for Major 'Nipper' Wordsworth to inspect our battle readiness. I can't remember if he was impressed

over which the enemy were supposed to withdraw. On the second of these occasions, it put the umpires in a pretty pickle, for it threatened to cut the whole scheme short by a couple of days. Naturally, they claimed that I must have crossed a dozen minefields or so. But when they inspected the areas that they assumed to have been mined, they discovered there were no indications of any such defences having been laid. (Of course there weren't, for I'd been careful to remove such indications while crossing them.)

Finally, they managed to persuade me that there had been an aerial bombardment by high altitude planes and, by a strange coincidence, the bombs had landed on my troop. This meant that we had to withdraw, and the scheme was thus enabled to continue in accordance with the plan. News of my exploits had been circulating on the umpires' wireless-net, so that congratulations began to filter down from the division, to brigade, to regiment, to squadron. I had no means of communicating my victories direct to Nipper, for my wireless had broken down. Yet, by the time I got back to my own lines, he must have received his due share of congratulations, for he was actually pleased to see me. In fact he was as perky as a buck rabbit in spring.

"Hello, Alex. Glad to see you in one piece. Jolly well done. Hang around. I may have something for you later."

He was so perky that it seemed to call for a little celebration. The only trouble was that he left me celebrating for a bit too long – until nightfall in fact. I was as pissed as an newt by the time he sent for me. And he was then in consultation with a major from the infantry regiment, with whom we were supposed to be co-ordinated. We were at their disposition, so to speak. As I approached the order-group, I could hear the major saying something like: "You must send a chap who knows what he's up to. It'll be a tricky job."

At that moment I had the misfortune to trip over a haversack, so that my presence was noticed. As I clambered to my feet, the lamp was turned towards me. I stood there swaying slightly and there was a dubious pause. Then I heard the infantry officer murmur: "Are you sure this is your best man?"

Nipper refrained from any reply by launching hurriedly into his orders. I was to advance into contact with the enemy through the murkiness of a black night and to keep in touch with them as they withdrew. A bloody ridiculous thing to expect any troop of armoured cars to perform! We'd never be able to see the enemy, unless they jumped up to sit on our gun-barrels – and there was no reason to suppose that they would oblige. Still, it didn't really matter. It wasn't as if their bazookas would be armed with live ammunition.

Roaring off into the darkness now, we made our way forwards to where the enemy had last been reported. I had sent a scout car way out ahead of me, so that I could relax in my armoured car hoping that my head would eventually begin to clear. But Nipper kept on coming up over the wireless, making all his usual comments, which struck me as being even more absurd than they normally were. I decided to imitate him, spluttering with laughter after every attempt. Just an occasional "Jolly good!" or "We'd better get a move on – and quickly too!" But I felt that I was being so incredibly funny and Nipper was becoming so excitable in his replies that I slightly overstepped the mark. "Nip! Nip! Nip!" I cried and followed it with the imitation of a crowing cockerel. I then switched off my own wireless set, which made me feel as if I was safely beyond the reach of retribution. But my operator, Callan, had to deal with the incoming signals and for the next ten minutes the poor man was apologising his head off.

Later he told me that he'd been intending to clout me one over the earhole if I'd come up with any more Nipper-talk. I was saved from this act of insubordination by what happened next – suddenly there were flashes and bangs exploding all round him, way up in the front of our armoured car. I went to give an order over the wireless but found it was no longer working, which was nothing unusual. I'd forgotten that I had switched it off after my final ribbing of Nipper. I now decided that I would have to rely upon the power of my lungs.

"What are you waiting for? Don't just sit there. Charge!"

There was no response from any of my troop – except for some mutinous rumbles from someone in the car behind. I think he said: "Stone the crows! Can't one of you put a cork in him?"

This irritated me. "Go on!" I roared. "Charge! Get moving you idle sods, and charge. Charge! Charge!"

Suddenly the whole battlefield came to life with the commotion of human voices and engines starting up all round. I sat there slightly bewildered, no longer quite certain what might be happening in the vicinity. I might have been sounding a bit more pissed than usual, but I'd hardly been anticipating any of these effects. The night was too dark to see more than a few yards. There were definitely vehicles on the move, and some of them were large ones, but they were now quickly receding into the distance. After a considerable pause – now feeling definitely subdued – I switched on the wireless and suggested that we might proceed with the advance.

Armed and ready to defend our country...
except that we were in Wiltshire

On Patrol: Trooper Wintrop was never convinced
that my camouflage skills would fool the enemy

Ronnie Ferguson and a bunch of other officers watch
the troops repair our vehicles

Bogged down while on manoevres –
the local female talent proved too much of a distraction.
Nipper was not amused that we were out of radio contact

By this time, however, rumours of a full-scale onslaught of tanks, with infantry support, must have been circulating through the enemy lines and they never allowed us to come within striking range a second time. As soon as the sound of our engines was heard approaching in the distance, their outposts were hurriedly withdrawn. I had long since abandoned such futile practices as snake patrolling – except when Nipper was around. This enabled me to fulfil his instructions "to get a move on, and quickly too". But the faster we advanced, the faster the enemy retreated. And by first light, there was no sign of where their armed forces could be hiding. In fact, we had broken right through to a wood where their supply column had been harboured for the night – wonderfully defenceless and still snoring happily in their tents. Having upset all their radio communications (twiddling the knobs and pulling out the pigtails) we were able to awaken them with a fusillade of thunder flashes. Then I came up over the air to report that armed resistance was at an end: that the brigade was free to launch its full-scale offensive, or whatever else they wanted to do.

It took me some time to persuade Nipper that I was now quite sober, but I did so eventually, and he became reasonably polite in his retorts. After a little while he even became complimentary and, later still, effusive in his praise. Somebody must have been doling him out great dollops of congratulations, to make him so appreciative. By the time I returned to base he wasn't looking at me quite squarely in the eye but there was a gigglish air of complicity in the enjoyment of undeserved praise, which made him appear more human than I'd ever seen him before.

> With tedious obedience, building bridges over muddied
> puddles, I'd slaved so gravely my behaviour had shuddered
> to a muddled halt – till I threw this gruesome rule-book
> sky high, trying instead to fly.
> Bred to tread reality's sordid boards,
> I'll shed those shackles for a slackened attention to facts,
> and track a rainbow's train of fantasy, panning
> to grand vision of heroic feats in battle.
> I'll rattle a sabre in my hollow scabbard, bellowing
> yells of cavalier bravado, whooping
> like a stupid cowboy, with reckless disregard
> for farcical, sham distributions of death.
>> For war is just a festival of fun
>> when blanks (instead of bullets) fill the guns.

A few days later, the Colonel received a congratulatory telegram from the divisional commander (General Harding, I think it was). Apparently we were the best armoured car regiment that had ever manoeuvred with the Rhine army. To be strictly modest, I believe there were a few other sabre troop leaders who had excelled themselves in other parts of the battlefield. But I was able to feel that I had wiped out a debt of honour to the Regiment, which I had incurred by my contribution to the Midhurst fiasco over the Very pistol and other incidents.

I seemed to be rising in the general esteem. Nipper came shuffling up to me one morning after parade and muttered something about me signing on for an additional year's service with the Life Guards. I thought he must be joking, so I laughed. He was careful not to press me any further. It seems that he had been ordered to make this suggestion by the Colonel, who later called me into his own office – along with various other subalterns who were considered to have done well – and the suggestion was put to me more formally. I hadn't the slightest intention of letting myself in for more of the army than I was obliged, so I turned it down without hesitation. But it was nice to have been asked.

My self-confidence was rising too. There was a morning when one of the Corporals of Horse – Gardner – who currently had his own troop, made some derogatory comments in public about what some of the officers in the squadron had said. He had been getting away with this kind of insolence for rather too long, so I called him to one side after the parade and told him fiercely that he must watch his step. Such an assertion of my authority would have been unthinkable a few months previously. It certainly took CoH Gardner by surprise, but I knew that he respected me for it.

I still wasn't quite where I wanted to be, however, in terms of having found my feet in the Regiment. I'd established that I wasn't quite so low down the pecking order as some of my peer group might once have been assuming. I had also displayed how I could bluff my way along with the best of them in the attainment of mock military advantages. I still didn't feel that I was accepted yet, even liked, by the general rank and file within the Regiment. But I was to make good headway there, too.

I was pleased to observe that those under my command were actually boasting about our prowess. At last some troop spirit was developing. I heard Rose saying how he was proud to be the only trooper who had survived from the previous batch – as if there was no question in his mind of the blame for past confusions being attributed to me. And I heard Fowler – who had been temporarily attached to my troop at the time when things had been going very wrong for me at Combermere – telling the others how I had at some stage gathered the troop together to tell them that once I had got the hang of things, they would get better. I was now even receiving the occasional verbal request for a transfer into my troop. This was from troopers under Nick Buckley or Bruno Shroeder, who had newly joined the squadron – two more friends from Eton, it should be noted.

When it came to the final scheme of the summer, I was discomfited to hear that Corporal Alexander would be rejoining the troop. And, just as I had feared, he began to pull the carpet of authority out from under my feet, trying to make a fool of me in the eyes of the troopers to elevate himself in their eyes at the expense of me. Yet now I had the measure of him, as well as the standing with my troop, so that I could take him to task on his behaviour. I spoke to him sharply, in the hearing of all the others. And I was aware that I carried their sympathy with me and how he had clearly lost out on their support. He resorted to buffoonery in declaring that he couldn't give a bugger for my reprimands, since he was due to be demobbed the following week. So it wasn't worth my while to take the confrontation any further.

I had this boxing course coming up in the autumn, so there was some sense in trying to revive my proficiency in that field. I made enquiries through the Squadron Office to see if there was anyone interested in having some sparring practice with me. I suppose I might have expected it, but the only interest that appeared was from one of the company – the trooper that I had transferred from my troop some six months previously over personal antipathy. He left word at the office to say that he'd be very happy to spar with me in the gymnasium.

So spar we did: with each of us doing his best to bluff the other that we were more dangerous in the ring than our reputations suggested. I remember him claiming that he had fought several fights professionally – though I very much doubt that to have been true. When sparring, it soon became apparent that, despite him being a good stone heavier, he was no match for me. I knew that I could put him down virtually when I pleased. So I took it to the point of saying that he must tell me when to desist, before starting what could well have been my final attack. I staggered him and he was quick to suggest that we take a rest.

Gone was the cheeky insolence that had formerly characterised his relationship with me, nor was it ever to recur. I suggested he bring along a friend to the next sparring practice and he eventually found someone to oblige. I proceeded to take on the two of them simultaneously – landing more blows to each of their heads than I received. Once again I could see that I had impressed them; moreover, I was aware that stories about my boxing prowess were now circulating amongst the other ranks.

Chapter 3.2

Activities: nursing the creative flame

The business of being a soldier didn't bring with it too wide a variety of activities – though perhaps that statement needs to be examined a little more closely.

I had brought out *Roger the Rover* with me from Britain, which allowed me to travel where I pleased. It also meant that others had to rely on my company when they wanted, for example, to eat at local restaurants that were not within walking distance. When we first took over from the Blues, there was still plenty of winter snow on the ground and there was skiing at Bad Harzburg in the Harz mountains. I had yet to learn how to ski, but I spent a couple of weekends there. All that surprises me now is that I didn't break a leg – at least. Army boots are hardly conducive to quick learning. But worse than that, in the absence of any instruction, I had got it into my head that beginners should come straight to grips with the task of shooting headlong down a slope, more or less as if they were tobogganing. I took the inevitable tumbles in my stride, without it occurring to me that such antics should be reserved until a time when I had mastered some control over my skis.

There had also been the shooting competitions for the British Army of the Rhine shortly after my first arrival in Wolfenbüttel, when I had in fact been picked as the only officer on the Life Guards team. And there had been no favouritism in my earning that place, which I had won on merit with scores that were consistently high – around the 85 mark. But come the competition itself I somehow went to pieces, to the extent that I even suspected someone had tampered with my sights. After trying to correct them, I found I did even worse. Then, during the lunch break, I was irresponsible enough to anaesthetise my anxieties with a few gin and tonics – predictably my aim in the afternoon's Bren gun shooting became reckless and erratic. My final score was so low that it put the whole team to shame. This black spot on my army record must rank as the last setback before my bullish future in the Guards was consolidated.

Several months later, during the course of the summer manoeuvres, I was at one time posted on the banks of the Rhine to supervise a life-saving post. A night crossing of the river was to be staged but, as there was very little for us to do during the days of gradual build-up for the crossing I had brought my twelve-bore shotgun with me. I'd had no opportunities to use it since our arrival out in Germany but this struck me as a suitable one – we had seen partridges in the neighbouring fields. I decided I would try to bag some for the pot. So I drove off in a scout car with a handful of troopers to act as beaters, and we began to drive to one of the open fields where some partridges had been observed to settle.

We flushed them out from the corn stubble and I got off a couple of shots though without actually hitting one. But I had fired just as the covey was approaching a hedge. And to my alarm the hedge suddenly came to life, spewing from behind it a swarm of high-ranking officers with red-tabbed epaulettes and their aides. It suddenly dawned upon me that we'd flushed the central order group for the whole river-crossing exercise. So we took flight and legged it back to the scout car, only just managing to get mobile before a jeep started out in hot pursuit. What would have happened to my career if we had been caught, I dread to think. But our scout car turned out to be faster than their jeep. Well, on this occasion, with a dragon breathing down our necks, it so proved.

We had taken over from the Blues their stable of horses and a pack of hounds. There was a coppice or two in the vicinity, amid all those rolling farmlands, but the sight of a fox for hunting was a great rarity. There were quite a number of dedicated huntsmen in the Officers Mess – with Sunny Blandford, now the Duke of Marlborough, as our Master of Hounds. He had antagonised the German population of this neighbourhood with a story in the local press how, in the absence of foxes, the Life Guards were hunting the farmers' cats. I wasn't myself a participant within their sport. But I sampled a taste of how outraged the inhabitants of Brunswick were at the Life Guards on the first occasion that I went to visit that city – unwisely dressed in full uniform. A man who saw me approaching along the pavement made a point of barging into me, full frontal, taking me by surprise and thus forcing me to step aside. I have never known for sure whether his action was in response to his having read that piece in the paper, or to some more general dislike of Germany being subject to occupation by the Allied Forces.

The tennis courts in the barracks at Wolfenbüttel were virtually wasted upon me, too. I had played it just occasionally at Eton, but without any great proficiency. And it was much the same out here. I preferred to spend my spare time in other pursuits.

Most evenings there was a game of poker being played in the mess and the habitual gamblers were eager to persuade newcomers to play – for that was where the potential killings lay. One problem, however, was that some of the higher subalterns – the captains and the majors – were comparatively wealthy, since it was not unusual for them to have already inherited capital from their fathers to avoid the ultimate payment of death duties. With such funds behind them they could afford to play for higher stakes than most of us. And they could afford to bluff, although in doing so they also ran the risk of losing out. I tried to match them at their game, with fluctuating fortunes. A run of wins was followed by a run of losses. But when it came to the day of reckoning, the mess steward came to us all with the book in which our debts were recorded. A page had been torn out – leaving the faintest traces of the tear – but it was the one that logged my run of wins and, without any other record, I was left with my debts alone in evidence.

It wasn't a vast sum – let us say £50. But it was a loud wake-up call to face what I was doing: could the thrill of the risks in gambling justify the misery of accumulating debt? There was also the realisation that one of the officers with whom I had been playing must be dishonest, if not a thief. After reflection on the whole matter, I decided to eschew such pastimes. Gambling was not right for me. So henceforth I refrained from participating in their games of poker.

There was no purchase tax to pay on alcohol or cigarettes while serving with the Rhine army. So it was not unusual for me to have a gin and tonic in my hand when sitting in the mess. Plus I was smoking as well, though probably no more than five cigarettes a day. It's not that I ever managed to enjoy the feeling of smoke in my lungs, it's just that it was such a ubiquitous habit at the time that it was easier to smoke than not. Whatever we might be doing, we stopped for a smoke break – so, along with all the others, I smoked. I would have been left standing idle and fidgeting if I'd chosen to be a non-smoker.

I made good use of the NAAFI's travelling library van, reading for the most part accounts of military valour – as in *The Dam Busters* or *The White Rabbit*. But I was also concerned to hear about a more bohemian way of life, as in the fictionalised biographies of the Impressionist painters: Van Gogh in *Lust for Life* and Toulouse-Lautrec in *Moulin Rouge*. I regarded the life of the soldier and the life of the artist as being greatly in contrast to one another and something that I felt I needed to get sorted out.

I had brought out my painting equipment with me to Wolfenbüttel, and found time enough to paint just a few pictures – a self-portrait in army uniform being the most notable. I have given myself a fiercely militaristic expression on my face, which may be indicative of the personality that I vainly hoped my Squadron Leader might recognise within my features. I knew that people didn't really see me like that and it was far more a case of wishful thinking.

There was in fact a great deal of time spent in my own room, working at my own devices, for the truth is that I had never been a really good mixer. The company of my friends was something I tried more to avoid than to cultivate – and I say this without the slightest intention of being offensive to them. But I seldom felt truly at ease in the company of others; my concern was to establish some peace of mind, rather than shine in entertaining others – or even to enjoy being entertained by others. I always felt safer when I was in a room on my own.

The occupation that engrossed me more than any other was in the writing of my first (completed) novel – *The Millions and the Mansions*. It never got published and, on examination today, rates as trash. But it was the product of much labour and, as I learnt a valuable lesson from it, I want to touch on it in passing.

Chapter 3.3

Activities: my first completed novel

My general intention was to write a novel on the subject of opening a stately home to the public. I had been galled by the successful utilisation of this theme by Adam Fergusson and John Mander, two of my friends at Eton who had written a play that had been performed at M'tutor's with some measure of critical acclaim. Of course, I knew far more about the subject than them and I saw no reason why I shouldn't make even better use of it. The predicament of the aristocracy was that to generate sufficient income to meet the costs of maintaining their stately homes they had to put themselves on public display. In humorously dramatising this I also hoped to show my reader that their reputation for being condescending stems from a misinterpretation of their manner.

The plot was concerned with two families, both of whom had a single child. One of them is called David and was based upon me; the other, based on Xenia, is called Rowena. The final outcome that I intended was of course obvious from the start. Before such a betrothal would be successfully concluded however, I availed myself of the idea that the two families should fall out with each other as a result of their competition in attracting tourists to their respective mansions.

I went on to sketch a tale of mini-warfare breaking out between the two families, conducted in a manner inspired by the farcical situations arising throughout my own experience of military manoeuvres. Campaign plans are unfurled at headquarters, observation posts are established prior to commando raids, there are counter-attacks, the capture of prisoners, rescue missions, secret agents and espionage, pitched battles, negotiations for peace and a final armistice.

Meanwhile David and Rowena are pulled hither and thither before true love triumphs.

As far as literary inspiration was concerned, I was modelling the novel on the style of P.G. Wodehouse. I was hoping to carry my readers on a wave of hilarity concerning the absurdity of attitudes and events. But I still did not possess adequate insight into what does make people laugh and most of my attempts to arouse such mirth were merely facetious. The novel is replete with clichés, caricatures and stock comedy plots… in a word, it is a pot-boiler.

David's stately home is owned by his parents William and Julia (I based them on Henry and Daphne) and they are depicted emphasising the Henry's egocentricity, ill-temper and despotic bombast, and Daphne's scatterbrained volatility. The manner in which they speak is an exaggeration of their personal idiom, but it still strikes my ear today as being fairly authentic. In a passage where William is planning the first day's opening to the general public, he lectures his wife and son on their duties:

> "The first sight the public will have of the house will be myself. I shall be standing in the doorway, framed by the stone pillars."
>
> "If you remain here, you'll miss our first visitors," said David.
>
> "Damn the first visitors!" said William. "I'll meet them later."
>
> "You won't get very far if you just go round the place damning all your visitors," said Julia.
>
> "Stop interrupting," said William. "I'm trying to teach you the important task of guiding a party round the house. So don't interrupt."
>
> "May I have a map?" asked David.
>
> "No you may not," said William. "If you don't yet know this house like the back of your hand, you ought to be shot. Yes, you ought to be shot!"

Later in the novel William is fuming about his commando unit failing to be up and about at breakfast time and he is outraged to discover that one of them is being served breakfast in bed. His response is drawn from comments actually uttered by Henry:

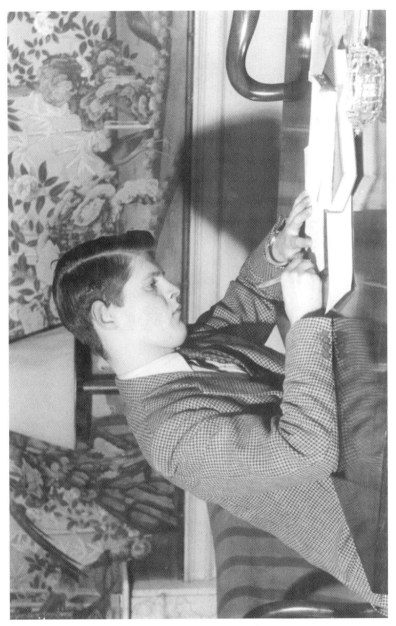

Writing by hand – the only way to write verse and the proper way to write letters

> *"Damn it!" said William. "Anyone would think that this house was run for the benefit of others. Well I tell you that it isn't, It's run for me, me, me, and ME alone!"*

William owes a lot to the real life Henry. There is another scene in the novel when the two families meet and the subject of religion comes up:

> *They were really discussing religion, and William appeared to be attacking all such faith. Or rather Susan seemed to think he was attacking it just because she was defending it.*
> *"Anyway we must all turn fascist," cried William boisterously.*
> *"Why?" she asked.*
> *"To beat communism," said William. "They are the only people who'll give you any action. We need bags of action."*
> *"Which are you talking about?" asked Susan. "The communists or the fascists?"*
> *"Both," said William. "Do listen."*
> *"I was," said Susan. "But I thought we were talking about religion."*
> *"I was," said William. "But we've moved on. Christ!" he exploded, "Doesn't anyone understand me in this house?"*
> *Giles attempted to interpret. "I think he means that religion can't defeat communism, so the only alternative is for us to support fascism – which is capable of defeating communism – so that we may ultimately reintroduce religion."*
> *"No!" shouted William. "Damn religion! We've got to support fascism, and continue to support fascism. Religion can be practised on the sidelines."*

Later still at the same dinner party, Julia is portrayed – from a remembered incident – as offering amyl nitrate capsules round the table for the other guests to break open and inhale. After the high, one of the guests comments about the low:

"On second thoughts, perhaps it was not quite so nice."
Julia sat limp and gasping for breath. "Never mind," she
moaned, "it was worth it while it lasted."

By adult standards, the love scenes between Rowena and David are pretty boring. I depict her as enticingly naughty whilst still prudishly virginal. The concept of the cock-teaser, or professional virgin, had yet to be registered as undesirable within my values.

David's heart was pounding. Where Rowena was now seated, she could not be seen distinctly out of the corner of his eye. He could gather an impression of what she was doing, but he couldn't see her with any precision. And seeing her was for the moment all important. Surreptitiously, and with the greatest care not to be noticed, he gradually turned his head a few inches to a position where he might continue to study her.
But Rowena had seen. "Stop staring at my legs!" she remarked sharply.
David winced like a small boy caught stealing sweets. "I'm not staring at your legs!" he lied – thankful that the night concealed his crimson cheeks.
"You have been staring at my legs for the last two minutes," said Rowena in biting tones.
David swallowed twice in quick succession with the result that he almost choked himself. Flustering for an excuse, he realised that none was at hand. Then to his joy he found that his anger was returning. He turned as best he could and looked at her squarely, waiting while his temper kindled a new light in his eyes.
"God! You're just a bloody conceited little tart!"

This opens up into a full-scale altercation and David might have been better advised to escape from the prospect of any betrothal at this juncture. But of course, that's not the way in which the tale finally gets resolved. As a potential novelist, I was aspiring to present to my readers the tale of a premarital relationship – respectful of a virgin's inhibitions and yet revelling in all the unfulfilled, tantalising anticipation of fully fledged

Henry's abrasive rhetorical style served as inspiration
for my first novel – *The Millions and the Mansions*

copulation. It was a case of not having worked out the subject within my
own mind, so my literary flow was to that extent impeded.

What really comes to the reader's attention is the naïvety of my outlook
upon life. Yet, despite the laborious pace at which the tale unfolds, I still
regard it as an achievement to have completed the arduous task that I had
set myself. Before the end of my National Service, I had this manuscript of
some 50,000 words in my hands. Throughout my life I have met people
who are constantly talking about the book they will one day write –
without ever putting pen to paper, or no more than a few pages. Whatever
my natural talent in these matters – or the lack of it – I now knew that, if
I embarked upon such a task again, I could be sure that I had the tenacity
and perseverance to see it through. And that was an achievement in itself.

At the same time, I had grave doubts as to whether I had written
something that might be appreciated by others. I knew that my friends in
the Life Guards would only ridicule it if I were to show it to them. So I
kept it hidden away in a drawer – fearing greatly that someone might sneak
into my room and set me to ridicule by quoting passages from it in the
officers' mess. Thankfully, this fate never befell me.

Chapter 3.4

Sex: establishing my sexual repute

When I arrived out in Germany at least the whole business of losing my virginity was safely behind me. But I knew there was really very little prospect of developing my sex life any further while I was posted out here at Wolfenbüttel – not with the assistance of genuine girlfriends, that is to say. But the same officers who had made regular trips up to London to visit *The Bag of Nails* soon discovered where they had to go to receive similar services out here.

Actually, it wasn't really the same kind of service. At *The Bag of Nails* we had participated in a pleasant evening, at a night-club, in the company of a young woman who was both pretty and sociable. And what occurred afterwards was in her own private apartments. Here in Brunswick there was a special street where the whores sat at open windows – or lounged against the wall outside – dressed in the flimsiest of underwear, while a crowd of males prowled the cobbled street swapping lewd comments to one another in anticipation of the libidinal meal. After chosing a partner, the financial transaction was quick and, by London prices, cheap: in marks, just a couple of pounds sterling. The curtains were then drawn and copulation delivered, with no time to be lost on what could be her next customer.

As it happens, the street was officially out of bounds to all British troops. If for any reason the military police had stopped me to ask for identification, I was told that the best excuse was to say I was checking up on a rumour that my troopers were visiting the alley… Not that such a showdown was ever likely to occur. The military police were wary of officers, even those who were young and unpromoted.

It was so much a part of traditional upper class behaviour in Britain – that as a young man I should resort to prostitutes if alternative intercourse was not available – that I never felt any pangs of conscience on the issue. I have only seen cause to question my values in life subsequent to this; even then, none too severely. It happened and I leave it at that. And there was no shortage of companions on these trips that I made down to Cobblers' Alley, as we called it.

I had become very friendly with one of my old public school colleagues who hitched lifts with me up to London more frequently than most. We each had our favourite girl in Cobblers' Alley. Mine was called Sonia and it was a help that she could speak English. I could have liked her quite well, if the circumstances and the opportunities had been different. And I think that she took an interest in me, too – probably because someone in the Life Guards must have spotted me visiting her and then told her something about my background. Other officers revealed how she would sometimes enquire after the Herr Baron. It pleased her no doubt that I was always at pains to treat her with respect, in a manner that she informed me she encountered all too rarely.

But there were occasions when Sonia was either occupied or absent. And this led to a variety of questionable experiences – if quite humorous on occasions. There was the time when the lady in question was attempting to get me to enthuse with her on our performance, exclaiming, "*Prima! Prima!*" But in those days my knowledge of German was even less than elementary. *Prima* should be translated as superb or wonderful, as I now know. But at the time I thought the word must relate to the Latin language and that she was asking me if this was the first occasion that I had ever copulated. So I was full of indignation, fiercely retorting: "*Nicht prima! Nein, nicht prima!*" The poor lady looked quite disconsolate.

There were other occasions when I picked up memories that were even less savoury. One, in particular, resulted from my politeness of disposition, in feeling that I had to go through with it after discovering in the full electric light of the room that I had made an error of judgment in my choice. The lady was far older than I had first supposed and I was left with a distasteful record of what followed, a memory that had the vitality to conjure up unpleasant recollections.

Sagging her shrivelled skin and flagging breasts,
she wrestles to embrace my glacial face in a slug's
hug, while I struggle to flick the fingers of her clasping

114

grasp on my **shoul**ders, **heavi**ng to re**trieve** their **freed**om.
Speedily **spun** into **dream fabric**, the **gleam**
of un**sight**ly **night**mare **sears** my **fearful visi**on
with de**risi**on, **cack**led in a **harri**dan's **hard featu**res,
re**plete** with de**caying teeth** and **slime** on the **tongue**.
Her **spongy cunt spews goo**ey **spid**ers,
which **slide side**-step on **gall**oping **hairy legs**,
to **peg** my **palpi**tating **heart** to the **floor**
in a **naus**eous **pool**, con**vuls**ing in **shudd**ers of re**vuls**ion.
    Beneath me lies a skeleton that's mute,
    with flesh disrobed from ribs like rotten fruit.

Brunswick wasn't the only town with a special street like Cobblers' Alley for prostitutes. I took a couple of weekend passes to visit Hamburg and discovered that there was a more elegant class of alley to be found, where some of the ladies were really quite glamorous. But I won't dwell further on these matters. I estimate that there were no more than about ten occasions when I resorted to this method of sexual relief. For the rest of the time it was, as before, masturbation.

In any case the whole novelty of having a prostitute for sex soon palled on me. And towards the end of my time in Germany, I was beginning to perceive that there was too much indignity in resorting to this manner of intercourse. But what it did do was reinforce both my personal and public image as a heterosexual copulatory male. And here one should bear in mind just how vulnerable I had felt on this issue. Stories of my being seen entering Cobblers' Alley certainly reached the ears of my own troopers and there were ribald conversations when they tried vainly to draw me out on what I got up to. In any case, there were no more snide comments from anyone in the Life Guards about my sexual orientation.

But there was a dearth of any sophisticated entertainment, such as might have been available to us if we had still been within easy reach of the London scene. So there was occasionally an element of crudity within the entertainments that we devised for ourselves – as when a group of officers (sometimes including a few of the wives who were stationed out in Wolfenbüttel) would go down to Cobblers' Alley and pay to see a sexual exhibition, consisting of lesbian love-play between two of the fattest and ugliest ladies on the street.

Or there were other occasions when something of an equally crude nature was set up spontaneously within the officers' mess – like the time when Ben, who was an officer's springer spaniel, was furnished with a stool so that he could gain sufficient height to mount Calamity Jane, who was another officer's Great Dane. But as soon as he had achieved his orgasm, someone sadistically kicked away the stool – leaving poor Ben in a vain endeavour to retain his position humped upon her back. Despite falling off, they were unable to disengage from the act of copulation. The only happy note to this story is that Calamity Jane did get pregnant.

I found it interesting to note how the spirit of debauchery was resisted at first by my friend Laurence Kelly. He saw it as contrary to the spirit of Catholicism – such of it as he had acquired during his schooling at Downside. At the time when he was commissioned, he spoke about the fornicatory habits of some of the other officers in terms of them being lapsed Catholics. But it didn't take very long before such judgment ceased… he too had fallen from grace.

I had my own contributions to make to the crudities within the officers' mess: composition of blue verses sung to well-known tunes of the day. I had best draw a curtain over some of these, so as to avoid giving unnecessary offence to the memory of particular contemporaries whom I ridiculed and lampooned in verse. But on a milder note, I furnished the words for a rendering of the song "Sweet Violets" – some of them were taken from a fragment that one of the officers had heard sung in a London cabaret, but I composed the rest of the verses so as to complete the song's bawdy intent.

> There once was a farmer who sat by a rick,
> teaching his nephew to play with his...
> catapult and arrows and such things of yore,
> when over the yard came what looked like a .....
> milkmaid called Mary, who walked like a duck;
> she persuaded the farmer to have a good .....
> look for his cows, as an organized hunt
> would find them, and then she would sell him her .....
> Chorus:
> Sweet violets, sweeter then all the roses,
> covered all over, each little bit,
> covered all over with .....
> sweet violets.

It continued in the same vein for another two verses.

It was one thing to have acquired a reputation as an officer who "liked his bit of skirt", but it was quite another to be someone who could count on getting "a free roger". There were not great opportunities for such things out here. But many of us held high expectations for what might happen when we took a holiday up in Scandinavia – in Copenhagen, to be more precise. There was much talk about free love being a way of life up there and the thought of it excited us British, especially the ones who had only recently left school. It was as if we had anticipated that the end of the war would have thrown open the doors to revolution in sexual matters, but we were finding it to be disappointingly slow in its appearance upon the scene.

Anyway, I teamed up with Bendor Drummond and Rivvy Llewellyn-Davies in August for a trip to Copenhagen. We were travelling the 400 odd miles in Bendor's car and he was a most dangerous driver. There was one particular point where we all felt lucky to get round a corner on screeching tyres, where to have left the road over the edge of a steep drop would have meant probable death. But I dare say we valued life less at that age.

Another memorable episode was on one of the ferry crossings. There was a fierce little skipper in charge of the ferry and he gesticulated to Bendor to move his car into a preferred position, which provoked Rivvy to exclaim, "What a bastard!" The ferryman, who couldn't have been much more than five foot tall, obviously had a smattering of English and took offence at this and started screaming at Rivvy, "What? You call me bastard? I understand you! I fight you! Stand up here! I hit you!"

This was all most un-British and took Rivvy completely by surprise – especially in that the man had now reached in through the car window to grab him by his tie. Rivvy was apparently looking to me to do something about it, given that I had a certain reputation as a boxer – but I was damned if I was going to fight other people's battles for them. It was Bendor who redeemed the situation. With an expression of supreme complacency, he enquired of the ferryman: "Now what's the matter? I think there has been some mistake. Nobody has called you a bastard. All he said was: 'We've passed it!' You know – the line. You were telling me to park closer to the line."

The ferryman was now drowning in this foreign language. He released his grip on Rivvy's tie and the tension lifted. But it had been a close shave and one that impressed me considerably with regard to the sparky ferocity in the Danish character.

By the time we arrived in Copenhagen it was late in the evening and we had quite a problem to find anywhere with a room left vacant, so we ended up sharing one between the three of us. We had only two nights to our credit, so we launched straight into the business of trying to find ourselves a free roger. I won't dwell at any length on our frustrations. After visiting half a dozen bars and night-clubs to no avail, we were becoming depressed. Scandinavian girls appeared to be no different to any others that we'd met, when it came to declining sexual advances. Bendor and myself eventually decided to waste no further time by returning to the hotel. When we were finally joined by Rivvy, however, he spun us a tale of the marvellous sexual adventure he had experienced shortly after our departure. We had him recount the story in all its details to us.

Apparently he had gone to sit in a late night cafeteria, where he had espied an attractive girl reading a book at a neighbouring table. He had asked her what book it was and the conversation led on to her inviting him to come back to her flat with her. Shortly after that, she had changed into "something more comfortable", which turned out to be a nightdress. And shortly after that, they were making love.

It didn't really occur to me that Rivvy might be making it all up as he went along. And in response to my lascivious questions, the story was embellished with even more exciting detail – like the positions from the *Kama Sutra* into which they had experimentally ventured. He made it all sound so easy that, amongst other things, put Bendor and myself to shame. So we were both very much on our mettle when it came to the second night's outing. We needed to display our seductive proficiency or we stood to lose face when the stories were recounted back in the officers' mess.

We kept to our own devices on this occasion. My own endeavours met with abysmal failure, similar to my previous experience. Bits of it were quite humiliating – like the way women were cadging drinks off me at the bar and then slipping away with absurd comments about just having spotted that their husbands had arrived. And there was one tart who kept asking me if I was a *"bucker"* – which I failed to comprehend until it dawned upon me that she was mispronouncing "bugger". I was being taken for a homosexual once again. There was something too passive in my whole approach to this business. It discouraged me greatly and I didn't wait around for much more of it.

Once the others returned to the hotel, however, I had them both telling me how they'd scored successes in their seductive attempts. Bendor claimed that he'd had a virgin in the back seat of his car and Rivvy had the nerve to claim that he'd had the best roger of his life. I was told how he'd gone back to a girl's flat only to find that there was a second girl waiting for them. My constant questioning as to what exactly had taken place soon laid me open to Rivvy's ridicule. "Why are you so interested, Alex? Is it that you've never had a free roger?" I hoped that in replying that I probably hadn't had as many as himself, I was managing to circumvent the need for an admission.

Back at Wolfenbüttel, I sensed that not all the officers were prepared to swallow Rivvy's vaunted account of his sexual exploits. In fact, he became strangely silent in the face of their cynicism. But it was my sheer insecurity that rendered me so gullible. I was unable to discount the veracity of all that he said as, especially in this unknown territory, I perceived myself as deficient in sex appeal.

Only one officer noted the nature of my inner discomfort and this was Jan Barnes. He told me that he, too, as a young subaltern, had doubted that the day would ever arrive when sexual seductions would come easily to him. He was now a captain and he assured me that the time would come when the complications would disappear. "You'll have successes all right. Everything will eventually fall into place for you." I noted his words, but I wondered if he really understood just how much ground I had to make up before my techniques in seduction might be regarded as mature.

It was the absence of sufficient womenfolk out there in Germany that rendered my sex life so frustrating. It is true that there were the occasional visits from girls back in London, invited to stay by one of the officers' wives who had accompanied the Regiment to Germany. I wasn't really in a position to suggest that anyone should receive such an invitation. I just had to sit back and watch whom the others might persuade to come out and visit them.

One of my principal concerns was to ensure that my name didn't simply get forgotten by all those hostesses in London... after all it was through them that I was going to meet beautiful young debutantes once I was back on the scene. So I felt that I should try to make some impression on their memories, from my distant exile, with eccentrically worded answers to the numerous invitations to dances that were sent to me. They took the following form.

> *Lord Weymouth thanks Lady Xenia for her kind invitation to... but he regrets that his Squadron-Leader is being exceedingly troublesome at the moment, refusing all his applications for leave until such a time as his inefficiency as a troop-leader has decreased. So Lord Weymouth is extremely unlikely to be able to attend – although there is still a remote possibility that he might.*

I was always careful to keep the possibility open that I might suddenly turn up on the scene, imagining that it would give them something to think about, or even hope for. In any case it would keep them wondering about the nature of my personality and encourage them perhaps to issue other invitations at a later date.

What came as a setback, however, was a letter from Caroline Child-Villiers to say that she was engaged to Gibby (Viscount) Melgund, who was Dommie Elliot's elder brother. I didn't know him personally, but it came as a surprise to me that things in Caroline's life could have moved so fast during this brief spell that I had been away. I regretted it of course, inasmuch as it cut back on my options. The truth of the matter, though, is that my sights were set upon Xenia, so I knew how I had no right to feel slighted. Indeed, I wrote Caroline a warm letter of congratulations.

Chapter 3.5

Worship: agnosticism

The two years that I had spent in the army certainly were not a time for spiritual development. But, anyway, I was no longer sure of my commitments in that field. I had gone through my religious phase comparatively early in life – around the age of eleven. But I had been veering towards agnosticism since then. Let me contrast this with the attitude of one of my contemporaries, Alaistair Thompson. We first met when we both arrived as Potential Officers from the Household Cavalry for that first period in our training at Caterham.

Most of us slept the nights in our army underwear of singlet and pants. Alaistair was one of the few who had brought his pyjamas with him, and actually saw fit to wear them. This could easily have laid him open to ridicule, but he was more "together" – more mature – as an adult than most of us. And he had a sense of dignity that, while it sometimes bordered upon pomposity, rendered him less vulnerable perhaps to the taunts of lesser mortals. Though falling just short of a grading that would have got him awarded the Stick of Honour at Mons, he still managed to pass out above the rest of us. But this story concerns his very first days of National Service, when his self-confidence might have been expected to be at a low point.

He had mentioned in conversation how someone of his school acquaintance (from Winchester) had boldly set the pattern of conduct for the Brigade Squad of his day, by kneeling beside his bed in prayer each night for a full minute before going to bed. It was an example that others gradually took upon themselves to follow – until the whole squad had adopted the habit of praying beside their beds last thing at night. Now, the story was told to us as an example that he assumed we'd all admire, but all that I noted was a nervous giggle or two.

What we hadn't anticipated was that Alaistair probably intended to attempt the same act of leadership with ourselves. In the event, the experiment didn't work out quite so well. He kept it up for about three nights, without anyone following suit. Then the Trained Soldier – who must have concluded that he was losing out on his example-setting role – decided he should put a stop to it. So he said: "What the heck does Thompson think he's up to?" And Alaistair eventually replied: "I'm saying my prayers, Trained Soldier." There were some scoffing and mutterings, but that was the last time that Alaistair put on such a public performance of his religiosity.

In spite of the fact that he had made a fool of himself, I admired his courage in sticking out his neck like that. At the same time I felt critical of his stand. What his action had amounted to was a bid to shame us into an affirmation of the Christian faith, through our fear of getting left out from the drive towards conformity that he had inspired. There was something in this attitude that militated against individualism. It didn't seek to win such affirmation by reason, to promote understanding; indeed, by its call to follow the believer's example, it was contrary to the demands of rational debate. Alaistair might well have interjected that Christ only set an example. But as an embryonic individualist, I already knew that this was probably not the right kind of religion for me.

After I had rejoined the Regiment, first at Combermere and then at Wolfenbüttel, the two friends of mine who were the most concerned about their Christian faith were Tim Sainsbury and Laurence Kelly: the former a Protestant and the latter a Catholic. I observed their positional stances when in argument with interest, but without any wish to take sides. But the gist of it was that Tim saw his religion in the light of social example: the Church as the mode of promoting the right kind of values within the community and something in which we should all play our contributory part. But Laurence saw his as the only true vehicle of Christ's message and was anxious to bolster his own doubts by persuading us all to come over to his viewpoint.

It would have been much more appropriate if the likes of them had been ordered to attend the Christian Leadership course but, as so often happens in these matters, the choice of who should go was dictated by the Squadron Leader's convenience. I was detailed to go – along with Miles Burkitt from C Squadron – because at that time I was the officer in D Squadron whom Nipper was most happy to dispense.

But I wasn't happy at being sent on this course. Somehow I didn't feel that I was ready in my own mind yet for a discussion on the subject of religion. I wanted to be left free to observe the world for a while, without being required to dispute what I should or should not believe. Nonetheless, the padre expected me to respond to his talks by airing my own views on the subject. This I was reluctant to do. The nearest that I came to participating was in leaving a letter for the padre in which I explained that my greatest inhibition against accepting the Christian message as anything more than great moral teaching, lay in my inability to accept the divinity of Christ. I regarded it as absurd to suggest that any man, born of a woman, should somehow be the son of God. And I preferred not to open myself to contrary conviction on that issue – not for the time being, that is to say. Until I might choose to raise such subjects for debate of my own accord, I preferred to be left to my own doubts.

Other than that, there is little else that I can add with regard to my beliefs over this period in my life.

Chapter 3.6

Parents and siblings:
rumours of pending divorce

When I first arrived at Wolfenbüttel, I hoped there might be a chance to get released three months early from the Life Guards, which would have enabled me to go up to Oxford in October of that year. My demobilisation at the beginning of January wasn't going to suit my plans very well, in that it would leave me with nine months on my hands without any specific ideas on how best to fill them. I had, in fact, explained all this to my father before leaving home and he had promised to enquire from his friends in White's Club if any strings could be pulled to excuse me from those final months of my National Service. And he did make some enquiries in this direction through his friend Anthony Head, who was then a Tory Minister.

But it turned out that things were no longer quite as they once were – my reasons for a remission of my National Service term would have to be better than any I could offer. It was evident that I would have to give some deeper thought to the problem of how to spend the period between my demobilisation and my going up to Oxford. I raised the question in a letter home, in April.

> *About the army, I have really given up by now the hope of getting out early. It is probably all for the best. If I am going to try for the diplomatic service, I shall need to speak French pretty well. And the best way to do this would be for me to live in Paris for a while. And as an*

occupation during this time, I'd like to go to an art school – so that if I fail for the Foreign Office, I'll have something for which I've trained for me to fall back on...

It should be noted that the idea was still in my head that I was going to try to get into the Foreign Office. To become an artist was merely a second string to my ambitions at that time. On the other hand Henry was beginning to feel that he should discourage me from the whole idea. He wrote:

If you are really adamant in wishing to get into the Diplomatic Service – which I don't personally agree with – then you really must work now you are in Germany, and learn to speak German, because you will find it will take much longer than three months even to learn a smattering of that language.

It is curious that I made no effort whatsoever to learn to speak German while I was out there albeit there was time on my hands to do so. On the other hand, no one else in the officers' mess did either and any roles that demanded such a facility fell to those who could speak German before they arrived. Henry's own idea as to what I should do with my life after leaving the army was that I should get quickly into a real business concern – so that I could start accumulating money for Longleat. He wrote:

I want to have a long talk with you about your future plans – including the whole question of you going up to Oxford... We must have a lengthy discussion about your future life as a whole.

This looked a bit ominous. But I confined myself in my reply to the issue of going to Paris.

I still think that Paris would be the right place for me to learn French. And I'll want something to keep me occupied while I'm out there. So that something might just as well be an art school.

125

These issues were shelved for the time being. But it is noticeable how my relationship with Henry, now that we were not actually required to see one another, appeared to be warming up nicely. The subject of health perhaps, is discussed rather too frequently in our exchange of letter. There had always been this tendency towards hypochondria in his attitude to life and it could be that dutifully I was beginning to follow in his footsteps. I had written in March:

> *Please ask Donald to send me out a large size container of Carter's little liver pills. And I recommend them to you Dad, provided you don't keep up the prescribed dose for too long, as that would give you dia-rear – however you spell it!*

Henry's reply was full of his own complaints.

> *I have just come back from a fortnight in the South of France, seeing the doctor who was supposed to be able to cure my sciatica. Unfortunately he has not done me much good, although I am a little easier. I am beginning to get desperate, as I feel that I am going to be perpetually lame for the rest of my life. I am still trying however to see other doctors, and hope by the next time I write to you, things will have improved.*

The note of hypochondria even infringes upon what are intended as humorous uttering in my letters back home – as can be noted in the one I posted as an Easter greeting. There is an element of facetiousness which strikes a very wrong note when I come to read it today.

> *I hope that all the Easter blessings will cause the ills of the flesh – and of the spirit – to depart from you for this life henceforward, and for ever more!*

I should point out that this merely reciprocated the element of facetiousness that Henry himself displayed, although in his case it was generally delivered with a more discernible charm.

What troubled me somewhat was that all of my mail over this period came from Henry, and none at all from Daphne. My letters home display repeated enquiries as to what had happened to her. I knew, in fact, that she was away in Crete with Xan Fielding and I rather suspected that this was something that Henry didn't wish to talk about. So I left it at that. But it was most unlike her to communicate so little with me. All I received was the occasional postcard – almost as if she was using the relative silence as some kind of a smoke-screen to prevent me discerning what was truly happening in her life.

It was in a letter from Caroline that I gleaned the only real news – and even then it was only hinted. She wrote something to the following effect:

> *Won't it be horrible if the divorce really takes place? Mum and Dad have been married for such ages that it's impossible to think of them otherwise. Anyway I doubt if all the rumours are true.*

Well, this certainly put the possibility in my mind, although I continued to discount it – notwithstanding a comment or two from the likes of Nick Beaumont, on return from leave in London, that my parents weren't supposed to be getting on very well together. I was too far removed from the scene to worry about these matters.

Caroline's first baby – Harry – had been born in May. So they now had a son, who stood to inherit Badminton House and the dukedom – third in line after David and David's father, Bobby Somerset, that is to say. But the present Duke of Beaufort, their cousin, was still very much alive.

The news on Christopher was less good. He had been in trouble previously at Eton, for making copy in his own handwriting of some pornographic limericks, which were taken from one of the first editions in Henry's personal library at Sturford. And he was careless enough to leave these lying around in his room, where they were found and passed on to his tutor. I know not what punishment he received, but he was treated with lenience. Perhaps Jaques saw it as being similar to my own past crime, harbouring *The Encyclopaedia of Sex Practices* within my boot locker. But there was now a second incident, which got him into further trouble. Christopher told me about it in one of his very rare letters to me. Once again it can be viewed perhaps as an attempt on his part to recreate my own former glories.

> *The 4th of June was terrible. After the first procession of boats, the cox ran over my straw hat – [for he now had his Lower Boats] – and I shall have to buy a new one. The Lord Londonderry gave me about six Pimms, laced with gin. At Masters I got hold of a bottle of what I thought was cider and, having drunk it, was told it was*

champagne. I thought I was quite all right, but Mr
Herbert insisted on helping me into the boat. I told the crew
that I was going to swamp them, so Barnard, who was the
captain of the boat, ordered me not to row. So I didn't, and
just sat there. But when we got to the top and turned round,
they threw away my oar and told me to swim and get it. I
did, and they tried to set off without me. But I managed to
get back into the boat – without my oar. I did not stand up
when told to by the cox, and then shouted at him saying that
he had forgotten about me. I nearly pushed Barnard
overboard, but after that all went well. But Herbert insisted
on helping me out of the boat again.
After the Procession, we went to the Burning Bush, where
Tom Brocklebank was stopping anyone from getting near to
it. He told me to go away twice, and said he would give me
a Georgic [lines: usually copying out untold verses of Virgil].
Then an Old Etonian tried to take my hat, and there was
rather a fight. After that I went and climbed up the statue of
the founder, and then we pulled down a wall near
Martineau's After this I went to bed. I was woken up by
Jaques at 1.30 saying that I had been reported, and he
wanted to know what I had been drinking. I was on the
Headmaster's bill, and have had my Henley leave stopped,
and have to stay here until 1.30 on the Friday of Long Leave.
Nick Vivian has had the sack for going to drinking
parties, and Charlie Wilson has had the sack for getting
tight at Marlow. Isn't our family doing well?

I know not if these events had any direct bearing on Christopher's decision to leave Eton at the end of the half – one half earlier than had originally been intended. But there was certainly some additional reason for taking such a course in that his godfather – Brendan Bracken (a close colleague of Churchill during the war) – had been asked if he could find an English lord to join up with a party of university students, who had been invited to tour America as some kind of a publicity stunt for Sears Roebuck, the well-known mail order firm in the States. Christopher was delighted at this chance of joining their number and spent the next few months travelling around America with them.

The news on Valentine had been rather more enigmatic. He had been at Eton for more than a year now – having passed in at Middle Fourth, as I

Henry always encouraged us to shoot.
I eventually turned against it – in the army!

myself had done. But I learnt he was now in Henry's bad books because he had gone on a letter-writing strike. Henry was unused to such tactics and had tried nearly every possible device to oblige him to send letters home. Both fines and bribes had been attempted; he had even been put to do extra work in the woods during the holidays. But little Valentine remained stubbornly disobedient, so that Henry was now at his wits' end. It was at this juncture that I wrote to Henry, urging him to take a softer line.

> *Poor Valentine will be having dismal holidays. You should consider this. You have always argued that character is the product of treatment rather than heredity. And you complain that his behaviour at Eton is hopelessly idle. So you take repressive measures against him. In fact you have been taking increasingly repressive measures against him for several years. But the net result appears to be increasing idleness. So doesn't this indicate to you that the treatment may be wrong? That his stubborn idleness is actually caused by the treatment? That reverse treatment might produce the reverse effect? You give Valentine no time to recover from all the discipline he encounters at school. Indeed, he experiences more punishments in his home life than he does in his school life. Consequently, you find him in a continual state of opposition.*

In his reply of 15th August 1952, Henry wrote:

> *I have earnestly and seriously considered the suggestions made in your letter about poor little Valentine, but I'm afraid I still have to disagree with you. He started his three weeks work in the woods last Monday. I am very glad to have to tell you that he has improved beyond all recognition lately. He has at last developed a mind of his own!*

This last point was a reference to the jokes we all made about him being little more than Christopher's sidekick. It had indeed seemed at times that he didn't have much of an independent personality. But with Christopher now touring America, the situation had apparently been transformed. It had little to do with the imposition of additional holiday work, as it pleased Henry to suppose.

PART FOUR

FINAL
TRIUMPHS

Chapter 4.1

Authority: on the turn of the tide

I was actually beginning to enjoy myself in the Life Guards, and I should have been quite content to stay out in Germany for the remaining three months of my National Service. But I had put my name down for the Boxing course – something that I regretted once I had been informed that the whole business culminated in having the honour to participate in the Army Officers' Boxing Competitions... But I couldn't possibly withdraw at this belated stage without losing face. And in my appreciation of the fact that I really had no alternative but to go through with it, I decided that it was best to do so with an air of apparent indifference.

When I returned home it was to find that Chris had just arrived home from the States, much thrilled by his travels and full of stories about how different the Americans were to us British. He had brought home for me a gift: a gold watch, which he had been sold on Brooklyn Bridge! As I saw it he was fobbing off on me the stigma of his gullibility – not that he admitted it. I accepted it without gratitude and never, in fact, wore it.

All the entrants had to undergo a fortnight's intensive training at Aldershot, which provided us with ample time to size up our potential opponents. But there were so few entrants this year that it was decided to promote only two contenders for each weight. I didn't manage to get myself eliminated on these grounds and so I faced one fight for the championship.

Chris came to Aldershot with Henry to watch me win my weight. He took some delightful photographs of the bout that I still treasure to this day. They told me that I was emitting snarling noises whenever I swung my punches. My one disappointment was that Daphne was still abroad and so couldn't be there to witness my triumph. But I knew the others were greatly impressed, and it was always so important to me that I should succeed in impressing Henry.

I suddenly found myself being hailed as the new Army Officers' welterweight boxing champion for 1952. Then the press got hold of this information and made a big thing of it – "Viscount wins title" and all that kind of nonsense. Congratulations began to pour in, and I was careful not to disillusion anyone as to the amateurish tenor of these competitions. But I regret making one comment that was reported. An evening paper phoned me at Sturford to check that it was indeed myself who had been listed as the winner. When the reporter was chatting with me he was using boxing jargon, which I was unaccustomed to following and, in trying to, I used an unfortunate phrase. The paper quoted me as saying, "I just couldn't finish him off." Which must have infuriated my opponent, David Townshend, who had put up some fierce opposition to me in the ring.

There was one letter in particular, though, which warmed the cockles of my heart, in that it came from my former drill-sergeant at Caterham. It is worth quoting.

> *Dear Viscount Weymouth,*
>
> *I am writing to congratulate you on becoming the officers' new Welterweight champion. I was delighted to read of your success as printed in 'The Star'. Trained Soldier Stapleford and I have often laughed and chatted about yourself and the remainder of the squad. I said to him on Friday: "Well we have trained a champ. His reply was 'Blank-blank! Xxxxx!'"*
> *I see you are spending a spot of leave at home now. I trust that you will enjoy yourself, sir. Once again my hearty congratulations, and best wishes for your future.*
>
> *I remain sir, your obedient servant*
>
> *D.McMahon, Sgt.*

But the role of champion had fallen upon me somewhat too suddenly for me to feel comfortable with such an appellation. I knew too well that I had only got there by default, on minimal effort, and that I wasn't the courageous bruiser that people seemed to expect. I certainly wasn't going to let myself in for any of the club's fixtures, as they also semed to expect – to fight against the other armed services, such as Oxford and Cambridge and other such institutions. I steadfastly refused all such demands. I had paid the price of obtaining for myself a few weeks in England and as far as I was concerned that was the end of the matter. They could damn well find their pugilists elsewhere.

Then I fell sick with glandular fever. I was bedridden for several days without Dr Graham-Campbell diagnosing precisely what it was. Sore throat and earache were the principal symptoms. But I found it most uncomfortable, and lay in my bed groaning. I was now using a bedroom on the front side of the house, relatively near to the drawing-room, and Henry complained that my groans were disrupting the peace of the household.

The upsetting part was that he seemed to believe that I was faking the whole illness. He had never forgiven me for obliging him, three years previously, to fly me back from the South of France with, what had been proclaimed to be a broken neck, but which his own doctor later pronounced as nothing more than torn neck muscles. And, with slightly better justification, he might choose to remind me of the high temperatures that had laid me low at the time when I was about to take up my duties as a newly commissioned officer. One thing he had always hated was to be conned (It made him feel so silly). So he was most unsympathetic to my display of suffering on this occasion. Nor was he sufficiently apologetic once the ailment had been fully diagnosed.

I never managed to identify any particular friend who had given it to me, but I decided – as this malady is usually transmitted while kissing – it must have resulted from a recent visit to a prostitute. The encounter occurred during one of my trips to London immediately after the boxing competitions. Incidentally this turned out to be my last such visit: as my personal sex life was now on the brink of becoming slightly more successful, I could now dispense with prostitutes. But the fever turned out to be a blessing in disguise. While recovering from it, I learnt that I was entitled to some sickness leave – quickly authenticated with a signature from my doctor on an appropriate form, which was then dispatched to the Adjutant back at Wolfenbüttel. This meant that as soon as I felt well enough I could begin to live it up again socially; but I will come to that in the next chapter...

There was one unexpected call that added a slight counterweight to my present balance of good fortune. I received a surprise telephone call from Captain Taylor, who was the secretary of the Army Officers' Boxing Club. I had made it quite clear to him when at Aldershot that it was really just

My bout with David Townshend, which I won on points. My younger brother Christopher, who was at Eton at the time, took the photographs

an accident of circumstances that I found myself as their welterweight champion and that I had no intention of representing the club in any of their fixtures. But he was now phoning me to apply the pressure in getting me to change my mind – with some particular contest lined up for the coming week. I iterated that I could not be persuaded. So, he enquired with a sneer in his voice, "So you're scared, are you?" And in what must rank as one of the braver responses in my life, I replied, "Yes!" – and rang off.

But the truth of the matter is that his taunt had got through to me. I felt emasculated by it and thoroughly uncertain as to what my innermost state of mind might be. It hadn't actually occurred to me to tell him that I was in the process of recovering from glandular fever, so wouldn't even obtain medical clearance to fight if I tried. In any case, that would only have postponed the issue. He would simply have waited until I had recuperated and then rung me again. But I didn't like it that my courage was thus being held in question – motivated though the taunt may have been. In fact, I was in two minds about telephoning him back to say that I'd do as he wished. I was at least thinking about it and I discussed the matter with Henry over dinner.

His own line was that it would be sheer madness. But I balked on agreeing with him, putting it in doubt as to what my intentions might be. Henry was now growing angry with me, but he now made the error of becoming authoritarian. "Well if you won't listen to reason, then you must listen to me as your father. I order you to say *no* to them."

This brought me up short and I didn't like it. His issue of a directive like that threw us right back into the kind of relationship that I had been hoping had been left behind. Maybe I did want to be persuaded to that end by reason, but I'd suddenly been wrong-footed in this entire discussion. What I now needed to do was to disobey him. Yet that would entail my acceptance of Captain Taylor's challenge – when I didn't actually want to do that. Suddenly I realised the impossibility of continuing with the subject in any manner whatsoever, so I just got up and left the room. But it had left me feeling badly inside, for more than just one single reason. And I knew that it must now remain a subject that was closed between the two of us. It was clear to me, though, that I had to await better opportunities to display my disobedience.

But the news of my success was well received by the Life Guards. On returning to Germany, I was hailed as a bit of a hero. And the less I said about my achievement, the more glorious they assumed it to be. My silence was even interpreted as modesty. People suddenly discovered that traits they had formerly attributed to eccentricity were in fact rather endearing. And they began digging for other qualities in what had previously been regarded as barren ground.

I also had the satisfaction of receiving an apology from CoH Bobbit, who had been scurrilous in his comments about me when acting temporarily as my Corporal of Horse during those manoeuvres at Combermere. He had then blamed me wholeheartedly for all the misfortunes that had come his way and he had gone round the squadron giving everyone his undiluted opinion of me. Well, he now came up to me, during a visit to the NCOs' mess, and insisted on buying me a drink. He was a little tight but he wanted my assurance that I bore him no ill will – something I gave him readily enough. He also made it clear to everyone that he had "misjudged" me.

It was much the same with Corporal-Major Radcliffe, who had once booked me for being late on parade. He didn't actually apologise – he would never do that – but he talked about the matter indirectly. "You know sir, there are two sorts of officer. Some are good on the parade ground, and some are good on the battlefield. I think we all know which category you belong to, sir." Well, that was good enough for me.

As far as my own troop was concerned, I could do nothing wrong now. They considered themselves to be the finest unit in the squadron and they seemed to think that this made me the finest troop-leader. During my last few days with the Regiment, at the NAAFI party on Christmas Day, they gave me a rousing farewell, trying to hoist me on their shoulders while singing "For He's a Jolly Good Fellow", and all that kind of thing. I managed to transform it into some kind of "Ring-a-Ring-o' Roses" dance, in which we could all equally participate. But the flattering signal they were communicating was clear enough for everyone present to read. And they could all take note just how very different our present spirit was in contrast to what had once prevailed. I felt quite sentimental at the idea of leaving them.

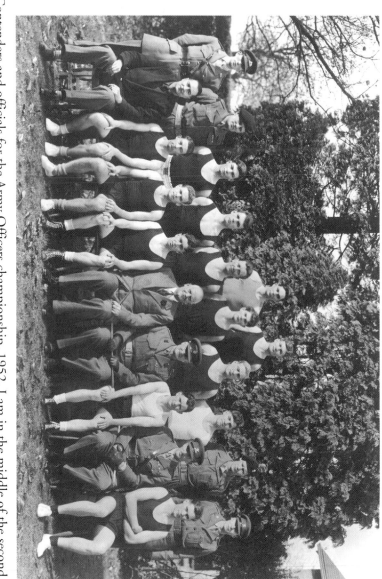

Contenders and officials for the Army Officers championship, 1952. I am in the middle of the second row – my opponent Captain David Townshend of the Royal Engineersis behind me and to my left. We are still friends

Turning an eye to each uncertain face,
I placed them in mind like a new deck of cards;
hard lidless expressions, dressed to assess
the measure of my own humanity and power of command.
Granted the insight of fretful retrospection,
direct from recollection of details where our feet
were ground down into rolling stubs, and our bodies
trodden in shit, it's fine that smiles can shine.
Entwined together in a single silken skein,
it's plain to see that confraternal bonds,
fondly – if without affection – unite my troop's
grouping to a comrade fellowship in arms.
    It never fell to us to fight a foe,
    but if we had, such butchery they'd know!

It would be difficult for me to claim that I had actually made a success of the army. But I knew that the tide of failure had been turned. If I had remained with the Regiment for an additional year, I might yet have emerged as the best subaltern that the place had ever seen. There may still have been those amongst my peer group who regarded me as an utter cunt, but I knew that I had won the esteem of my own troop and of the senior NCOs. In time I felt that the others would surely have followed suit.

The stigma of the low grading at Mons had now, in my own judgment, been absolved. Things had been pretty tough for me at one point and my self-confidence had certainly been shaken. But I had no reason to conclude that my former faith in myself had been misplaced. The old pattern was emerging again. I had the capacity to succeed – no matter where or in what. And the feeling of relief was enormous.

Chapter 4.2
Sex: in quest for love

The Boxing course at Aldershot furnished me with an opportunity to discover how things now stood between myself and the various girls I'd left behind. There was nothing that I could do about it until after the competitions. But then I was due to take a fortnight's leave and after that we would see.

There were two other cavalry officers in these competitions – Cecil Paynter and David Weir. And it was they who suggested that we go up to London for a celebration binge once the ordeal was over, with each of us inviting his girlfriend to attend. My own secret problem was that I didn't really have a girlfriend, upon whom I could rely to accept such a date. It turned out to be a vain hope that Xenia might accept the invitation when I telephoned, although I cannot remember what excuse she found to decline. So I then tried phoning Venetia, with greater success – despite the fact that I hadn't even written to her while I'd been out in Germany. But, accept she did, so my face was saved.

The evening hardly ranked as a success. For one thing I arrived late at the theatre, so that Venetia got the impression that I was standing her up or even passing her off with a blind date. Apparently there had been some icy exchanges of conversation before I belatedly took my seat. But the atmosphere thawed out now that I had arrived. We even went on to *The Carousel* afterwards, where it was evident that she was endeavouring to be most attentive to me. But when the evening came to an end, I had to arrange for the others to give her a lift back to the flat where she was staying – since I was dependent for my own transport on the motorbike that I had borrowed (*Roger the Rover* still being out in Germany). Venetia looked at me with wide, reproachful eyes – after which the relationship once again ran out of gas. Nevertheless, the effect of the new title upon my sex appeal was indubitably advantageous – despite the fact that Venetia had proclaimed that the three of us fell far short of the pugilistic stereotype that she might have expected.

What really boosted my sex appeal was being mentioned in the press as the Army Officers' new welterweight boxing champion. The difference it made became apparent when I accepted a weekend invitation with the Crawleys. Just one year ago, Sarah seemed to have precious little time to spare on me. But everyone now seemed to recollect how I'd been quite a glamorous figure at Eton; they were equally prepared, as well, to give me all the encouragement that I might demand with regard to my future aspirations.

I made quite considerable progress with Sarah sexually, on the evening we were left alone together in the drawing-room, after the others had gone to bed. But she stopped me gently when I moved to climb on top of her and she didn't volunteer any genital stimulation for me. As I see now, it was a situation that I mishandled through inexperience. And as a result I think it was an opportunity missed.

Caroline and Gibby Melgund's wedding took place up in London at this juncture, and the Mayfair set were all present. I caught her eye as she walked back down the aisle on this stranger's arm and it struck me that her expression was apologetic. In any case, I wished them well. I failed to win the attention of Xenia at the reception. But I did obtain an invitation to join a theatre party that was being organised for Serena, Neil Dunne's older sister; I was invited as her date in particular.

I had always liked Serena but had never felt romantic towards her. But she was full of animation at the nightclub to which her father took us all afterwards and this increased with the quantity of champagne that she was drinking. Indeed she was known to have been drinking a little too much over the course of the London season that year – though I dare say I was not far behind her. Anyway, there came a point when she looked at me with sparkling eyes and exclaimed that she thought she was about to fall in love with me. Unwisely, I told her that this would be delightful. And later, when dropping her back home in a taxi, I kissed her briefly.

Next there was an invitation from Serena to come over to Stock Farm, her mother's house in Wiltshire and – joy of joys! – it was said that Xenia would be bringing along a party of friends. I accepted with alacrity. I discovered that we had the run of the house to ourselves that evening. But my problem, as indeed I should have anticipated, was that Serena intended me as her partner, rather than Xenia's. This led to complications of course. And when Serena discovered that my attentions were not for herself, she began knocking it back – and she was very soon quite plastered.

Meanwhile Xenia, who had brought over with her (amongst others) a lugubrious young man, was flirting with me discretely enough not to antagonise Serena. She kept on telling me earnestly – while gazing at me with those huge, deep set, grey eyes of hers – that I ought to go over and give Serena a little encouragement. Finally, there was a bit of a scene that led to Serena seeking sanctuary in the kitchen, reportedly in tears. So I was able to sit there in silence – whereupon Xenia decided that she ought to take her own party back home. Before she left, however, I was able to fix up a date with her in London; after which I was able to return to Sturford in an elated frame of mind.

During the short time that remained of my sick-leave, I took Xenia out on two occasions – ending up at *The Carousel* each time. She was definitely encouraging me and I responded fervently. When taking her back in a taxi the first time, to the address where she was staying, I did get round to kissing her. But I did it too roughly – as she subsequently informed me. Apparently I clutched too savagely at her breast, and she felt nervous about letting me go further – even wondering if I had sadistic inclinations. But she still accepted my second invitation. And when I kissed her this time, I was at pains not to be rough with her. She promised to write to me when I was back at Wolfenbüttel. I was now in a state of ecstasy since it did truly seem that there was someone (at long last) whom I could describe as my girlfriend.

In point of fact, there wasn't much time at all before my demobilisation was due to take place. I was even hoping that they might decide it wasn't worth all the trouble and expense of transporting me out there again. But I was hoping for too much on that score. I went out there for what really amounted to nothing more than the Christmas and New Year festivities. And indeed, it was a glorious time for me in that I had the pleasure of savouring all the revised estimates of my worth, so I was able to feel that I was a popular and esteemed human being once again.

Not that I was left without any cause for anxiety, however, because I received one piece of information that I found quite disconcerting. There was a lot of toing and froing between England and Wolfenbüttel. One friend of Xenia's, Mariette, was one of our crowd who came out regularly. The previous summer she was said to have been greatly smitten with Christo Phillipson, which unfortunately was unrequited. But when Christo went back to London for a spot of leave, I suspect that he excused his lack of attentiveness to her by claiming that his heart was taken by Xenia. So Mariette was much subdued by the time she came out for her Christmas visit.

I must have told her that I was in love with Xenia and was probably enthusing too openly to her upon her rival's qualities. Mariette's initial line was that I ought to be careful, as there was madness in her family. But I replied quite cheerfully to this one: there was also madness in mine. So she went on to warn me against her in more authoritative terms, claiming that she was only telling me what came from Xenia in person. It seemed that Mariette had approached Xenia to discover how definite the relationship was that Christo had proclaimed was theirs, only to be told that there was virtually no relationship whatsoever – or only an amicable one. To reinforce the point, Xenia had told her that everyone knew how she was in love with someone else.

Who my rival might be was kept a secret from me. But I wrote to Xenia intimating what Mariette had said, while probing to discover more. She wrote in reply that she had met Mariette and told her that the rumoured engagement to Christo was a fantasy. But it turned out that my original suspicion of the source of the rumour was wrong. It was not Christo who had told Mariette that his heart was taken by by Xenia but Denis Daley, who was infatuated with Mariette himself, in a desperate ploy to put her off Christo!

Regardless of the qualms that had been raised in my mind – and it did occur to me that my real rival was probably [M] – I rejoiced in the fact that I was now corresponding with someone that I could openly avow as my love. I knew that Xenia wouldn't endorse such a description as yet, but that hardly mattered. The most important thing was what I knew from my own senses: she had given me a fair amount of encouragement. And I felt confident that time would take care of the rest.

A few days after the New Year, I drove homewards in the Land-Rover – along with Tim Sainsbury and Angus McNeill. We stopped for the night in Brussels and then next day made our way to the ferry that would take us over the Channel. For some reason we were badly delayed, so that it wasn't until about midnight that we finally arrived back in London. I had been fretting badly all the while, since I'd made a date with Xenia for that very night. But it should have occurred to me that there comes an hour after which it is politest – to the entire household – to postpone a telephone call until the next morning. It is perhaps a measure of the degree of my infatuation with Xenia that I could not restrain myself from attempting to get through to her at this belated hour. I must have been aware this was a disturbance to the peace that might have gone down badly with Brigadier Sale's household, where she was staying, because when the telephone rang I suddenly panicked and hung up the receiver. I know not if my guilt was detected

I did manage to get through to Xenia on the following morning. And she was to tell me later that she was *uncertain* whether she really liked me, until she heard my voice over the telephone that morning. Then she knew that she was "pleased". This was the message that she chose to give me – but it does leave a little to be explained. For the tone of her previous letters did indeed already indicate that she *liked* me. So it was unclear whether she was inclined to display a false front in her letters or just wasn't so good at giving an accurate analysis of her own state of mind at any given juncture.

There was also some confusion as to whether I might get a chance to see her before I drove down to Combermere later that day for my official discharge. In the event, I went round to Brigadier Sale's house in Eaton Place, only to find that Xenia hadn't returned when she said she might. So I was ushered into their drawing-room for a chat with the Brigadier and his wife. It turned out to be an unfortunate experience, which I prolonged in the vain hope that Xenia might yet arrive. In fact, I was to hear later that I'd created an unfavourable impression. It is difficult to recollect how the conversation went, but I think my mistake lay in a display of military disloyalty. He was enquiring about my immediate superiors. And while I had only good things to say about Colonel Jackie Ward, I may have been less favourable in my tributes to Colonel Gerard Lee, who had just recently arrived at Wolfenbüttel to replace him. Worse still, I may well have told some funny stories about Nipper. Anyway, he decided that I wasn't the kind of young officer that he would ever want to see on *his* staff. And that was the gist of the message that he passed on to Xenia and her parents. So I was to find it more difficult than I might otherwise have done to arrange my next date with her.

In any case, my immediate task down at Combermere Barracks was to obtain my official discharge from the army. We all put in our appearances at the appointed hour and I remember in particular how we were required to hand in our pass-books and identification papers at the same time. If I had been a really efficient young officer, I would have insisted on these being destroyed before my eyes. But I was content to leave them with the corporal at the desk in the Orderly Room. I mention this in passing, in that

I was to hear much later how my pass-book had come to be in the hands of an impostor, claiming himself to be the real Lord Weymouth. But that is a story to be told in a later volume.

It was several weeks before I actually managed to fix up a date with Xenia, largely because I went down to Cornwall for a while. Indeed, before I saw her again, I got invited to a party by Sarah Crawley. Now I liked Sarah and I found her attractive. But there can be no doubt that my sexual interest was currently focused upon Xenia. It eventually transpired that we were both invited separately to a small cocktail party that was being given for Henrietta Scott, on her birthday. I was there for Henrietta – as I was told later – and [M] was there for Xenia. And the whole idea was for us all to go on to dine somewhere together. But I was sufficiently insensitive not to appreciate any of this. In fact I was so besotted by this opportunity of seeing Xenia again that I hastened to invite her on to dinner with me almost as soon as I arrived. I did this in full hearing of the others and she accepted in full hearing of the others.

So what, I might venture to ask, was the real intention in her mind? She could so easily have nudged me back towards agreeing to participate in a collective outing. But she accepted to go on with me in [M]'s hearing. It could be that she was wanting to goad him into greater attentiveness – or it could be that she wanted our relationship to develop and knew I was on the verge of going to live in Paris for a while. In any case, there *were* developments on this particular evening, which might almost be counted as the start to our affair.

It was when driving her back home, after dancing until a late hour at *The Carousel*, that I stopped the car in a dark mews and started kissing her in earnest. Xenia was making a shameless bid to get me to fall desperately in love with her, in my view, without any real intention of matching what she was encouraging. Indeed, I was to observe in time to come how she was apt to employ those tactics to ensure the attentiveness of other admirers, who were not (as I judge) of especial importance to her. Yet I supposed that I was succeeding with her very well, when she looked at me from her over-earnest wide eyes to enquire: "Would you mind very much if I fell in love with you?" Taking her words at their face value, I responded with kisses.

Once I was back at Sturford Mead, I tried to assess the situation. Clearly, there were some factors that might indicate that I was going overboard too quickly. I knew too little about this whole courtship business. Besides, I was due to go to Paris in a couple of weeks time. So I wrote a letter to Xenia being very careful not to scare her off, but earnestly advising that we step back a pace and reflect before advancing further. Her reply was warm and reflected feelings in agreement with my own.

I counted the receipt of this letter as a great success. Nor did it occur to me that there might be an element of insincerity in it. But the truth of the matter is that there may have been only partial sincerity in what either of us uttered or wrote concerning our feelings about love. For in the absence of knowing what it could or should be, we both needed to experiment in the expression and description of such emotion.

> Shedding our shreds of chiffon sprightly as we prance
> the dance our ballet demands, leaping aloft
> in tropical warmth, we race in graceful circles,
> berserk, on the open ocean-washed beach.
> Each of us bearing gifts for the other, snappily
> wrapped in colourful paper with happy patterns,
> we chatter, enjoying our new generosity -
> which costs us nothing, and we know not what they contain.
> Remaining at the keyhole of a door, we seek a secret
> space to place ourselves inside, where we ride
> tip-toe in excitement, playing hide-and-seek,
> peeking from fairytales – where nothing's real.
>   "Knock, knock…!" For others in the world can share
>   the game of guessing that we too are there.

Chapter 4.3

Parents and siblings: the parental rift

At the time of my last argument with Henry – when he had ordered me not to take up Captain Taylor's challenge – I did thrash out with him the question of what I should do with myself after the completion of my National Service. What I didn't realise then was just how closely the divorce between my parents was looming. The time was approaching when Henry might be very glad to have me at a little distance from the home scene – at least until the appearances in the divorce court were safely behind him. So his resistance to my wish to study art in Paris was much diminished. In any case, he was prepared to discuss the matter in an open-ended fashion. He would have preferred if I had agreed to go to some provincial part of France, where I would have been less likely to meet up with other people from Britain. But I held out for Paris – because of the art school potential. And he eventually agreed to ask his friend Russell Page to look round for a family that might be prepared to take me in as a lodger.

But the conversation then became a lot heavier when Henry asserted that we should discuss the more long-term prospects. In particular, he wanted me to drop the idea of going up to Oxford. He didn't think it was in my best interests to deceive myself into supposing that I might be an intellectual. The Thynne family simply didn't produce intellectuals. Well – there were the Stanley cousins perhaps, or some of them. But it wasn't our genes that were responsible for any of that. A university education would be wasted upon me. And a man must acknowledge his limitations in life or he'll suffer from setting his sights too high.

The conversation then led to Henry asking me to tell him what I thought might lie within my limitations. But this whole idea of having limitations declared for me was getting under my skin. It offended me that he should want to perceive such limitations for me. So I became arrogant in my replies – all in an attempt to get him to appreciate that I was a far more talented young man than he gave me credit for. So I began naming some of the fields where I felt that I might conceivably succeed in life, if I were to put my efforts in those directions. I could become an ambassador, a Cabinet minister, an acclaimed author or artist – even a professional boxer, which I was rash enough to add to the list.

Henry was unimpressed. "Well now I know that you're lying," he declared. "You're just living in a cloud-cuckoo-land. You've got to come down to earth."

> My **straining fingers stretch out to reach**
> the **peaches, bulging from boughs** at **treetop height.**
> You **frighten** me, **pointing** out that I **lack** the **stature**
> to **catch** them in **clasping clutch.** Yet **trees** can be **climbed!**
> Sublimely **disregarding all** you **say,**
> I'll **play games, saddling** the **grey mare**
> for a **fair-weather** adventure. And **do** not **daunt** me
> by **flaunting** the **taunt** that I **never learnt** to **ride.**
> **Wide** is the **range** of **fancy dress** I **could**
> (and **should**) acquire, inspiring **colourful** behaviour
> to **brave out** this **lacklustre life.**
> But **trust you** to **knife** me with a **failure** to **notice!**
>> So tell me now, in all this lidless sky,
>> is any spot too low to be too high?

It stung the way he discounted me: that he could never display sufficient faith in my own sense of identity to enable me to feel that we were indeed thinking about the same person. On the other hand, I knew very well that he did hold my future happiness at heart. He thought I was competent to succeed in life all right, as a businessman or whatever – provided that I didn't get any high-falutin' ideas that might take me out of his own intellectual orbit. He wanted me to admit that I was the same kind of species as himself. But then – I don't suppose that's very different from many a father's visionary prospectus for a son.

Anyway, the net result of the discussion was that Henry accepted that my intention to go up to Oxford in the autumn remained unaltered. He stressed that I would have to pay for it myself and that he wasn't going to increase my allowance. But I don't suppose he really thought that was going to change my mind.

By the time that I returned home in January with my demobilisation papers in hand, he had fully come round to accepting the idea and there was a greater feeling of concord between the two of us. Russell Page, a celebrated landscape gardener, had found a family in Paris that would be happy to lodge me and Henry himself was generously offering to pay my boarding fee. It was as if he feared the disruptiveness of all the discord that was about to break over our heads and just wanted to reassure himself that our own relationship wasn't going to prove troublesome over this period.

Even so, there were some dangerous pointers that he had no intention of being flexible in the relationship where it might really count. I had requested a duffle-coat from him for my previous birthday. And he indeed supplied me with one. But he now made me pay for it. I feel sure there was a reason for this and I suspect that it was that I had given him an unsatisfactory Christmas present. I had brought some pornographic items back home from Hamburg for him – items like contraceptives dressed up to look like showgirls. He handed them back to me a few days later, saying that he had no use for that sort of thing. I hadn't intended to irritate him: it was merely a case of mistaken judgment on the level of his taste in these matters. But I regarded it as definitely on the petty side, yet somehow typical that he should then present me with a bill for the birthday present he had given me.

Daphne was back from Crete, but had been spending Christmas with her friend Oonagh Oranmore at Luggala, in Eire – in the company of Xan, of course. And Christopher, too, was away from home, having just started his two years of National Service in the Life Guards. (I could only feel sorry for him as he first had to undergo the Caterham experience.)

And this was the situation when Henry assembled all of us who remained at Sturford to make an important announcement in the drawing room. He kept it all brief and to the point. We were told that after a long period of trying to make the marriage work, he and Lady Weymouth had finally reached the conclusion that it would be happier for everyone concerned if they divorced. This would take place in a few months time. And they would each then remarry – to Mrs Tennant in his case and to Mr Fielding in Lady Weymouth's case. Sturford Mead would be sold since Mrs Tennant didn't want to live here. And we'd all move into Job's Mill – where the estate agent, Mr Algar, currently lived with his family.

So that was just about the size of it. I can hardly say that it took me by surprise – but that was only with half of my mind. With the other half, I'd been hoping somehow that life would continue much as before. As for young Valentine, the disbelief was written all over his face in a smug little smile – as if he saw quite plainly through the trick that we were playing on him. He was to tell me years later how it was Nanny who had eventually persuaded him that it wasn't a joke. He had supposed that this was another of those occasions when the family was inventing a tall story just to tease him. (Reminiscent of my own mentality, on the occasion shortly after my arrival at Eton, when I'd refused to believe a letter from my mother telling me that she'd had a miscarriage!)

It wasn't so much the divorce itself, or even Daphne's pending remarriage to Xan, which surprised me most. It was the identification of Virginia Tennant as the person my father was going to marry. He had somehow been far more discreet than Daphne with regard to the existence of an affair. I was aware of her being a most attractive woman, on the rare occasions when I had seen her at Sturford. But it had never occurred to me that Henry might be on such intimate terms with her. Caroline would have known of course, for she was far closer to the hub of London gossip – and closer to Daphne too, when it came to discussing matters of concern in their lives. But it made me feel a bit stupid in that I'd missed out completely on what he'd been getting up to.

Others in the household, such as Donald and Mrs Sims, were severely shaken. Donald seemed to take a dim view of Mrs Tennant trying to fill Lady Weymouth's place. "Well I ask you," he said, "do you really think she'll be able to cope with all the parties and the Women's Institute, for example? She'll never be able to fill your mother's shoes. She's simply not in the same class." And as for Mrs Sims, despite her disloyalty to the family in terms of the way she gossiped round the village about the goings-on at Sturford, she knew that Daphne was her special friend. The uncertainty was now plain to read upon her features. But we were told that the household would remain unaltered, once we had all moved into Job's Mill.

I wasn't too happy about this last point, either. I had my own room at Sturford and the privacy had become an essential part of my life. But Job's Mill was smaller than Sturford and Virginia had two daughters of her own. So how were the rooms going to be shared out? When I raised this subject with Henry, he declared that the boys would all have to share one room together – as we did when we were in Cowrie. Well, I didn't like the sound of that. But it was a matter that I'd need to cogitate for a while before coming up with any of my own suggestions.

In truth, though, my innermost feeling on the subject of a pending divorce was by no means one of dismay. There had been too much tension building up over the past few years in the relationship between Henry and myself. I worried about it sometimes in that I didn't see how I was going to loosen his stranglehold on my development. But with a divorce on the horizon, that might just give me the opportunity that I'd been waiting for. An opportunity to establish my own identity as something separate and apart from the rest of the family. The notion that I might set up my own household at Longleat was taking shape in my mind. But I wasn't quite ready to suggest it at this juncture.

Daphne had, in fact, written to each of us separately on the subject of the divorce, so that the letters arrived the morning after Henry had made his public statement on their plans. And she was due to come back to Sturford in a couple of days time to collect all her things and take them down to Cowrie. I realised how she would be working herself up into a terrible state over there at Luggala, so I hastened to write her a letter to lessen some of those fears. I told her that I understood how the marriage had been going badly in recent years and the important thing was to get her settled in a happy relationship once again. When she finally arrived back at Sturford, I could tell she was grateful that I had seen fit to communicate with her in this fashion. She told me how she'd had the feeling that everyone was saying awful things about her behind her back. So it helped.

The de Vulpian family in Paris had agreed to take me on as a paying guest from the beginning of February, so I didn't have very much time left. But I did accompany Daphne down to Cowrie for a while. I found somewhat of a paranoid atmosphere prevailing there. Daphne was terrified that she might be reported to the Queen's Proctor – by Miss Prokinar in particular – and the evidence used against her in court. Xan wasn't even staying in the house. He had taken lodgings locally – in Polperro – and used to sneak over for visits once the cook had gone home. If this was really the way that adults were obliged to conduct their amorous affairs then I regarded the whole business as unpleasantly hypocritical. But it was important that Daphne should feel that I was close to her over this period – as indeed I was. My love for Daphne was not altered by the pending divorce in any way at all – although I wasn't used to the idea of having to regard Xan as being of such importance in her life.

I took the opportunity of this visit to give Daphne *The Millions and the Mansions* to read. But she wasn't an ideal critic. She lacked the capacity to pick up on essential aspects of what was either good or bad in my approach to writing a novel. Her wish was more to identify with my aspiration to become a novelist – and, inasmuch as she had always been the instigator of my literary and artistic ambitions, she now found it in herself to praise what I had written. She thought it would need polishing up a little, but declared it to have the makings of a novel. Encouraged by this judgment, I returned to Sturford feeling that I might yet astound Henry by emerging as the youngest author of my generation.

Henry, predictably, was not happy to hear me talking that way. He felt that he knew me quite well enough to know that he did not have a precocious literary genius as a son. Moreover, it offended him to hear me talking as if I might be that kind of thing. It was just another instance of me showing signs of aspiring to outgrow him and it wasn't a thought that he was going to encourage. There came a point one evening when we disputed the issue in terms of a bet. He even offered me odds of one hundred to one that I'd never get this novel published within a period of three years; and this wager was written down on a piece of paper, and signed by both parties. I only stood to lose my £1 stake. But it was somehow a lot more important to me than that. I daresay he regarded it as a good incentive for me to improve on whatever I had written. But I stood to lose face so badly if I failed – and I knew it.

PART FIVE

SAVOURING
PARIS

Chapter 5.1

Career: cutting my teeth
as an art student

At Russell Page's instigation I flew out from London to Paris on 2 February 1953 to stay as a paying guest with the de Vulpian family, who lived near the Gare St Lazare. She was an impoverished widow, a Comptesse, with two teenaged children, Michelle and Jocelyne, and an elderly aunt who went by the name of Tante Marthe, all dwelling in the same flat. I had a room to myself, but there wasn't much feeling of living space and there was an atmosphere about the flat which, if in London, I might have classified as Edwardian. I was expected to take my meals at home with them, but to occupy myself with my own studies for the rest of the time.

I came to know the de Vulpian family quite well over these next four months – my return to Britain having been planned for the end of May, in time to attend the Coronation. But I never really accustomed myself to this idea of living under somebody else's roof. Both at Eton and in the Life Guards, I had been accustomed to greater privacy – somewhere that I could really feel I was on my own territory. In the little room where I slept, which was separated from their drawing room by a thin partition door, I never felt truly at home. There was a small table that acted as a desk and I did indeed engross myself for many hours each week – especially Sundays – revising and rewriting my novel, *The Millions and the Mansions*. But my lifestyle was distinctly cramped in that room.

Something that I was always anxious to avoid was the daily session after dinner, or after lunch as well on Sundays, when the household would sit themselves round the drawing room for interminable polite conversation. I certainly wasn't accustomed to this kind of communication – not at home, nor anywhere else for that matter. I had never developed the skills of being a polite conversationalist, nor in fact did I want to. I rather hoped to keep a distance between myself and such intrusions.

Nor did I find it any better when the two girls tried to persuade me that I ought to practise dancing with them – accompanied as it always was by one or other of the scratchy tunes from their sparse collection of records. *Le jive* was very much the in-thing on their dance floor, but I discovered that the French approach to it was utterly different to what I had experienced in London. It seemed to be all a question of neat little steps, to be performed in sequence, while only taking up the beat lightly on the stretch of the arms – whereas in London the beat was always more heavily stressed, to the disregard of any special foot play. In their company, I simply couldn't dance. And they were quick to pronounce that I conformed to their ready-made, stereotyped notion of Englishmen as lacking a Frenchman's innate sense of rhythm. Personally, I didn't see things that way. But I knew that I couldn't enjoy myself when trying to dance their way.

I did find it refreshingly different, however, to be dwelling in a French family who could be relied upon to behave in a most un-English fashion. Particularly memorable for me was the way in which Michelle and Jocelyne were liable to fling bread rolls and glasses of water at each other across the dining table to fortify their disagreement with one another during whatever the dispute of the moment was. After an initial verbal skirmish followed by their raising their voices to a shriek, it seemed like the only natural step in escalation that either of them could take. Mme de Vulpian usually made an attempt to restore law and order but, on recognising that matters had got out of hand, she would revert to the task of making polite conversation to me – seemingly oblivious of the missiles that were ricocheting all around us. It always struck me as so very different from the environment that I had known at Sturford Mead.

At other times, it was my behaviour at which the de Vulpians might look askance – largely over the quantity of wine that I took great pleasure in consuming at meal times. (I think that I did this, in part, with the attitude that it would be a pity to set aside what had already been paid for in my lodging fees.) This was usually noted in quiet comments on the side, but sometimes more fiercely. On one occasion, Jo had invited me to accompany her to a surprise party at the home of one of her school friends.

And I might have become bored stiff at such a juvenile gathering, if it hadn't been for the champagne. The father of the family was treating it as a bit of a corny joke to find an Englishman who was so fond of his wine instead of asking for beer. I certainly wasn't drinking excessively by the standards with which I had been acquainted in the Life Guards, but Jo was quick to let me know that she felt I had put her to shame. "*Il est complètement soul!*" she said, when Mme de Vulpian came to fetch us. But I think we all drifted thereafter towards the conclusion – stereotyped, again – that the men in English society drink rather more than their counterparts in France. We left it undetermined how English women might be expected to behave.

I hadn't been with the family for very long before we were joined by another lodger – a Dutch boy of approximately my own age, whose name was Eughien. He didn't take quite so kindly as myself to the antics of the two sisters and, while excusing Michelle for her part in these exchanges, he eventually made it his business to tell Jocelyne that she was a spoilt brat. This didn't go down at all well with Jo who felt that she had the right to behave as she pleased in this, her family home. She promptly got up and fled the room in tears. And henceforth the two of them had to be seated at different ends of the table.

But I acquired my freedom from their home environment with the purchase of a Velosolex. It looked like an ordinary bicycle, if slightly more solid, with a small motor on top of the front wheel. It was a most practical and inexpensive way of getting round Paris and, over the course of time, I journeyed to almost every corner of the great city, visiting all the museums and other tourist sights, or sometimes just getting a feel of its geography and seeing for myself how it fitted together.

My daily routine involved attendance at *Le Cours de Civilisation Française* each weekday morning at the Sorbonne, the purpose being for me to improve my understanding of the language by listening to the lectures. I had after all obtained a Credit for French in my School Certificate and the subject of French civilisation was something that any foreigner spending extended periods in France needs to know. The lectures gave broad coverage, but mainly within the subjects of France's history, art and literature.

That was where I went – by the Metro – each morning and, after re-crossing Paris to 26 Rue de Turin for lunch, I returned each afternoon to the Left Bank to attend an art school. The choice of where I went was largely on the advice of Vanessa Stourton, who was a niece of Russell Page and a former lodger with the de Vulpian family. She herself was due to return to Britain shortly, but she was invited over to lunch and volunteered to show me a bit of Montparnasse that same afternoon. And the art school – or *atelier* – that she especially recommended was the Academie Ranson in the Rue Joseph Baras. She regarded it as more authentically *student* in its atmosphere. The two better-known ateliers, the Academie de la Grande Chaumière and the Academie Julien, were the haunts of a more middle-aged crowd – in addition to their student members. She showed me these as well, but I did initially follow her advice by signing on at the Academie Ranson.

The main problem for me to overcome at this art school was my excruciating self-consciousness. I had a dread that others would single me out as someone who simply didn't belong within this assemblage of young bohemians. My upper-class Englishness was something that I was wearing like a ridiculous hat. I didn't know how to blend in with everyone else. I had faith in my ability to paint, but I craved a little time to get myself organised as an art student without the eyes of others being focused upon me. That was not to be allowed to me, of course. It never is, no matter whom I might have been.

I was just another anonymous young student, as far as any of the others were concerned. But there was always curiosity to see what kind of a painting style I might display. And the work I had been doing the most recently, when at Wolfenbüttel, was decorative more than plastic, patterning my subject – as can be seen in my painting of a potted plant that I did at that time. Well, I set out trying to do the same thing, here in the Academie Ranson, with my subject matter being a young model. It didn't take me long to realise, however, that this approach was far divorced from the line expected in this school. I was dragged up to show this effort to Roger Chastel, who was the art professor presiding over the weekly session of criticism. And from the way he talked to me, I was painfully aware that I was being treated like a total beginner.

Hastily I started another painting in a totally different style – far stronger and more sculptural. But the construction within my initial sketch accentuated the lines of her vagina. I was bitterly embarrassed at the way two young French girls were spluttering with uncontrollable giggles when I took it up for Chastel's comments. Aware of the way they were getting at me, he did make some comment intended to reassure me – about it being a big improvement upon my first effort. But I knew I wasn't matching up to the minimum requirements of a serious art student – and I just wished that the earth could swallow me up.

The inhibition I felt about having others see what I was creating, heightened my inner tension. There was so little space in this atelier that we were all on top of one another and with only one model posing up on the dais, I discovered – within the feverish urgency in which I was undertaking the work – that I was often completing the task in hand without something else to which I could turn my attention. But I was indeed learning. I was painting with a sudden realisation that there were new criteria that I had to satisfy, more concerned with the mechanics of making the viewer's eye move round the painting and creating impact at given points that still had to remain in balance with all the rest of the composition. The notion of draughtsmanship was utterly different as well. I was not liable to be told that I had drawn a particular figure incorrectly, but how the lines in the picture didn't cohere into something that was sufficiently interesting to study. What would formerly have been castigated as bad drawing might, here, be praised as a valuable contribution to the completed picture. It was a question of having to rethink my artistic position all round.

But as I endeavoured to loosen up my style in accordance with these new requirements, I was still blundering with regard to the type of style that might seem acceptable within the judgment of my peer group at the art school. In one of my early efforts I painted the model with exaggeratedly flagging breasts. I had no wish to be offensive to her, but I happened to see things that way. The trouble was that the youngish woman kept addressing remarks to me while she posed. And she eventually asked me to hold up my painting and show it to her, continuing to make this request so that there was no escape. And then of course she was offended – turning to the other students and asking them to reassure her that her breasts were in no way like the ones I had portrayed. I was squirming with an even greater embarrassment than her – especially when the dominant young male in the group spoke up to champion her cause, telling her that she should pay no attention to me, that I was mad and that my art work was absurd. Once more I felt acutely that I wasn't accepted within this throng: I was someone who had implanted himself from outside.

It was this general feeling that I stood apart within such a relatively small group, combined with the notion that I required more than one model to keep me busy, that persuaded me that I ought to try out one of the larger ateliers – opting for the Academie Julien, which was in the Rue du Dragon. The atmosphere might be less serious from an art student's point of view, but the two studios were indeed spacious and fairly crowded.

I love painting, but if I had to choose between
that and writing I would choose writing

This gave me a far greater anonymity in which to find my feet – to work out a new painting style for myself, before contending with the task of making friends with anyone.

I could still take my paintings back to the Academie Ranson for Chastel's weekly session of criticism. The difference in his general approach to art had shaken me, but I respected it and I wanted to succeed in impressing him within the criteria that he demanded we meet; in contrast, my first impressions of the criticism at the Academie Julien was that of a far inferior quality – more concerned with academic detail as to correct or incorrect draughtsmanship. Having by now shifted my sights with regard to my intended product in art, I had no wish to shift them back again.

On each successive session of Chastel's criticism, I was gratified to hear him expressing his astonishment concerning the rapid progress that I was making. He was of course totally unacquainted with the prowess as a painter with which I had formerly been credited at Eton. And I knew only too well that he wouldn't have admired those styles very much, even if I had shown him some examples of such previous work. I realised I was starting from the bottom rung of a different ladder – but my relief was enormous in that I could now feel that I was beginning to climb up it. And it was my artistic temperament, in particular, for which I was being praised. Chastel was careful to point out that it wasn't the paintings themselves about which he was enthusing, but the zest and dedication in my effort to improve. I could sense, too, that the others were beginning to take notice of how he was praising me.

This stood in sharp contrast, incidentally, to the angle that Henry had taken when attempting to dissuade me from going out to Paris as an art student. For he had quoted Russell Page in saying that what I lacked, as a potential artist of distinction, was the artistic temperament. I am inclined to suppose that Russell Page had envisaged me as being too much of a typically well-behaved young aristocrat – someone without sufficient fire in his belly to create his own path to creative self-fulfilment.

I was making good use of my time while I was out here in Paris. I owe much in my current appreciation of art to the visits that I paid to galleries and museums over this period. I visited virtually everything that was important to see, acquainting myself for the first time with the art movements that were in vogue at that time. Work by any of the big names in Abstract Expressionism was now something I might hope to recognise on sight. Indeed the importance of bright colour and variant texture was now upgraded in my own approach to painting. But my real favourites

163

were from the Expressionist school. The paintings of Van Gogh were something that I had long admired. Yet I had never heard of Soutine. In fact it was only after Chastel had commented that my own painting was very much in his style that I sought out some of his paintings in the Musée d'Art Moderne. And other names which featured high on my list for admiration were Chagall, Rouault, Picasso, Kokoschka, Munch and Nolde.

Then came the Easter break, when the Sorbonne, if not the art schools, closed down for a week. I decided to make good use of it by going on a trip round the châteaux of the Loire. The first part of the journey was by train, but all the rest was on my Velosolex. It was to be a painting holiday, so I had a suitcase together with the rest of my working equipment. In retrospect, I realise it was all quite dangerous owing particularly to the canvas boards that I had strapped to my back. For my trip coincided with a spell of foul and windy weather, so the boards acted as sails, catching every gust of wind and propelling me across the road at unexpected moments – sometimes when I was being overtaken by a car or with an oncoming lorry approaching me. But I have lived to tell the tale.

I probably got to see about twenty-five of these châteaux in all. Two that I painted were Chaumont and Le Moulin, and I remember being greatly impressed by Chambord, Chenenceau, Villandry and Azay-le-Rideau. This was my first opportunity to see how Longleat compared with equivalent stately homes in France. While I recognised that the Italianate influence of the Renaissance had reached the Loire some fifty years before Sir John Thynne brought that style to Britain – minus the high rooftops which give these châteaux their distinctive character – it was also evident to me that few of them could match Longleat in its quality of being a place that still possessed a residential atmosphere. These other places were often sparsely furnished, after being gutted at the time of the Revolution. There was no longer any living family's spirit to be discerned within them. All this made me the more appreciative of Longleat.

I had been deceived by the mildness of the weather during the weeks prior to this trip into bringing all the wrong clothing with me. For it had suddenly turned freezing cold and there were days when I was lashed with hailstones while I was painting. This happened to me at Chaumont, I remember: it tickled my fancy how tourists would rush up with their cameras, during any lull in the storm, to snap me as I painted. I wasn't doing this expressly to catch their attention, but I was aware that I was behaving in a manner that few others would choose for themselves. It entailed a display of artistic temperament such as fitted me well in my new guise. I was *being* the young artist, undaunted by all the discomforts that nature could devise. And I threw myself into this role with zest.

I was also sleeping rough and economising on my meals. The single blanket that I had brought with me was insufficient to keep out the cold at nights, when I was dossed down in a hay-barn or wherever. The first night I shivered until the dawn enabled me to get up and be on my way. It is revealing for me to quote from a letter that I wrote to Henry, describing my recent holiday.

> *I must have looked something like the Cheddar caveman, hair on end, straw in my clothes, and oil paint – or woad – on my hands and face. When I arrived at a small village in the early hours of the morning, to try and buy some bread, the village policeman questioned me as a suspicious character. It didn't help matters when I was unable to produce any papers to prove that I was employed. A passport had to suffice...*
> *You have often asked me what is the modern method of asking a girl to go to bed with you. Well I have now witnessed the American method. He was a serviceman, as I imagine. I was sitting in a café sheltering from the rain, when in he walked. Already present were two French women – not prostitutes, but a bit tarty looking. The G.I. stated that he didn't know what there was to do during the evenings in this village, and asked one of them if she could tell him. Not much progress. He then said that he hadn't anywhere to sleep that night. Still not much progress. He then asked her if she would like "a hard proposition." She asked him what he meant. "Well," he drawled, "it's about this long, and this round – and it's hard!" Progress established. Exit G.I. with both of the tarts. But for personal use, I have concluded that the method is a bit un-English!*

I discovered that my impersonation of a tramp over the course of this week had its rewards at times. I was genuinely hungry and dishevelled but I had not been anticipating that, after a display of ravenous appetite at an auberge where I had been dining one evening, the proprietor would actually take pity on me and offer me the use of one of his rooms free of charge. The idea then entered my head that I had only to give the appearance of such deprivation and people would come forward to offer me shelter. It didn't always work out that way however.

I remember one occasion when my clochard appearance merely disturbed the proprietor of a small gourmet restaurant on the banks of the Loire, where I had been hoping that my air of impoverishment might serve to obtain a reduction in the final bill. It must have crossed his mind that the *Michelin Guide*, or whatever other publications might send out inspectors to sample the fare anonymously at such reputed gastronomic paradises, were quite capable of dressing up their representatives in this guise in order to test the tolerance of their host. In any case, for whatever reason, the proprietor – with some hesitation I must admit – permitted me to sup at a table in the far corner. But he served me in histrionic fashion, at arms' length and with his face creased into lines of petulant disapproval. In vain did I guzzle greedily at the chunks of meat barbecued with herbs. In vain did I wolf down the delicious garlic bread and a whole third of the cheeses that he had so rashly left upon my table. In vain did I seize the fruit with both hands and munch as though my life depended upon it. At the end of my repast, I proffered my payment with a forlorn gaze at my host. But there was no offer of a free bed and board forthcoming at this establishment.

By the time I returned to Paris, the de Vulpian family commented that I was looking magnificently robust and healthy. Contending with the elements had done my complexion some good, it would seem. But I was conscious of a psychological boost within my personality as well. I had that feeling that I had just been living the life of hardship such as every artist worth his salt should suffer. And I had shown that I could take it in my stride: that my individualism could flourish no matter how harsh the environment. It might be nothing more than self-delusion, but I felt as if I had at last earned my spurs as a bohemian.

It was in this same spirit of exhibitionism, that I now set up my easel in the streets of Paris; in the Tuilleries Gardens to be more exact. I was doing a painting with the Arc de Triomphe up on the horizon – in a style vaguely reminiscent of Soutine. People were coming to stand behind me as I painted and some of their comments were really quite flattering. (The feedback from a French audience is characterised by their desire to appreciate the work of any artist, whereas in Britain there is a dubious distrust of anything even faintly modernistic.) But on this occasion I had the misfortune to become the object for observation from a horde of young schoolchildren. They began wisecracking to each other about my painting. But when I heard one of them declare that I was *"un vrai Picasso,"* I retorted that Picasso didn't paint in this kind of a style in any way at all. *"Heureusement!"* said the schoolboy – which set off the assembled crowd into hoots of laughter.

Repartee had never been one of my strong points, so I quickly reverted to silence. But the schoolboys were now stimulated by the idea that they had drawn blood and were emboldened into taunting me more actively – by picking up the tubes of paint which were resting upon my easel and scattering in all directions with them. I started out to retrieve them, but rapidly (and wisely) perceived that this would open up into a ridiculous game of piggy-in-the-middle, with the tubes thrown from one to the other of them over my head. So I promptly desisted. And when they saw that I was declining to rise any further they lost interest, dropping my paint tubes on the ground and running off in quest of their next victim.

When painting at the Academie Julien, the urgency in this whole business of trying to emerge as an artist was becoming virtually obsessive. And, in retrospect, I can see that my behaviour was becoming quite ridiculous at times. The habit I had developed of grinding my teeth while I worked was but one example. I did so under the illusion that nobody could hear me. But I gradually became aware from people's expressions that they could indeed hear me. So I stopped it.

There were other ways too in which my conduct might have been regarded as eccentric. The manner in which I ferried all my wet canvases across Paris on the metro was, perhaps, an example. It seems obvious to me now that people might complain at the menace I created for them at rush hour, in that the mirror images of the busty ladies who graced my canvases were liable to get transferred to their own clothes. I was even aware of this happening. And it shouldn't have surprised me when a man made it his business to give me a public rebuke on the subject.

I mention all this because it did perhaps stand as evidence of the development of an artistic temperament – inconsiderate though it may have been. Indeed, others may have seen such conduct as nothing more than a determination on my side to behave at odds with the world. What was significant for me, however, was that out here in Paris, distanced from the company of all former friends, I felt at long last as if my inner individualism was breaking through to the surface, vibrantly perceptible, conscious of itself, constant and unchangeable.

Inured to the **drab rags** of diurnal **ted**ium,
I **greed**ily **flight** my **sight** from a fleeting **keyhole**
to **treat** my **vision** with **feathered hats**, and **pend**ent
medals, glittering **glory** on beribboned **breasts**.
My **testicles ache** with **unslaked yearn**ing
to **spew** the **bloated congestion** in a **blocked gut**
to **such** explosive **height** that **rocket clusters**
will **bust open** as **beckoning beacons** in the **sky.**
A **fright**ening intensity, **pillared** like a **waterspout,**
swirls all **whirling** trivia into **trumpet shape,**
cramped in a cranium aflame – if **unfulfilled** -
with **willing, galvanising aspiration.**

      Then like a planet with a molten core,
      I'll sprout with foliage for evermore.

Chastel latched on to my individualism, making it the subject for his praise. That was a form of recognition that was so important to me. By the time I wrote home about it, it seems to have gone to my head. Or rather, I was attempting to enthuse Henry with this recognition of my natural talent, so that he might finally endorse my ambitions in this field.

> *I am going to horrify you by making a conceited comment. The professor who criticises my work seems to regard me as a potential future genius of painting. I don't expect you to believe this. You will just think that he must be a pansy – or a pretty rotten art teacher. He is not a pansy, and his name is Chastel. And he has just been made an officer of the Legion of Honour – which is an honour awarded to all the most illustrious of French artists, authors, poets etc.*

But if Chastel took kindly to the oddities in my behaviour, there were others who most certainly did not. I didn't make a favourable impression upon the professors at the Academie Julien. There was one – called Schultz or Schwartz – who, after ignoring me for a number of weeks, tried to take me vigorously to task on the excess of colour and general indiscipline in my paintings. But he was exercising his subjective judgment as if it consisted of objective rules to be learnt, and I wasn't going to stand for such a dismissive approach. I answered him back as fiercely and as loudly as he had chosen to speak to me – telling him that, to my eyes, the colours that I used were brilliant. Because the exchange was all so public, he stood to lose face – and authority – if it were to be continued, so he just turned his back on me and walked away. But I was aware that my standing up to him had not passed unnoticed – indeed, was admired in some quarters.

It may be because he had been informed about this episode that Chaplain-Midi, an established artist and the professor who came in to offer weekly sessions of criticism at the Academie Julien, was distinctly wary of me from the start. His own style of painting was far removed from anything I might personally wish to absorb – being pale of colour and too academic in spirit – and it was some while before I actually took up a painting for him to criticise. A whole lot of the students had their paintings lined up against the wall, waiting for his comments. But he was studiously ignoring mine. So when the session was finally drawing to its close, I asked him openly what he might have to say about it. He merely looked at me with a weary smile and excused himself on the grounds that he was now too tired.

Chapter 5.2

Identity: discerning my Englishness

On first taking up my abode with the de Vulpian family, I was made to feel self-conscious about my immaturity. Their brother Alain, who since he had married – surprisingly early at the age of twenty-three – only came to lunch occasionally had developed all the air of a full participant in the adult world. But there was still something lacking in my own outlook on life, which showed up as a basic uncertainty as to how I should be behaving; coupled with the freshness of my complexion, it gave the impression that I might be years younger than I in fact was. It was almost as if I had reached the age of seventeen, in the company of all my school friends, at which point my development had been arrested.

This had left me with a constant urge to open people's eyes to the fact that I was older than they imagined. As soon as I discerned that they were getting my age wrong and treating me as if I were still a juvenile, I wanted to wag my finger at them and inform them that I had already served as a commissioned officer in the Brigade of Guards and was still the British army officers' welterweight boxing champion. But I was far too inhibited to be so boastful; modesty was also required of me. Nonetheless I felt torn between the two modes of behaviour, with some unresolved schism splitting me up inside me on the issue.

Out here in Paris, in the bosom of a French family, the deficiencies in my development were perhaps all the more noticeable, due to the cultural contrast in our respective upbringing. This cultural contrast was an eternal subject for discussion at our meal times – that the French do things like *this*, whereas the British do things like *that*. It was all an exercise in probing where our identities might lie. Some of my conclusions seem curious in retrospect. Or perhaps it said something about this post-war decade. As I wrote home to Henry, early on:

> *French habits are amazing. I may be wrong but, as far as I can make out, they only have a bath about once a week. And then they advertise the fact by leaving black grime clinging to the enamel of the bath. I have now Frenchified my habits to the extent of taking only two baths per week.*

My upbringing under Henry had indeed been greatly concerned with the question of cleanliness – with a bath taken regularly each morning. Not that I had matched these standards at Eton or during my National Service in the Life Guards. And in any case, I was beginning to identify Henry's attitude to cleanliness as symbolic of his whole regime in life, and something from which I should establish my sense of distance.

The fact that I had withdrawn myself from the ranks of my peer group - Eton and the Life Guards - was now perhaps serving to fortify my eccentric outlook. It had thrown me back upon my own individualism – which had in fact always been the key note to my development. Out here in Paris, I was struggling fiercely to perceive what I was, and to define myself in contrast to all this foreignness around me. This certainly didn't have the effect of making me revert to a stereotyped version of Englishness. I saw that too as something from which I was striving to distance myself. It was more a question of discerning those building-blocks of Englishness from which I could construct my own brand of identity.

It wasn't just the de Vulpian family against whom I was endeavouring to measure my Englishness. I also contacted Mr and Mme Decroix, with whose family I had gone to stay at Trouville when I was seventeen. It was to their house in Paris, near the Pont Alexandre III, that I was now invited on a fairly regular basis to come and dine with them. It was so kind (and so typical) of them to bother – although if truth be told, we never really felt close enough to one another for psychological comfort. The effort was painful on all sides. But it all helped to remind me of the distinctions that I had originally observed between the French and English way of life. And there was one episode in particular which, when I recounted it to them, became their reference point concerning behaviour which they regarded – mistakenly I think – as being typically English.

Mme Decroix and I, on the beach at Trouville when I was seventeen

My Palm being read by a Gypsy while on holiday in Grenada

It was in early March that I went to cash some travellers' cheques at Thomas Cook & Son on the Place Madeleine. On a previous visit, I had noticed there was an Arab with a beret, surreptitiously displaying a packet that he kept trying to sell to passing tourists. It was impossible to get a close look at it, but the package evidently contained photographs and we tourists were intended to suppose that these were the *"feelthy* postcards" we all assumed must be on sale somewhere or other in this notorious city.

Anyway, on this second visit, I decided to inquire how much he was asking for them – whereupon he became even more secretive, ducking into a side alley and beckoning me to follow him. He was in a tremendous rush to get the transaction completed, as it seemed. He whispered to me confidentially that he would let me have two packets for 2,000 francs (something less than £2). I murmured that this was rather more than I'd been expecting. And seeing that I was holding a 1,000 franc note in my hand, he quickly agreed that I could have them for that. Taking the note, he thrust them into the pocket of my duffle-coat – and disappeared round the corner rather too rapidly for me to feel that things were all above board.

Well, as soon as I'd had the chance to open the packs, I found that they were nothing more than photographs of paintings from all the Parisian museums – admittedly with a nude or two featured in each, with titles like *Adam and Eve* or *Leda and the Swan*. But there was nothing especially "filthy" in material of that ilk. I felt truly diddled. But the Arab had now disappeared from the vicinity, so there was no opportunity to ask for my money back.

I wasn't going to leave the matter there, however, so I kept returning to the Place Madeleine until I found him. When he saw me coming, he adopted the *vieux copain* attitude, feigning to suppose that I'd only come to purchase some additional packs. Indeed, he appeared well-accustomed to fobbing off his dissatisfied customers – adopting an obtuse expression as soon as I mentioned that I would like my money back in exchange for the packs he had already given me. *"Mille francs? Quel mille francs?"* So I became gruff in jogging his memory, whereupon he said he'd go and fetch the money. But I announced that I'd go with him. He claimed that this wasn't necessary – but I insisted.

So he took me a little distance and then introduced me to "his friend" – an Arab with grey crinkly hair who was far better dressed than himself and looking more like the man who ran the enterprise than any mere salesman. He said that I should wait with him and, since the latter shook my hand in greeting, I supposed that our business might soon be successfully concluded – so I permitted the other to depart. As soon as we were on our own, however, the one with the crinkly hair disclaimed all acquaintance with the one who had departed. I was now feeling utterly stupid, but I could think of no appropriate action that I should take. So I went back home to fret upon the manner that they'd been making a fool of me – until my umbrage became too much for me.

It wasn't until the following Sunday that I needed to collect some more money from Thomas Cook & Son. So too did Eughien, my fellow lodger with the de Vulpians, so I was not on my own this time. I took the precaution of warning him, as we approached the Place Madeleine, that I might have to make a bit of a scene if I found certain people ahead of us. And sure enough, there stood the Arab with the crinkly hair on the same spot where I had previously conversed with him, this time he was chatting with a small group of others.

I took the initiative by going straight up to him and demanding my money back. He then made the error of trying to frighten me off – shouting contemptuously at me and suddenly raising his fist as if he were about to strike me. My reaction as a boxer must have looked adequately professional, as I ducked to one side with my hand coming up to shield myself from the blow. He stopped it short and I was then standing in fighting stance and quite ready to counter with whatever punches might be necessary. He was now just standing still, so I seized him by the scruff of his coat collar and shook him.

This wasn't doing his status any good in the eyes of his friends – and they were quick to distance themselves, now that it appeared that violence was threatened. He had reassumed a reasoning demeanour, stressing that he really didn't know what I might be talking about. But I shook him once again by his coat collar and declared that he'd better explain all that down at the gendarmerie. People were beginning to gather round and he liked this even less. He tried to persuade me to let go of his collar, but I merely shook it the harder. He declared that he would accompany me, if only I let go of his collar. So I released him. And he did accompany me to the police station, which was some little distance from the Place Madeleine.

What had slipped my mind, however, was that the gendarmerie would be closed on a Sunday. We went right up to the door and he pointed out to me that it was locked. Once again I felt that I'd made a fool of myself – although not so badly this time. I was still in a position to make threatening noises and tell him that this wasn't going to be the end of the matter, and that I'd be returning to demand my money back from the Arab who had sold the photographs to me. And I let him depart.

Eughien, meanwhile, had been following us from a distance – never actually at my side, even at the moment when it looked as if blows were to be exchanged. But when he saw the Arab emerging alone from the alley that ran down beside the police station, without any sign of what might have happened to me, he suddenly became quite scared – he told me later – supposing that the man had knifed me once he'd taken me out of sight. I was aware of his relief and how my cool had greatly impressed him.

But this still wasn't the end of the story. I kept up my inspections of the Place Madeleine until I espied the small scruffy Arab with the beret, the one who originally accosted me. When he saw me approaching, he immediately started shouting: *"Je ne vous connais pas! Je ne vous connais pas!"* – which was an unusual comment to be making to someone who had yet to speak to him. And as I came nearer, he turned round to run. So I followed suit and caught him by the hem of his jacket, which he immediately shed – like a lizard's tail. I tried to get a further grip on him and he immediately fell to the ground, calling out to the passers-by to witness that I had assaulted him.

People came running up to join the crowd of spectators and the police, too, were soon on the scene. When they arrived, the Arab tried to make out that he was the injured party and that I was a great big bully who had struck him down for no apparent reason. The police wanted to know what I might have to say about this. I explained that I hadn't struck him but had paid an exorbitant price for some photographs and therefore wanted my money back. The Arab promptly produced his very un-filthy postcards and showed them to the police, protesting that I had no right to complain about such innocent pictures. The crowd now began to mutter their sympathy with the poor man, while I was being portrayed as an absurdly prudish Englishman who regarded such pictures as immoral. One of the gendarmes even remonstrated with me to be more reasonable. Why should I be so offended? There was nothing indecent about these *nus des musées*. That was precisely my complaint! And I eventually managed to get this point over to him – that they were not sufficiently pornographic to warrant the price that I had paid.

The two gendarmes now saw that there might be some substance to my sense of grievance, so they bade us to accompany them to the police station. While we were being marched along there, the Arab played the game of trying to make me lose my temper – to prove that I was the unreasonable one – by whispering the grossest of insults to me in such tones that I realised perfectly well the kind of things that he was saying, but wisely responded by claiming that I could not understand a single word of this odd dialect.

By the time that we had arrived at the police station, I had decided to take a different tack. I told the gendarmes that, as a tourist, I'd had many superb experiences in France, but that *this* experience was *"un mauvais souvenir"*. And I looked at them with maudlin eyes, hoping that this might arouse in them some innate sense of national chivalry. It worked. They immediately displayed sympathy for my cause. My adversary was also helpful in that he suddenly became petulant, even disagreeable, to all and sundry. He now appeared to accept that he was in the wrong and was merely concerned cheekily to display his lack of any repentance. They ordered him to turn out his pockets, and finally to remove his filthy shoes and socks. A 500 franc note was discovered in one of the socks, and offered to me, but I declined it. The final outcome was that they released me, but detained the Arab for further questioning. And on that basis I felt that I was emerging from their custody as a marginal victor.

Then as I was making my way out, one of the gendarmes came after me and handed me a package of saucy postcards, such as had been circulating in Paris during the earlier part of the century. He declared with a sheepish smile that they had been confiscated at that time, but had now been lying around the police station for so long that no one had any further use for them. If they were any use to me, then I was welcome to take them. I assured him that this generosity of spirit transformed a bad experience into a magnificent one. And I have those photographs to this day – fully aware, as I am now told, that their value far exceeds what I originally paid for the two packs of nus des musées.

Anyway, this was an experience which I recounted in some detail to Mr and Mme Decroix over the course of one of my dinner invitations. And it was their view that the stubbornness and perseverance which I had displayed were entirely typical of the English character. A Frenchman might have flared up in instant anger and taken more effective steps to regain his money at the time. But he would never have sustained such a prolonged effort to bring the man to justice. The story was repeated on subsequent occasions, too, for the appreciation of other guests – until the notion of my Englishness seemed to be contained within that anecdote. Not that I saw any reason to object: I had after all finally emerged as the victor.

The idea that I had been attempting to buy myself some filthy French postcards prompted Mr Decroix to explore that particular vein of conversation with me. And I indicated that I was curious to know what his compatriots called one another, if they were hoping to register a sexual insult. This led to him dictating a list of such words, while explaining their meaning to me. It is a list that has survived to this day, so I shall take this opportunity of revealing its contents, which read as follows: *"Pederaste! Homme enculé! Tante! Tapette! Inverti! Gousse! Gouine! Macquereau! Putain!"* If I wished to be particularly offensive, then I should call someone: *"Con de carron!"* – or cunt of rotten meat! But he did warn me that I should be most careful in the choice of occasion when I might display a knowledge of such vocabulary.

The effort of making polite conversation with the Decroix family generally turned out to be a strain, though. And it was perhaps unfortunate that they appeared to recall how, when I had been on that earlier visit to them, I had posted home some postcards whose humour was distinctly scatological – even coprophagous (I had been endeavouring to fulfil Daphne's request for saucy French postcards, but had misjudged what was required and Jean-Louis, their son, who was then staying at Sturford Mead, no doubt reported back to them this evidence of what was liable to amuse us). Anyway, Mr Decroix now did his utmost towards the end of each dinner to keep me amused by recounting dirty stories – while Mme Decroix looked on anxiously to discern whether they were scoring any points in my appreciation of such humour. And I was desperately anxious to please them by appearing suitably amused.

"Mais il n'est pas amusé," Mme Decroix would murmur reproachfully to her husband. *"Au contraire, je suis très bien amusé,"* I hastened to reassure them – with my face grimacing into a less than spontaneous grin. *"Mais tu vois cherie, il est très bien amusé,"* declared Mr Decroix, quite evidently relieved. And the sequence of dirty stories would be prolonged for a further quarter of an hour. The truth of the matter was that I found it very difficult to grasp the point at which laughter might be appropriate. I am obtuse enough when such jokes are recounted in English, but I was invariably lost when it was all in French.

I did make some terrible errors when attempting to converse with other people on this subject of the English versus the French archetypal character. There was an occasion, for example, at a dinner party to which I had been invited, preceding some society ball. This was prior to the occasion when Mr Decroix had been at pains to explain the meaning of such terms, and I had been hearing, at the lectures that I was attending at the Sorbonne, how Marcel Proust was *"un inverti"*. Unfortunately I took this word as meaning introverted, rather than it being the French way of referring to homosexuality. So I rapidly got myself into a hopeless confusion when explaining earnestly to my British hostess's assembled company of French dinner guests that the important thing to understand about Englishmen was that they were all *"invertis"*. As their expressions became quizzical rather than intelligently comprehending, I sensed that my communication must somehow be incomplete. So I persisted, putting forward the same word indefatigably in combination with other phrases – until my hostess broke in, to change the subject to something of her own preference. I was never invited to grace her table again.

It was the Decroix family who took me to my first opera – which was Rameau's *Les Indes Gallantes*. It was a production orchestrated for the appreciation of foreign tourists, as I later learnt. But it furnished me with a valuable first glimpse into that particular cultural scene – a start upon which I might later build. And in a sense I saw this as a move in the direction of absorbing a more continental attitude towards the cultural scene – coming as I did from a family in which Henry's own philistine view upon life outweighed at times the artistic influences which had emanated from Daphne.

A word or two upon any utterances that throw light upon my political views at this time might now be offered. The de Vulpian children were eager at the start to discern whatever bias I might possess on the political spectrum. In the scoffing overtone to her enquiry, I may accurately have discerned that Michelle, who was in her final year at a lycée, had Communist sympathies. She and Jo had once tested me to the extent of enquiring if I knew the theme of "The Red Flag". I couldn't remember it – and realised that this branded me in their eyes as being dangerously right wing.

Eventually, it was Michelle who came more exactly to the point, in stating: *"Mais Alexandre, il est sûrement un royaliste?"* I endeavoured to duck the question by pointing out that in Britain, royalism was hardly one of the political issues. The Royal Family had all-party assent. But they wouldn't leave it there.

"What are your politics?" asked Eughien more emphatically.

"Vous verrez!" I retorted – without really perceiving what a conceited remark I was making.

"So you think a lot of yourself?" declared Eughien – to the accompaniment of some sniggers. I just withdrew into a silence. In fact, the whole subject of politics was something that, at this juncture in my life, I felt uneasy about discussing with anyone at all. I knew quite simply that I wasn't ready for it.

When it came to the May Day celebrations, which took the form of two large political rallies – with the Gaullists gathering in the Place de la Concorde and the Communists in the Place de la Bastille – I chose to put in my attendance with the latter. But it was far more from curiosity than from any sense of participation. I was frightened of the Communists and of all that they stood for. But they represented a side of life with which I wanted to acquaint myself.

Chapter 5.3

Parents and siblings: the divorce

While I was conveniently out of touch with everyone in Paris, my parents had to face up to the media coverage of their divorce. Whatever may have been written just passed over my head in that I read none of it. I had already accepted the inevitability of the event itself. There was nothing that I could either do or say that was going to alter any of that. But there were still some things that I could do to affect the planning of how our lives should now be organised. I had already done my share of brooding upon the whole issue of going to live at Job's Mill. There seemed little prospect of me being furnished with a room of my own, which was something in life that had become very important to me. But I realised how such privacy would be lost to me, if I didn't hasten to speak up on the subject. My best bet was to angle for a different solution, which I broached for the first time in a letter to Henry in February 1953, after I'd been in Paris for some three weeks.

> *The idea has just occurred to me that it might be an easy solution to the accommodation problem, if I were to have a room at Longleat. It would save you all from a lot of untidiness at Job's Mill, and would enable some of the others to have rooms of their own, instead of having to share. And to move all my belongings into a new house, just to move them out again a year or two later, does seem an awful waste of effort. I could get accustomed to the atmosphere of Longleat, ready for when it is to be my home. It will really need a number of years to do this*

satisfactorily, since there will not be that many weeks during the year when I am at home – what with Oxford and travel.

The last thing that I would want is to make Virginia think that I didn't want to live in Job's Mill because she was there. If that were the case, there would be the more obvious solution of going to live down in Cornwall with Mum. This would just be a case of having my own bedroom and study at Longleat. But if you strongly disapprove of the idea, then I will of course forget about it.

Henry's reply was not entirely encouraging:

With regard to your suggestion about living at Longleat, I am afraid that I cannot agree to this in the manner that you suggest. I am all for you having a room at Longleat where you can go and paint, or do what you wish, but under the present staff arrangements there, it would be quite impossible for you to have a bedroom and breakfast, since I know Mr Chapman [the retired policeman who was the resident caretaker at Longleat] would not relish the idea of having to take your breakfast up every morning. I think that by far the best thing would be for you to sleep and live at Job's Mill, and take sandwiches – if you wish – over to Longleat and stay the day there. I quite appreciate your remarks about your reasons for wanting to do so, and I know they are true. Believe me, if you ever live at Longleat, it won't take you long to get accustomed to the atmosphere.

But Henry went on to have second thoughts about the matter. My guess is that he wrote the first letter without actually consulting Virginia on the matter – perhaps specifically so as to shield her from all responsibility in taking such a decision. But it looks as if, on being shown a copy of the letter he had posted to me, she perceived how it might be wisest to accommodate my wishes. A week later he wrote:

About the matter of having a room at Longleat, I have
since been talking it over, and I think you may probably
have gathered some wrong impressions regarding the new
house from Donald. Therefore I feel that my former
decision of stamping on your idea from the start may be
a little hasty, and I think when you come back we could
discuss the matter to our mutual satisfaction.

The whole question was then shelved until my return to England in May
– by which time I was to discover that the idea of me living at Longleat was
more or less accepted by everyone concerned. It was only a matter of
having to make the final arrangements, ready for the day when the shift in
residences was finally to be put into effect – that would be in the summer,
after both Daphne's and Henry's nuptial knots had separately been retied.

The real concern over this period was as to how the divorce would be
treated in the media, after the dirty linen had been washed in court. Not
that my parents intended to be seen wrangling in public concerning the
division of wealth, nor in maligning each other's reputation when it came
to the question of apportioning blame. It was all to be conducted in
gentlemanly fashion, with Daphne's petition for divorce undefended on
Henry's side – their respective lawyers had come to an agreement on their
behalf before it ever came to court.

In the meantime I was informed of some of their domestic problems
through the letters that they each wrote to me. Daphne wrote to tell me
that Miss Prokinar the cook had walked out on her, down in Cornwall,
giving as her excuse that her doctor had said she was too ill to work due to
her "fatty degeneration of the heart". But the excuse didn't look quite so
plausible when Daphne soon discovered that she was working for someone
else. The parting was in fact quite bitter for Miss Prokinar walked off with
various items of electrical equipment from Cowrie, claiming that Henry
had given them to her. And even when legal proceedings were threatened,
nothing could persuade her to return the property.

Then she developed a paranoid obsession that Daphne and Xan were
going out of their way to persecute her. She retaliated by heaping curses
and insults upon them and spreading scandalous stories round the
neighbourhood about the goings-on during the divorce. Fortunately she
had never acquired the reputation of being a reliable source of information,
so her testimony was largely discounted. But it meant that Daphne was
unsettled for a while and found it difficult to get someone appropriate to

replace her; this problem was eventually resolved in the appointment of a charmingly unprofessional couple from Lancashire, who went by the names of Danny and Beryl Owens.

I also heard from Daphne how Valentine had won his weight in the Eton boxing competitions. And I think it was this year that he made a courageous stand in the Quadrangular Tournament against Ashdown of Bedford College – subsequently to be identified as Paddy Ashdown former MP and leader of the Liberal Democrats and, in 2002, appointed the new High Representative for Bosnia & Herzegovina. Paddy later told me that there was much blood all over the ring, but that my brother survived until the final bell.

Valentine's victory in the Eton Championship was a triumph for me in other ways too. Before leaving for Paris, I had been disputing his qualities with Henry who had been running him down. His argument was that Valentine had no backbone: that he would go from bad to worse. But I was sticking up for him, saying that he was really quite gutsy. This had developed into a dispute as to whether he would ever box for Eton and, as usually happened with Henry, a bet was offered. It was all laid out on a little piece of paper that "Dad bets Alexander £5 that Valentine will never box for Eton". Winning that bet was important to me for I wanted to bring home to him that he continually underestimated the natural prowess of his sons.

There was no special news relating to Caroline or Christopher. The former was establishing her own position within the London social scene, while Christopher was still suffering the rigour of training as an officer-cadet at Mons – mild as it might seem after the experience of the Guards' Depot at Caterham.

While the divorce ordeal drew closer, it seems that Henry was still planning to treat the occasion of my 21st birthday as something that should be celebrated upon the Longleat estate. There was after all a tradition of such celebration within the family. It had been described to me when I was working in the woods how, at Henry's own 21st birthday, a special wooden bridge had been constructed over the Half Mile lake for him to walk over from the garden and be fêted by his tenants on arriving at the park end. The way I imagined it to have been was the creation of two segregated parties. Well I knew that my own party wasn't going to be anything like that, but there were still plans afoot for one – as indicated in Henry's letter of mid-April.

> *I have arranged for a very small and non-elaborate Coming-of-Age party for you on Saturday June 6th. I believe the tenants and employees will be making a small presentation to you. I shall have to make a short speech, the presenters of the gift will also make a short speech. And by short I mean that it won't have to take more than ten minutes.*
>
> *After that the Beer Tent will be open, and I am not quite sure what will take place from then onwards. I hope to get the Wiltshire Yeomanry band for the whole afternoon. I am sorry that I cannot do more, but this will be quite expensive, and I think it is essential for you to be seen by everybody – since 90% of the Estate hardly know what you look like.*

In all truth, I didn't welcome the prospect of such a party in any way at all. I had always detested having to stand up and make speeches in public. Therefore it came as a considerable relief to me when I heard that there had been a change of plan. As Henry wrote to me ten days later:

> *I am awfully sorry Alexander, but I have changed my mind about your Coming-of-Age party. It is hard to go into money matters at the present moment, but things are not too easy, nor will be in the near future – as you will gather when you come back here at the end of May. It would only mean that the whole affair might go off at half-cock, and people might say, or think, it was rather a poor "Do". I am sorry, as I should like to have done something for you, as my father did for me, but times and situations have changed. Maybe at a later date, which I hope won't be for many years – that is when you marry – we can conjointly get together and introduce your future bride and yourself at the same time. I do hope you will understand.*

In this same letter, Henry announced that he was currently in bed, suffering from chicken-pox…

> *…which I always thought to be a childish and simple disease, but have now discovered to be a most virulent and hideous complaint. The whole of my body and face is*

184

covered in spots, and I cannot shave in case they leave a scar behind. Heaven knows when I shall look respectable again, and be able to go out in the world once more. In fact I really feel rather depressed.

In my reply, I tell how the news was received.

When I was reading that part of your letter about you being inflicted with your childish and simple disease, I began to roar with laughter. The whole of the de Vulpian family were present, and enquired what it was that I found so funny. When I told them that you had chicken-pox, they were shocked, and said that if this was an example of the English sense of humour, then they didn't think much of it.

Despite my acceptance that there was to be no great festivity to mark my 21st birthday, I was still anticipating that my Coming-of-Age would receive some manner of recognition from home. But May 6th came round without me receiving a single letter or telegram from any member of my family. It may be that the de Vulpians took note of the neglect. But it was my fellow lodger, Eughien, who actually came up with an invitation – supposedly from his uncle (or godfather, perhaps), who was described as being the Director of the Casino de Paris – for him to bring a friend to see the show that night. So he took me along to it. And that's the way in which I celebrated my Coming-of-Age – savouring the privilege of being permitted to watch the spectacle from the wings. We saw ladies in crinolines rushing to strip off their gowns as soon as some act had ended and then prancing back on to the stage without any clothes at all, to pose as statues in the next act. Or some of them stood necking with the stagehands during the off-set periods. The presence of two strange youths in the shadows didn't seem to deter anyone. And the experience was memorable: a situation of this kind is unlikely to be on offer to me a second time.

I think it was Nanny who was the first person to recollect that I'd had my birthday. She had always been a constant if unappreciated letter-writer, in that her epistles were seldom tremendously exciting to read. Henry must have sent me a belated telegram, because there is no reference to my birthday in any of the letters he sent me. Then Daphne went so far as to apologise for forgetting about it in a letter dated May 18th – saying that she and Caroline would be combining to give me a joint present. Christopher and Valentine never got round to acknowledging it in any way at all.

It wasn't really surprising that everyone forgot because there were more important matters to occupy their minds – in that the divorce suit was then being heard. It was reported without any attempt to sensationalise it. The official citations were, I believe, against Henry and Virginia, with Daphne asking for the judge's discretion concerning her own misconduct with Xan. It was in her letter of May 18th that Daphne informed me that she had been granted a decree nisi with costs against Henry and the custody of Valentine nominally in her favour. And that was the end of the matter – for the time being in any case.

With regard to Henry's attitude towards my stance as an art student, he was careful to ignore the vaunted tones in which I had been describing my work to him. But he did make the gesture of letting me know that there were, at any rate, some people back at home who were appreciative of my paintings. He wrote:

> *Mr Chapman has tidied up the chapel at Longleat in order to entertain booked parties, and he has hung canvas on the wall, complete with flags and – believe it or not! – about a dozen or so of the paintings you did while you were at Eton, and in the Life Guards. Even Christopher said they looked quite nice.*

Chapter 5.4

Sex: Paris in the springtime

When setting out for Paris, my feeling with regard to the prospects for my sex life was one of venturing into unknown waters. I was to be much more of an isolated unit than when, for example, I first went into the army. In that experience I was enlisting along with quite a bunch of my school friends. Here in Paris, however, I didn't know if there'd be anyone out here that I knew at all. And I had doubts whether I would feel sufficiently akin to my fellow art students – few of whom would be British – for me to assert any sex appeal. I was nervous that, in this denuded psychological state, I might display no appeal whatsoever. So I was anticipating that these might be barren months for any sexual endeavours.

This was not too great a worry to me in that my heart was already plighted to Xenia. I felt for the first time in my life that I had established myself with a girlfriend on a reciprocal basis of loyalty and romantic commitment. We had agreed not to write to one another for a full month but I had brought her photograph with me, which I kept framed beside the bed – something which gave rise to a fair amount of curiosity from the de Vulpian sisters (*"Non, ce n'est pas ma soeur. C'est une amie"*). I had no intention of being unfaithful to her, although I may well have been hoping that some flirtation on the side would come my way.

But it was the discomfort with myself that really characterised the first weeks of work at the Academie Ranson. So I was unreceptive to such nuances of flirtatiousness that may have been on offer. There had been that model who kept trying to chat with me for example – until, that is to say, she obliged me to show that I had painted her with sagging breasts. And there was another one – a young English girl, whom I might well have responded to, if I had felt more certain of my own identity. A Japanese girl, too. I can see now that they were all offering me their friendship but I simply didn't feel assured enough of my own identity to behave naturally in these circumstances. Nor did I dare risk the potential inadequacy in attempting to play the traditional role for a male in self-assertive flirtation. I kept intensely withdrawn into myself, whilst I got on with the business of painting.

After I had moved to the Academie Julien, the young English model and the Japanese girl, on separate occasions, actually came over to the Rue du Dragon to seek me out. They came up to say hello, awaiting the invitation to go and have a coffee break with them. Both of them were attractive. But the feeling in my head was that I couldn't cope with it. I was almost gruff with each of them and quickly buried myself in my work. In retrospect, I can see how each situation might have evolved very differently if I'd had a wider experience at the time of handling sexual opportunities. Such memories have to be written off: put into the memory bank of hopes that were unrealised.

Associations of a different kind would have been all too easy for me to have developed. I hadn't been at the Academie Julien for long before an Englishman in his forties – a dentist with a twitchy expression, whom I perceived clearly enough to be lusting (nervously) after my body – tried to engage me in conversation over successive rest periods, finally persuading me to come out with him for a drink one evening. He made it with me as far as that – but no further. My coolness of demeanour was discouraging, no doubt. But it was a sad truth about my life at this time that I would have been a far more successful homosexual than heterosexual debauchee – if the inclination had been present. As it was, I felt excruciatingly embarrassed over the duration of our outing that I might be observed by someone who knew us and that thereafter my reputation would be sullied.

I also reveal in a letter to Henry that I had fears of being recruited as a toy-boy or some such ilk by an older woman. But I was rather more ready to write home about her, than about the homosexual dentist.

> *There is an awful old American lady who paints at the same atelier. She keeps on coming up to admire my paintings. Then she tells me that she likes me because I am such a nice quiet type! In short, I dread that she is trying to acquire me as her gigolo.*

There was in fact quite a large Anglo-Saxon group at the Academie Julien. There were American ex-servicemen studying art in Paris on governmental grants and there were some young English students too. It is really curious how I was never sufficiently at ease in their company for us to make friends. I can remember hearing one of these girls discussing me with an American student – not quite softly enough to escape my hearing. "He won't pay any attention to me," she was saying. His reply was, "I guess it's because you're not sufficiently melancholic." So I think it's evident that I did give people this impression of intense melancholia. But as I see it, it was more a question of me hiding behind the barrier of silence that I had created for myself. I had absorbed myself in the task of painting and I didn't want to step out as anyone's friend until I could feel that I had established myself with universal respect in that field.

When I had been out in Germany, there had always been the visits to Cobblers' Alley to relieve myself from further sexual desire. But I was never quite sure where such a place might exist here in Paris. There were a number of occasions when I commented darkly to the de Vulpian family after dinner that I was "just going out for a stroll". And I realised how my sexual intent was ill-concealed. But in the event I never enlarged upon my previous experience in such matters. I was now inhibited against the thought of taking a prostitute to bed with me, by some belief that I had by now evolved beyond the need to pay for sex. But there was little satisfaction in extolling this as a virtue when I wasn't actually managing to get sex for free. That was my intent, however, as I went prowling round the streets of Clichy and Pigalle, glancing in at bars to see if any young woman appeared to be unescorted and with similar intent to my own.

The truth of the matter is that my nerve was still not up to it. I can remember actually seeing an attractive young girl, sitting alone and unattended in a bar. She even looked up at me encouragingly. Then I panicked. I didn't have the self-confidence to go up and say something to her. I left the bar without even looking back at her a second time, excusing myself on the grounds that I ought to make a further exploration of the vicinity before returning to this bar. By the time I did return, she was of course no longer there. Secretly I felt relieved.

Then there was an occasion when I got myself into a situation when I was almost picked up by a man. I was standing on the central pavement that separates the two lanes of traffic between Clichy and Pigalle – standing still because I was uncertain which direction to take. A man approached me and asked if I had a light for his cigarette. I obliged. Then he asked me to come to a cinema with him. Only then did I comprehend the sexual nature of his intent, and said, *"Mais pourquoi?"* The man walked off swearing at me in French.

It was probably this episode more than any other that persuaded me that I wasn't really cut out for these night-time prowls. I had already reverted to masturbation during the latter part of my time in Germany. And I now renewed the habit while I was out here in Paris – to keep the unassuaged desire for sex within comfortable limits. On such occasions, I could feast my erotic imagination upon my memory of Xenia's delectable body – even if it had yet to be seen naked by my eyes.

I had in fact adhered to my intention of not writing to Xenia until a full month had elapsed. When I did write – in time for her birthday in early March – it was like an explosion of suppressed joy. I wish that the letters that I wrote to her had been preserved, but I have recently discovered that they were not. I believe that they were good letters for a young man of that age – full of effervescent *joie de vivre*, such as was sadly lacking from my real life. I availed myself of this opportunity of courting Xenia through the art of letter-writing and it may well have made a greater impression on her than if I had been wooing her face to face. There were quite a number of instances in her replies when Xenia praised my literary prowess.

Another factor that enhanced my chances with her was that Xenia told me she had just recently gone down with glandular fever. There is always the possibility that she had caught it from me, although I had been passed as fit before we were actually kissing for the first time. I think there had been an outbreak of the disease in Britain that year, so that is the more likely source of infection. But it must have had the effect of keeping her at home during weeks when she would have otherwise had ample opportunity of developing that other relationship – with [M] – if not a liaison with someone else. Indeed the source of the infection may possibly have been indicated in that first letter she wrote me.

There was nothing to make me suppose that there was any threat to our own relationship. It was only later, after my return to England, that I heard how there was more in this episode than Xenia had seen fit to disclose. For I then learnt how she hated Kerry St Johnstone – another suitor – because he went round telling everyone that she had permitted him to kiss her. Apparently he and Nicky Gordon-Lennox were competing against each other to see who could score the greatest number of points for seduction over the course of that term – with one point for kissing, two points for breast-fondling, three points for genital stimulation and a maximum of five points for a fully fledged copulation. St Johnstone had put down a claim for one point (or was it two?) and the following morning Gordon-Lennox had teased Xenia about it, in order to check that the points had been genuinely earned. But when I myself asked if she had really allowed him to kiss her, she took great delight in accusing me of jealousy – without ever answering my question.

If Xenia was only being true to me in her fashion, my own conduct was now hardly any better. The improvement in my sexual status came at the Sorbonne, rather than at the Academie Julien. As I have mentioned, I was attending *Le Cours de Civilisation Française* each morning in the hope that this would attune my ear to conversational French, whilst gleaning some useful information about France. The lectures were held in the spacious Salle Richelieu, with four large gallery sections placed in the upper storey of the auditorium. It was from a seat up there, in one of the gallery sections, that I surveyed the scene in the stalls below me: taking as much interest in the students themselves as in the theme which some professor would be expounding for our benefit.

It was in this fashion that I found myself developing a special line of personality projection, which suited my present line of introverted intensity. I didn't have to go up and make conversation with anyone. I just sat there with my head slightly lowered, fixing my thoughts upon this or that attractive girl, while imagining that we were coming together in spirit – or simply becoming aware of one another. And of course, if you sit like that for long enough, then the awareness does become mutual. Ideas about telepathy circulate as wishful thinking, which all serves to heighten the enjoyment of the game.

I know that I believed that I was becoming highly telepathic. And as the weeks went by, it seemed quite evident that I had opened up a whole network of such lines of communication. My excitement in the presence of certain girls was stimulated to a fever pitch by the realisation that (as I imagined) I was arousing a reciprocal excitement in them. And all of this was taking place without any words being openly exchanged.

In the light of our awareness of one another, it might have been anticipated that I would then avail myself of any opportunity that presented itself to go up and talk to one of these girls. I am confident that they would have been responsive to me. Yet such was my fear of rejection, I did not risk making an approach in person and I continued to remain aloof; in doing so, perhaps, I enhanced the excitement on their side.

Not all of the girls appreciated my telepathic attentions. I might make mention of one in particular, who was to be identified to me subsequently as Sarah Wignall. I never heard her speaking, but I knew from her demeanour and the way in which she walked that she was English. It was a new discovery that I could find out such information without actually approaching them. But she gave me some cross glances whenever my eyes found hers and I learned the dicretion of not making eye contact with her.

Besides, I soon discovered that I was being sought out by some English girls who had, in fact, recognised me. It turned out that Nick Buckley, who had been at Eton with me and who had joined the Life Guards in the Brigade Squad six months after me, had a sister called Jill who was here attending the same course as myself. Nick had even suggested that she look out for me in Paris, which led to her coming up to introduce herself. After this, she followed me up to my seat in the gallery to sit beside me, where she was subsequently joined by three other girls who were at the same finishing school as herself. And so the spot where I was sitting in the lecture hall began to resemble a private harem – which enhanced my romantic image even further.

It was Jill who persuaded me that the social life of the English group in Paris revolved around their attendance each Sunday at the British embassy's chapel services. So I decided to put in some appearances there so as to see for myself. I signed the visitors' book at the embassy at the same time – which led to me receiving a letter from the Ambassadress, Lady Diana Cooper, who was a good friend of my mother's. In fact, Diana had been something like the lifestyle model Daphne had taken for herself at the time when she was first emerging into society as a debutante. So it was not a great surprise to me to receive an invitation for a weekend visit to their château at Chantilly, which was officially on loan to them from the French government.

Other guests at this weekend were Anabelle York and a girl friend of hers – whom I was to get to know when I went up to Oxford. On this occasion, though, Lady Diana had selected Anabelle for me, no doubt after careful consideration of who would be suitable marital material. It came as second nature to the likes of Lady Diana to be matching young couples together for their subsequent voyage through life. I took a liking to both of these girls but it is curious that, at this stage, I never got round to taking their telephone numbers for the purposes of dating. It all indicates, perhaps, that I didn't really regard myself as being still available – or, when it came to the London social scene, not to any female other than Xenia.

The British embassy chapel services were indeed full of potential encounters. Camilla Crawley (Sarah's sister) was amongst those with whom I chatted in the street outside, along with her friend Claire Baring; this led to the occasional invitation to Sunday lunch with the de Castignac family, where they were paying guests. I flirted mildly with Camilla. And I was told that Sarah, too, would be coming out soon on a quick visit to Paris – causing me to wonder if there might be any notion in her head of taking up a romantic liaison once again with me.

I was not left much the wiser after Sarah's brief visit. I was invited over to dinner by the de Castignac family, with a plan for me to take Sarah on afterwards to one of the small night-clubs on the Left Bank. I was dressed to that end in my usual attire of scruffy grey flannels and sports' jacket. And Sarah rushed off upstairs to put on something she regarded as similarly appropriate. But the outfit she had carefully selected for herself back in London – a pair of jeans which were of a delicate pink shade – was far too chic for mingling unnoticed with the crowd of existentialist students on the Left Bank. It should be noted that the extrovert side to my personality was much in abeyance over this period. I told her that I certainly wasn't going to escort her anywhere dressed like that. So she promptly changed into jeans of a more sombre colour.

We spent an agreeable evening together at the Metro Jazz, after riding round Paris for a while on my Velosolex. Later we went down to sit beside the river, where I kissed her and probed to see if she wanted to take things any further. But she was gently resisting me. I didn't really know where I stood with her nowadays – so I dropped her back home. She was returning to London the following day.

There was another evening that I spent sampling a variety of Parisian dance halls in the company of Camilla. Nicky Gage – a school friend from Eton times – was then on a visit and he was accompanied that evening by Tilly Laycock. They were a younger couple than ourselves and we were both somewhat put out by the advanced scale of their overt courtship. Neither Camilla nor I had much personal inclination to follow suit, so we were left feeling like a couple of intruding chaperones watching from the sidelines. It was indeed brought home to me that evening that I was getting far surpassed in sexual adventure by those who had emerged from school even more recently than myself.

This notion that I was immature in my sexual outlook was reinforced on two other occasions when I was invited out to dinner only to find the girls I was re-meeting had now outstripped me in sophistication. Such feelings of inadequacy were even inflicted on me when I dined out with a younger cousin of Xenia's and her fiancé who were living in Paris. The experience left me feeling that it was not I, but they, who belonged to the senior generation. And there was an occasion when Camilla invited me to escort her to dinner at the Hoyer-Millers' where their daughter Liz was in attendance. Liz made it quite evident to all present that she now regarded me as being tiresomely juvenile, barely making even a minimal effort to converse with me at their dining table. I was aware that I urgently needed to develop my social skills in relation to women.

Meanwhile, Xenia had been recovering from her glandular fever and, during the course of her illness, her desire to see me appeared to have grown. A plan to come out on a secret visit to Paris was now being hatched – with the assistance of Serena who vicariously delighted in the sexual exploits of her friends. The plan was to wait until Xenia's parents were up in Scotland and then tell them that they were going to spend the weekend with a particular girl friend. But complications arose when Xenia was unable to find her passport. And she was still under the age when she might have applied for a new one of her own accord.

It may only be a coincidence, but Xenia's decision to abandon the idea of coming out to Paris was taken the same weekend that she re-met [M] for the first time since I had walked off with her at Henrietta's birthday party. This took place at a cocktail party given by Caroline Poole's mother. In her letter, Xenia only made casual mention of it, stating that their "strained relationship is now amicable". She also mentioned how her hostess accused her of getting drunk – which led me to suppose that she was patching things up with [M] rather more *amicably* than her letter conveyed.

But there is little justification for registering any complaint about her treating me falsely, since my own behaviour at the Sorbonne was now falling short of total fidelity. It pleased me to think that there were quite a number of attractive young girls down there in the stalls, who were endeavouring almost, but not precisely, to catch my eye in response to my own display of that kind. There was one in particular who seemed far more beautiful than the rest – with an elegantly graceful body, an olive complexion and long brown hair flowing freely down her back. She had only recently come to join the course, but I was fully confident that she was now aware of me. But on reaching the conclusion that I evidently wasn't going to seek her out for an introduction, she took the original step of shifting her regular seat from the stalls to the section of the gallery just beyond my own – so that we found ourselves quite naturally, at the end of any lecture, coming down the stairwell from the gallery at the same time. And on finding myself in such proximity to her, it seemed only natural that I should smile and ask her what nationality she might be – after which we went to have a coffee together at the Café Dupont.

It was evident that Lita came from a well-to-do family, without being ostentatiously rich. For my own part, I was dressed in paint-smeared grey flannels and I said nothing to disillusion her from the idea that I might be some truly impoverished art student. As such, I had her interest – arousing her concern no doubt, as to the degree of deprivation that I might have suffered in life. She also informed me that it was a superstition of hers that all the most wonderful things in her life had taken place on the ninth of some month. And this was the 9th of May! I took mental note of her superstition, while being careful never to make direct mention of it again.

Then came the question of where we should sit when returning to the Salle Richelieu after the coffee break. I realised that she was too proud to be seen joining the group that I regarded as my private harem. So I judged that it would be tactically advisable for me to go and sit with her – just for the rest of that morning. And I was aware how, in the eyes of all the others, her moment of triumph didn't pass unnoticed. There was even a splutter of laughter or two from the groups of girls who had been playing the telepathy game with me – even a gesture in her direction from one of them, which might have been intended to signify, "Hats off to you, Mademoiselle!" But I could see that the girls in my own private harem were looking just a trifle peeved.

On subsequent days I usually returned to my former seat, because I had no wish to appear disloyal to my established circle of friends. But the door to a developing romance with Lita had now been opened. I remained in the habit of pairing up with Lita in the coffee breaks, then I suddenly found that she had become acquainted with two of the girls with whom I had been playing the telepathy game. These were Martha, who like Lita came from Argentina, and June, an American girl from Boston. I never learnt precisely how it was that they now came to be acquainted, but I always imagined that the linkage had originated in me. Sometimes, too, they came to sit within my own section of the gallery, though they really formed a second group of their own with Lita as the nucleus. But there was still a sense in which I could feel that my harem was expanding.

The sense of romance began to take root in my relationship with Lita. It could hardly be said that I was at ease in her company: I was too self-absorbed and earnest for that. When we talked – sometimes in French and sometimes in English – it was in an endeavour to bridge what we both imagined to be the vast gulf between our respective backgrounds. We touched upon the question of values in life, while trying to divine the nature of this other individual with whom we were conversing. I sensed with awe that she fitted within that widely travelled international group, whose cultural background was far more appreciative of the arts than my own.

She knew about opera and who were the rising names in abstract art. While greatly interested in such matters, I realized that the briefest of conversations might leave me wrong-footed in my relative ignorance. But one card I could play was to show her some of my recent paintings at the Academie Julien… I was gratified to see that these evidently impressed her. She perceived that they were not the average product of a Parisian art school of the day, but something with an individualism apparent to her eye. And this enhanced the idea that I could be interesting for her to know.

Being English certainly wasn't something that in her eyes went to my advantage. She admitted to having no special liking for my countrymen, finding them cold and unfriendly. The idea that we were philistine, too, was dangerously close to her thoughts and, where Europe might be concerned, she identified France and the Latin world in general as the fount of all artistic culture. But I was the first young Englishman with whom she had found any opportunity to converse – being a mere seventeen years old herself. And my own lack of acquaintance with anybody from South America meant that there were mutual fields for exploration of each other's attitudes and outlook.

The importance to her of her Catholic faith was something that she had stressed to me from the very start. She stated this almost as a warning that I'd be advised to tread cautiously if I was thinking of developing on the theme of my own agnosticism – something I'd already admitted to her. So it was an area I left untouched. Nor did she share any of my own incipient doubts concerning the justification for wealth or, in particular, its display. She felt that being charitable and benevolent could be sufficient justification as well as compensation enough for any inequalities in the distribution of wealth. But she was clearly defensive about the whole issue.

Then came an evening when I was invited by Camilla to accompany her to one of the big society balls that year in Paris. This was the first time that I had seen her since my friendship had started developing with Lita. And it was not with the greatest tact, I dare say, that while dancing with her I was enthusing about this exciting young Argentinean beauty I'd met at the Sorbonne, when – lo and behold! – there she was in person, waltzing round the ballroom just a few yards away from us. Both Lita and myself cried out in mutual astonishment, although it may have been greater on her side than on mine. For she had never surmised that I might come from a background where I might mingle socially in the same affluent circles as herself.

This encounter had amused her, as much as stimulating her desire to find out more about me. And she arrived triumphantly at the Sorbonne a few days later to enquire if my parents were called Henry and Daphne. On confirming that this was so, she declared that my disguise had been penetrated: that friends of hers from Argentina had identified my family. And what surprised her, in particular, was the way in which I had portrayed my father to her as being an oppressive influence and a martinet for discipline: her friend had assured her that this was nonsense and that Henry was one of the most charming figures in English society! Well, it may be that my judgment was then held in some doubt – but these revelations had served to draw us closer together in some measure.

So it was in this atmosphere, with spring now in full bloom - waxing sunshine and lush verdant foliage - that the romantic aura hanging over my relationship with Lita was now heightened. It might be said that I was in love with her – without so much as the experience of a first kiss. The differences between us remained in their own way inhibiting. And I was far too cautious to put such progress as I had achieved at risk by any inopportune display of my inner lust. But I thrilled at her presence and all the aspects it opened up to me for flirtation with elements of a world unknown.

My **hands** caress the **gossamer glass tresses**
of a **brand new** bejewelled **ornament**,
which **rests** in a **scented nest** – an **object** to **peer** at
and revere, while **fearing** it'll **break** at my **clutching touch**.
Taking a **look** from a **high window**, a **winter**
garden **lies** itching at the **brink of Spring**,
and **tingling** into **floral life**, it **fascinates**
my dilating **eye** with **exquisite secret patterns**.
Statue-still, I **watch** the **movement** of a **plum**age-
blooming **bird** of **paradise**, **marital-minded**
in **finding adept steps** in its **ritual dance** -
then **prancing** to **wing**, perhaps **gone** forever.
   I thrill to what I might – but do not – dare,
    while balancing 'twixt ardour and despair.

It seems that I became negligent in writing home during these weeks that I was drooling over Lita. I refer to the subject in a letter to Henry towards the end of May.

> *I'm afraid I haven't written for some time. Sorry. I'm becoming Latinised and lazy under the influence of the sun. We are in the midst of a glorious heat-wave...*
> *I now go for paddles on the Seine with a ravishing Argentinean girl – who can speak good English. She suddenly turned up at the Sorbonne, and had every man within a mile rushing to sit at her feet. I even made the sacrifice of deserting my harem to do just that. But we have now compromised in that I go and sit with her group on one day, after which they come and sit in mine for the next. She is highly cultured, so I have to be careful about dropping any ignorant remarks. She says she is frightened of the English, because they are so cold. I regard it as my national duty to convince her to the contrary.*

I didn't feel any real sense that I was being unfaithful to Xenia in this flirtation with Lita. I had after all stopped short of even attempting to kiss her – for whatever reason that may have been. I don't recall whether I made any mention of the flirtation in my letters to Xenia. In any case, there was some hint in her replies that she was embarking on another flirtation, but this time the opportunity to develop it into a romance was denied, as shortly after this date the man in question departed on a voyage round the world.

In her last letter, before my return to Britain for the Coronation, Xenia broached plans for a weekend together at Stowell Park, taking advantage of an invitation by Serena. But the tone of her letter was later to strike me as being curiously devious. It was almost as if she was implying that she was being pushed into such a plan against her better judgment.

In these last few days before returning to Britain, I received a surprise visit from Bendor Drummond, who had just been demobilised from the Life Guards. He was driving through Paris, so came to look me up – inquisitive to see for himself what I might be getting up to in this romantic centre of Western civilisation. It was not without shame that I had to admit to him that I was living here without one consummated love affair to reveal. But I was glad to be able to inform him how, at long last, I was indeed experiencing romance in my life.

Interestingly, it struck me that Bendor's sexual attitudes appeared, almost in caricature, to be typical of someone from my former background, which now appeared immature in outlook despite all his assumed veneer of sophistication. The way in which he accompanied me to the Academie Julien to feast his eyes upon the nude models involved behaviour that I felt myself to have left long behind. So too did the flashiness of his sartorial display – with silk handkerchief lolling from the breast pocket of his Guards' boating-jacket. I found that I was deeply embarrassed to have him sitting beside me, up in the gallery at the Sorbonne. What made it worse was anticipating that he would have an instant success that might rival my own. Nevertheless, his behaviour was too close for comfort to the image that I had all too recently shed. But the distance with which I had now departed from it gave rise to hope that I might evolve indefinitely – until I had found my own relaxed and natural manner in female company.

In one way, however, Bendor was of great assistance to me, as I had been worrying how I might transport the large number of canvases that I had painted over these four months – it had risen to two per day – back home to England. They were still on their stretchers, so the problem seemed quite considerable. And it was with some reluctance that Bendor agreed to load them as freight into his car. So a few days later, on May 26th, I was then free to make my own return journey by plane.

PART SIX

CORONATION TIME

Chapter 6.1

Career: defining my future

It was virtually impossible to obtain a hotel room in London over the period of the Coronation, but Caroline had told me that she could put me up at 90 Eaton Terrace, provided that I was happy to sleep on the floor of David's study. Her spare rooms were already promised to others. In fact, Daphne and Xan were there briefly when I first arrived, on the point of departing for France, where we made plans to meet up after I returned to Paris.

Caroline told me how disconcerted she and David had been the week before, when on returning home one evening they discovered that someone had delivered in their absence a consignment of about thirty paintings without a word of explanation. It was only later that Bendor came back to explain how he had been doing me a favour in delivering them to their address – from where I would be collecting them in due course. The paintings had originally been spread all round their drawing-room, and David had immediately assumed that someone was playing a practical joke on him. In as much as David was now one of the directors of the Marlborough Gallery, it was hardly encouraging that he should have jumped to such a conclusion – nor tactful that they should tell me. But I took all that in my stride.

My anticipation that the Coronation was going to be an exciting event was never fulfilled. As far as I was concerned, it went off like a damp squib – with me sitting there in the rain, all on my own, occupying a seat in the stand near Westminster Abbey, for which Henry had passed on to me via his supplementary ticket. It was especially so that he might attend the Coronation ceremony that he had finally decided to take up his seat in the House of Lords. And having done so, he went through the ordeal with a certain panache – having the family coach transported up to London, so that he could ride up to the Abbey in style – but unaccompanied, since he was still officially unwed in the aftermath of his divorce. He told me later that he felt petrified during the coach ride, convinced that everyone was enquiring whom it could be who was putting on such airs. Clearly, when he arrived, my own attention must have been fixed upon others, since I never caught a glimpse of him.

The spectacle was a fiasco from my own viewpoint as, from the stand where I was seated, I only saw segments of the procession that arrived at the Abbey. The real procession, after the Coronation service had ended, took off from the Abbey in a different direction. So I saw none of that. All that I could do was to sit there in the rain, listening to the account I heard upon a portable radio. And it was a fair distance that I had travelled for such a dubious experience.

It was all so much of an anticlimax. And I felt indignant that some friends from Eton – like Dickon Lumley who, as the eldest son of the Earl of Scarborough, was less eligible than myself – should have been there inside the Abbey, as ushers, because their father had taken the trouble to put down their name on the list of applicants before the time limit expired. Henry had never been quick off the mark in such matters – but it had never occurred to me to suggest it.

This business of regarding it almost as a duty to turn up for the Coronation had given rise to a few discreet smiles, as far as Lita and her friends were concerned. From the South American point of view, it was all so typically British – this reverence for an hereditary monarch. And they were making comments like, "You must feel that you are tremendously lucky, to have such a beautiful queen on your throne!" – their mirth increased by my efforts to treat the statement seriously.

Given that the de Vulpian girls had also enquired whether I regarded myself as a royalist, I suppose that there must have been something of that attitude, which was apparent to a foreigner. But the real question was to what extent I saw myself that way. And the truth of the matter is that I did not. Or to put it another way, it may well be that there were others – the Royal Family in particular – and those who organised their lives for them – people like the old Duke of Beaufort – who might well have regarded me as the kind of person they were hoping to attract into the courtiers' circle, so that I would adopt it as my profession. After all, my grandfather Thomas, as Beaufort's predecessor, had been very much the representative of the monarchy within the various counties of the West Country. And Henry had also been tried out, until he lost the favour of the Prince of

Wales. But the role of a courtier had never featured upon the list of careers that I bore in mind: the required subordination to the royal will never did appeal to me as a life prospect.

At this time, however, I still featured prominently upon the list of young aristocrats who received regular invitations to attend royal functions. During this particular visit back home, I turned up for the Coronation ball at Buckingham Palace and I was there at the garden party too. That was a beautiful, spectacular event in that there were so many African chiefs and their wives in attendance, with robes and even their umbrellas truly resplendent in every colour of the rainbow. Being a mere Britisher, wearing a morning coat by way of traditional uniform, I looked very drab in comparison. Yet I regarded such attendance almost as my birthright, although I knew in my heart that I was shifting outside that particular orbit.

Something of far greater personal significance to my life, which was currently being drawn up by our respective lawyers, was the breaking of the family entail. I had only just reached the age when it was permissible for us to open such negotiations, and it was required by law that I should be separately represented. The general scheme had now been defined, so I was summoned to discuss the matter with the lawyer who was working on my behalf. He explained that the general idea was that I should receive a large portion of the family's capital investments, along with the 'outer' bulk of the Longleat estate – most of which would remain strictly within the family entail – in return for releasing a large portion of investments from the entail (some of which had already been squandered in tasks like the dredging of the lakes) for Henry now to spend the rest as he might see fit. And Henry would keep under his own control the inner core of Longleat itself in its surrounding park, to continue running the tourist business that he had created. But Cheddar caves would be amongst the properties transferred to myself – and it should be noted that Cheddar had always been the principal source of revenue for the Longleat estate.

What my lawyer needed to know was whether I approved of the scheme as it had so far been negotiated and whether I wished him to take a stronger line over the ownership of the chattels. My feeling was that I didn't want to seem greedy. I asked him whether or not he regarded it as being in my interest to agree to the scheme as it stood. He said yes, but that it was even more in my father's interests than in my own. I could hold out for a tougher bargain if I wanted to. But I had to bear in mind that this scheme would at least save me from having to pay any death duties –

provided that he was still alive after a period of five years. And it certainly wouldn't be comfortable for me if, with the matter unresolved, he were to oblige me to live without any financial support until the day he died – when the entailed property and investments would all come to me, *after* the payment of crippling death duties. I told him that I would accept the terms that he had negotiated, without requiring him to tighten up the clauses with regard to the ownership of the chattels. But this was something that I was to regret much later on in life!

The way Henry himself saw it was different, of course. He told me that his own lawyer, Sir Leslie Farrer, had indicated that there was no real need for him to hand over Cheddar Caves to me at this stage in life, despite the fact that my lawyers were insisting upon it. Their argument was that it wasn't worth my while to accept the transfer of the unprofitable portions of the estate, unless the gift was sweetened with something that really did make money. It should also be recalled that I might find myself having to pay crippling death duties on the transfer of such a remunerative business concern, if we waited until a later date.

Henry indicated that he had taken it upon himself to allow the transfer. But he held that we had a gentlemen's agreement between us that I wouldn't deny him funds for the promotion of Longleat and its estate, from out of the Cheddar reserves, if ever he found that he needed them. It was stated as if this was all a part of the official deal, though I was to learn later that Farrer had told him quite bluntly that such under-the-table clauses could in no way be part of the negotiated contract. Still, at this particular point I imagined that they were and I was certainly encouraged in this belief by Henry.

Of the two particular proposals for my future, which had formerly been controversial, both were now accepted without any need for further contention. That is: it was agreed that the next phase in my life was to be a spell of higher education at Oxford; it was also agreed that I should move into the Dowager suite at Longleat, just as soon as Henry and Virginia got married and took up their abode at Job's Mill. This was due to take place before my eventual return to Britain - that is, after my next spell in Paris.

But the question of my future career was still highly controversial. Henry had never really encouraged me on the idea of joining the Foreign Office – on the grounds that even if I were to rise high in the ranks there wasn't much money in it. And I think that I must have been retreating from the idea myself: certainly, I had refrained from asserting that this was my ambition when staying for that weekend at Chantilly, in the company of no less a mortal than the British Ambassador to France, Lord Norwich – or Duff Cooper, as he still preferred to be called, having built up his reputation both as a diplomat and as an author under the latter name. He had in fact enquired after dinner, when the ladies had withdrawn from the dining-table, as to what I might intend to do with my life. And I had told him that I expected to paint and to write. I daresay, too, that I told him about the novel I was currently writing.

He said to me, at this comparatively early age, the essential thing was to keep an accurate record of my life and that I should start a journal. He told me how, in his own autobiographical efforts, he had found that the task had been enormously facilitated by the existence of a journal. The periods during which he had been keeping one sprang far more vividly to life than when such effort had lapsed. No matter what the purpose that I might eventually bring to my literary endeavours, the best way now for me to be exercising such talent was in keeping a personal record of the life that I was living and of the problems that I perceived emerging in it. I took good note of all that he was saying, deciding that I should start such a journal on going up to Oxford. During this present phase, I felt that I had too much on my plate to contend with any additional material – for I was still involved in my revision of *The Millions and the Mansions*.

The revision was a slow and tedious chore and I never had my heart in it. But I was very much taken by the idea that I was making fast progress as an artist, so it was important that I should sort out the necessary arrangements for a return to Paris, once my agenda here in Britain had been completed.

I had already taken the decision that I would not be returning to stay with the de Vulpians. I had not fallen out with them, it was merely that I needed greater liberty of spirit than was possible in a household where I was subjected to the routines of family life. I wanted greater independence. In fact, Mme de Vulpian had raised the matter herself as to whether I intended to return to lodge with them – expressing the hope that I would. She explained how the friction between Jocelyne and Eughien necessitated that she should ask him to find lodgings elsewhere. It would render her task of telling him that he must leave much easier, she said, if she could point out that, while my room would still be occupied by me, his own room was promised to some Swedish girl. So, in response, I then explained to her how I intended to find lodgings on my own – ostensibly to be nearer to my places of work, which were all on the Left Bank. She had accepted that this was sensible, so it was all settled amicably.

My immediate task, now that I was back in Britain, was to secure the financial basis for me to continue as an art student in Paris. Already I'd seen the problem of making ends meet when relying upon the minimal allowance that tourists were allowed to take abroad with them at that time. Henry had obtained permission to transfer the sum of £40 a month to Mme de Vulpian's account, to cover my lodging fees, but the rest of my living expenses had to come out of the travel allowance that was legally permitted for tourism – which had just been raised to the figure of £40 *a year*. If I had to use this to cover whatever lodgings I might now find for myself, then I would indeed feel impoverished.

What I needed was a student's grant or at least some manner of official recognition that I was a serious art student, which would entitle me to transfer further sums of my own money to cover such expenses as that manner of life might warrant. But that wasn't so easy. When I approached the Bank of England on the subject, I was asked to come in and discuss the matter – and I found that they were treating me with the utmost suspicion. They were too well accustomed, I expect, to receiving applications for additional foreign currency on trumped-up pretexts, which were then refused. This claim that I was a serious art student required documentary backing. I hadn't seen fit to take art as one of my subjects for the School Certificate; it wasn't even as if I had been recommended for a course in Paris from some British art school. So I was advised to obtain some authentication of my claim from the Headmaster at Eton, before reapplying for such a grant.

I promptly wrote a letter to Mr Birley requesting such backing, but he in turn demanded that I should send him a report from my Parisian art school. It might seem that he, too, was wary of being used to legitimate a spurious claim for the transfer of foreign currency. Anyway, I dashed off a letter to Roger Chastel at the Academie Ranson, asking him to send me such a report on my potential as an artist, and he sent me the following – which I am here translating into English.

> *You ask me what I think of your work! It's rather more difficult to define your "potential" – as you put it so well – than to appraise your work over the course of one of my critical sessions.*
>
> *Nevertheless, I feel that you have displayed a character and a temperament which are exceptional, that the evolution of your style since I've known you has been*

*remarkable, and that there is no reason why this
evolution should not continue if you keep working on it.
I cannot tell you what manner of painter you will make,
because I am no seer! But I can say that you do possess two
of the necessary characteristics for a creative artist – the
faith, and the temperament. I have confidence in you,
and in your youth.*

Armed with this letter, I descended upon Eton to request Wilfrid Blunt to
now take up the matter with Mr Birley, so that he might furnish me with
the strongest possible reference. And I took along with me a batch of my
recent paintings. But I was unfortunate, in that Wilfrid was absent that
afternoon. Only Oliver Thomas was present at the Drawing Schools – we
both remembered all too clearly how he had recommended David Brooke
for the top art award, rather than myself. I found that he was now anxious
to make amends. While it was evident that he didn't really like the
direction in which my style was evolving, he did his best to treat it with
respect. Moreover, he intimated that, whereas originally he had judged
that Brooke was a painter with more potential than myself, he had come
to see that he'd been mistaken. The shallowness of Brooke's art had
apparently become evident, after my own departure from Eton. Well, it
was nice of him to be making this belated apology. But it never quite went
so far as to explain how he had placed me third in that final rating – after
both Brooke and Broad – when I was expecting, and had been expected,
to come top.

Now I rather forget *exactly* what transpired after this date. I think the
Headmaster did finally send a letter to say that I was a serious art student. But
this wasn't until after my return to Paris, and by that time I had finally made
other arrangements to transfer a little more foreign currency to France. Henry
had at first declined to be of any assistance at all in making it easier for me to
continue with what he regarded as a whim (He could, after all, have put me
in touch with any of his many friends who had the means to effect such a
transfer). Once I had returned to Paris, however, he relented; he wrote:

*I have also been reconsidering the whole question about
your allowance while you're in France, and I rather think
that, as I have in the past been prepared to pay Mme de
Vulpian £40 per month, I will continue to do so – and
you can draw it and be responsible completely for your*

*upkeep whilst in Paris. This I hope you will see is a very
big concession on my part!*

Well, if he wanted to see things that way, I wasn't going to waste any time
debating the generosity of his spirit. All I had to do was to continue picking
up this allowance from Thomas Cook & Son and I found that I could now
make ends meet in a manner that matched the living standards of my
fellow art-students.

It had in fact been through the agency of Thomas Cook that I found
my next lodgings. I had sorted this out shortly before the Coronation. I
had been given the address of Mme Pla at 49 Rue Falguière, who was
offering a room for 10,000 francs per month, which compared favourably
with the 40,000 francs that Henry had been paying to Mme de Vulpian. I
would now have to feed myself, of course, but I was in Montparnasse and
far nearer to both the Sorbonne and to the various art schools.

Mme Enid Pla was a delightfully eccentric middle-aged widow, a
bird-like creature, whom any sudden noise, one imagined, would send
fluttering from side to side in her cage. It was not unusual to see her
darting round her apartments, attired in nothing more than her long
woollen underwear. There was another lodger, a young Cambridge
graduate called Laurence Fleming. And it soon became evident that
Mme Pla was concerned about our welfare with what amounted to a
quasi-maternal regard. She had a particular liking for young men who
had been educated at any of the English public schools: Laurie had come
from Lancing. She was protective towards us, although occasionally this
did lead to inquisitiveness. But I found her endearing and I was pleased
with my new lodgings.

It must have been approaching the middle of June when I returned to
Paris, with only a month to go before the *quatorze juillet* celebrations –
after which Parisians would begin to drift away to their holiday resorts. But
I continued with my art studies at the Academie Julien, while attending the
Sorbonne each morning. And I put in a brief spell at the Alliance Française,
in the misplaced hope that this might give a sudden boost to my grasp of
the French language.

My style in painting was loosening up all round – becoming less
rigorously representational while I gave expression to what I had absorbed
from contemporary abstract art. It was still to the Academie Ranson that I
took my paintings to be criticised. But I was disappointed to discover that
Chastel had now left the school and his place had been taken by Henri

Goetz whom, at this stage, I found a poor substitute for my previous mentor. This may well have been because he was more reserved in the praise that he had to offer, in that he treated me as an average student like any of the others. But he opened up my eyes to the way I should view a subject as a visual experience in itself, and to create something distinctive from it, rather than to focus my efforts too closely on whatever might actually be there for me to see.

As examples of what I did over this period, I might single out a still life with copper tub, bottle and plums, an abstract conception of sunrise and a tangle of dancing figures inspired by the street scenes on the 14th of July. I should mention, incidentally, that the paintings I had taken home with me in May had by now been shown by Henry to some of his more artistic friends. His attitude to them was evidently softening, for he wrote:

> *Russell Page came down here the other day and had a look at your paintings, and I regret to say was very much impressed!! He naturally had criticisms to make, but he did say you were beginning to realize how to put on paint – whatever that may mean. Even Robin Campbell quite liked them, but let me tell you these are only two people.*

There was a model who often posed at the Academie Julien called Mme le Nivet. She had taken a personal interest in my work ever since I had arrived at the school, because she felt that I was the only person who had managed to capture some particular expression she saw in herself when I had painted my first portrait of her. I remember her hinting to me that she herself was endowed with magic powers, and she told me solemnly that one could see that I had *"quelquechose dans la tête"* – whatever that might have been intended to signify. Anyway, she was now urging me to take my paintings along to an artist for whom she often posed called de Jouvencourt. She said that he would understand what I was trying to express and I was given to understand that he was expecting me to call.

When I arrived at his address, I was far from certain that he had the faintest idea whom I might be or exactly who had recommended I visit him. But, with those difficulties surmounted, he was agreeably affable and was quite complimentary about my work. But he was really far more interested to hear that my brother-in-law was a director of the Marlborough Gallery in London and from that point on we were largely talking at cross-purposes.

His own style was curiously similar to my own at the stage when I was just about to leave Eton – when I had painted that large self-portrait, consisting of curling strands of flat paint, complementing each other within the cooler ranges of the spectrum. The difference in his case was that his colours were all drawn from the hot range. I don't think he liked it when I began to suggest that I had myself done something rather similar in time past, for he was the established painter whereas I was not. But he joked his way round that point and suggested that he might call in on David during a forthcoming visit to London; he would suggest to David that he might encourage me by arranging to exhibit some of my paintings at the Marlborough Gallery.

I realised very quickly that his real concern would be to investigate the possibility of obtaining an exhibition for himself at the Marlborough Gallery. He failed in that venture, but he did go round to see David at his home address, which I had given to him on the pretext of telling him about his brother-in-law's potential talent as an artist – over a drink of course. Then, on seeing that he was making no headway whatsoever to serve either of our ends, he had taken his leave of them. I was told all this over the telephone when I rang to enquire if any interest had been aroused.

Paris was already beginning to empty for the holiday season when I had an interesting encounter. I was sitting in a café when a couple strolled by, and it suddenly occurred to me that I knew the girl – who was none other than Caroline Blackwood, generally regarded as one of the great young beauties on the London scene and one of Venetia Murray's best friends. I had noted how attractive she was on the occasion when I had first met the two debutantes (as they then were) while I myself was still at Eton. And she now responded with recognition as soon as our glances met. The man with her was the artist Lucian Freud, whom she later married much to the fury of her aristocratic mother. Their relationship was a matter for considerable gossip at this time, for Lucian had recently deserted his wife, Kitty Epstein, to live with Caroline. I found myself eager to observe how they were getting on. Their behaviour was typical of young lovers, who had at last broken loose within the city where conventions counted for so much less. Anyway, they invited me to come and have a meal with them.

It was useful for me too to get Lucian's comments on my paintings. So we went along afterwards to the Academie Julien, where he took a look at them. He was quite encouraging in what he said, taking a particular liking to my painting of a nude model, which I had entitled *Ophelia*: a drowning girl, but almost cadaverous and transforming into a shell as she floated within a pool of water. This gave a pleasant boost to my self-confidence.

It was towards the end of July that I finally completed my revision of *The Millions and the Mansions*. This revision had in fact been a total waste of time, in that it added to the general length of the novel without improving it or making it more concise, which is what was required. It was only the first draft that I finally preserved for my future study. But I suppose I may claim some credit for my perseverance in pursuing the task I had set myself to its conclusion.

Daphne had suggested that I send it to Xan once it was completed and he would tell me whether he regarded it as something that might get published. So I posted it off to him, knowing in my heart that it simply wasn't good enough – that I was still far too immature as a human being to be able to treat my material in a manner that might hold my readers' interest. This wasn't something that I was ready to tell myself, however: it needed to come – gently – from someone else, whose opinion I might respect. And this was the disagreeable task that had been thrust upon Xan. He was quite prompt in his delivery of an answer, which arrived in early August.

> *I've just finished your book and want to tell you at once that I enjoyed it very much. Unfortunately I am speaking only for myself, and not for any old member of a general public completely unacquainted with the Longleat background etc. Whether the ordinary man in the street (i.e. the proposed reader) will like it as much as I did, I can't really tell.*
>
> *Technically speaking, I am afraid it couldn't possibly be published exactly as it is. Some bits are rather over-written (which a reader might take to be an insult to his intelligence.) Other bits are carelessly written, (And people don't like bad craftsmanship!) Oddly enough you've successfully accomplished the novelist's hardest task. By that I mean the architecture of the book as opposed to the decoration. Structurally your work's damn good; where you lose marks is on the decoration side: (descriptive passages, dialogues etc.) I think the reason for this is that you've attempted the seriocomic style, which is the most difficult of all to handle successfully. (P.G. Wodehouse is a*

fairly good example of this kind of writing, which, for want of a better word, I call the "facetious" school; but then he isn't everyone's cup of tea.)

That's my criticism, for what it's worth. As for suggestions, (not that I'm in any way equipped for making them,) I'd advise you to sit on the thing for a bit. Forget about it for at least six months; then come back to it with a fresh outlook. I think you would then see the essential alterations to be made.

Or have you ever thought of it cast in dramatic form? It strikes me as being good theatrical material... Then the playwright's job is pretty specialised, even though it appears to me, superficially at least, to entail less labour.

His judgment came as a disappointment to me, of course, but it wasn't exactly unexpected. For Xan wasn't the only person who felt that I should curb my optimism with regard to the likelihood of my novel ever getting published.

Evidently I felt no need to brood over the matter, in that there were other projects on which to focus my mind. For my current activities were more concerned with my possible emergence as a painter than as a novelist. My spell in Paris was now drawing to its close, but I had decided to spend a few final weeks on a painting holiday in the vicinity of Biarritz – departing by train, with my Velosolex in the luggage wagon. The real purpose of this trip was my own pursuit of free love, but I'll confine myself here to noting how I was hoping to repeat the stimulus my painting had received from that previous tour at Easter of the châteaux on the Loire. My idea was to live as roughly as I had done then, until I was churning out paintings with a zest for instant achievement. And I did get a few impressive canvases completed – one, in particular, that I liked was of an apple orchard with two hills in the background.

But my big error was in supposing that the beaches of Biarritz might prove to be a suitable spot to sleep. A policeman quickly informed me that I'd be arrested if I were found sleeping on the stretch of sand just in front of the town and advised me to try my luck on the beach just north of Biarritz – the beach where a fashionable swimming-pool had just been built. This was indeed better suited to my purposes and there was a small café where (as a regular customer) I could dump all my luggage. And on walking back up the beach a little way, to the spot where a headland protruded, I had it completely to myself.

My first night was spent in unspeakable discomfort, after digging a small trench for myself in the sand and depositing my sleeping-bag in this. No one had forewarned me that there was a species of sand hopper that infested this beach, and which took a savage delight in feasting upon me as soon as the sun had gone down. It was discomfort all right, but that was part of the whole business of being a creative artist, as I then envisaged it. So I determined to bear it with a grin, riding off to find an appropriate spot for painting just as soon as I'd breakfasted at the café.

I worked with amazing swiftness over that period, so that by evening, I was back at the café seeking to assuage my sharpening appetite. But while I was sauntering over to it, through the car park that catered for the clientele of the luxury swimming-pool, I spotted a large green Jaguar, which had caught my eye because of its sheer opulence. So I took a casual look inside – and saw, to my astonishment, Caroline was sitting there! Somewhat cautiously, I tapped on the window and said, "Hello Caroline."

I was looking a bit scruffy, I dare say – as was my wont – but I was still surprised at her reaction. She behaved as if she had seen a ghost, but hastily trying to adjust herself to the reality of the situation, while flustering for something suitable to say. "Goodness! Oh it's you, Alexander! Fancy meeting you here! I didn't know that you were in Biarritz." Then David came walking across from the swimming-pool and she added, "Look, it's Alexander."

David said, "My dear boy, so it is! Hello."

Caroline added, "What a pity we didn't meet up before. We're just on the point of leaving for Spain. Aren't we David? We're just off to San Sebastian."

David confirmed it, "Yes, we're leaving for San Sebastian."

"I've been sleeping on the beach," I mentioned hopefully.

But Caroline just replied, "Really? Was it comfortable? What a pity we didn't find out sooner. You see we're expected in Spain. And we mustn't be late. Come and see us when you're next in London."

David said, "Yes, we must now be on our way." I waved them a farewell as they drove off together.

It was beginning to sink home by this time that neither Caroline nor David would permit me to impose upon them. And I could forget about it if I'd ever seriously been supposing that he might endeavour to assist me in my profession as an artist. My thoughts at that moment, however, were more of cadging a square meal from them. But that wasn't on offer either, so I returned to the beach café for my fare. The food itself was good, but the nasty part was the prospect of another night on the beach, putting myself once more upon the sand hoppers' menu. I realised the trench had made things a lot worse for me in that the little beasts somehow delighted in collecting in underground crannies. Lying up on the surface was safer. But the weather now turned inclement – as indeed it does all too frequently in the Bay of Biscay. And I was awakened by a thunderstorm, which drenched my sleeping-bag – whereupon I took refuge in a small cave called, quite inappropriately, *La Grotte d'Amour*. It was a misery trying to get any sleep on that hard floor. And as if that wasn't bad enough, the whole place stank of urine.

By morning, my morale was sinking low. But it began to rise again as I got warmed up by the sun. And I was just dozing there in the sunshine, when I was accosted by a personable English lady, whom I had never met before, enquiring if I was Caroline's brother. It turned out that Caroline and David hadn't after all been due to set out for Spain that night, but on the following morning. And in the meantime, they had returned to the villa where they had been staying as the guests of Prince and Princess Radziwill – whose sister Jackie was to become rather famous – and where Lord and Lady Lambton – or Tony and Bindy – were two of the other guests. Tony was later to be engulfed in some sexual shenanigans that the tabloid press whipped up into such a froth that he had to resign from government.

But it was Bindy who – after learning I'd been sleeping on the beach – had taken the line that it was most remiss of Caroline not to have invited me to come back to the villa. So, with Caroline now in Spain, she had taken it upon herself to rectify this lapse, by extending to me an invitation from the Prince to come to dinner that very evening. And if I wanted it, I could avail myself of the wooden shed at the bottom of the Prince's garden, as an abode where I could pitch my sleeping-bag for the rest of my holiday. I accepted with alacrity.

I shall leave the remainder of this story for the moment. It will suffice here to say that it furnished me with an appropriate nook from which to make my sorties as an artist. And when it came to an end, I sold my Velosolex to the proprietor of the café where I had been taking so many of my meals, and travelled by train, first to Paris and then on to Britain and to Longleat. I had made things easier for myself on this occasion, by keeping my canvases rolled up together in one bundle, which I was able to take on the train with me. I was returning home in early September.

Chapter 6.2

Sex: fidelity in question

When I first came back from Paris for the Coronation, the day that I was really looking forward to was the one when I would see Xenia again. This was arranged for the dinner-party that my Aunt Vanda – Daphne's half-sister – was holding for a party of guests that would be going on to the Lycett-Green dance. I had written with a request that she be invited, which wasn't well-received. Vanda had pointed out that this was a debutante dance, where such girls would have the best chance for pairing up with eligible young men. There wouldn't be much point if all these eligible squires turned up with the partners of their own from the previous summer. The Lycett-Greens had also objected to the idea. But an exception was eventually made on the grounds that I was quite a close relative – with Vanda's mother being a Lycett-Green – and I was only back in Britain for a short period, so it would have been harsh to deny me this opportunity for seeing someone whom I really did fancy.

I did get a small rebuke, subsequently, from Vanda on the grounds that I had spent the entire evening dancing with Xenia and that we had left the dance far too early. I think we went on to *The Carousel*, for a spell of even more intimate dancing. But the part of the evening that I have reason to remember best came while I was walking her back home, when we sought out some nook where we might kiss more passionately. And we could find nothing better than the steps behind the Brompton Oratory. We were now behaving very much like an engaged couple and, while falling short of full-blooded copulation, this love-session marked a definite milestone in our relationship.

Then came the weekend at Stowell Park, which had been planned previously by letter. The other guests whom Serena had invited were Laurence Kelly, Michael Boyne and Markie Hills. But we had to drive over to collect Laurence from Oxford. (He was there already, since he had been demobilised from his National Service with the batch prior to my own.) And we found fortuitously that there was a party being given that very morning by old friends of mine from Eton days – Jimmy Skinner, who was now at New College, with Laurence. There were so many faces I knew that it made me appreciate how very much at home I was going to feel come October, when I would be going up to Oxford myself.

One of the friends that I re-met was Anthony Rouse. This was the first occasion that we had run into each other since he had sent me that letter of admiration, when I was on the point of leaving Eton. It had embarrassed me at the time, in that I didn't quite know how to answer it. But this went off without any awkwardness. I went over to chat with him, and there was a mutual and unspoken understanding that the letter would remain unmentioned. Xenia told me afterwards that she was fascinated by that fantastic person, who insisted on dancing with her at twelve o'clock in the morning.

During the afternoon we all gradually recovered by watching a cricket match. During the course of this, Laurence and I sat talking about Paris. In a fashion typical of ourselves when in the Life Guards, he wanted to know all about my recent sex life and I told him how I had been vainly pursuing a beautiful Argentinean girl. There followed a typical example of Laurence's disloyalty. He went off with Xenia for a long walk and when they returned, I noticed how she was behaving slightly coolly towards me – though I could not extract from her at that time what was troubling her. It was only much later that she finally intimated to me that Laurence had warned her how I was in love with an Argentine beauty.

Not that this put a damper on the progress that I was making with Xenia over this particular weekend. For we all returned to Stowell Park that same evening and, finally, when all the others had tactfully retired to bed after dinner, we were left with the drawing room to ourselves. And our kissing was now in greater earnest than it had ever been before. She eventually suggested that I should go up to bed in the room allotted to me by Serena's father, and that she would come and say goodnight to me. This she did – in her nightdress. And shortly afterwards, she was lying in the bed with me. Later still she had removed her nightdress. She would allow me to go no further than kisses and intimate caresses, however, pronouncing firmly that she was still a virgin and wished to remain that way – although it had now been established that our amorous sessions might culminate in my orgasm.

After a few hours spent in this fashion, Xenia decided that she had best return to her own room, which was the one adjoining Serena's. And once on my own, I was feeling greatly satisfied with life. Even if we were not yet fully fledged lovers, I felt such an event was something that I might hopefully anticipate in the near future.

Then, as I lay fantasising upon this theme, I heard the passage outside my door creaking. I watched as my bedroom door slowly opened – and there was Serena in her nightdress, gliding forwards with her arms reaching out towards me. I groped for something suitable to say. Then suddenly she dissolved into titters of laughter – with Xenia now emerging at the door and joining in the merriment. The two girls collapsed upon my bed, spluttering over their little joke. After this I was left in peace for the remainder of the night.

Next morning, I noted that Serena's father was now treating me with a lot of suspicion. He avoided talking to me when possible and, when he had to do so, avoided looking at me. I was to learn later that he had indeed heard the constant patter of female feet along the passages and felt that I was abusing his hospitality. I was to become one of his less favourite young men – a status from which I was never fully recovered.

Another person who appeared shocked by the nocturnal events was Michael Boyne – or maybe he just felt omitted from the romantic pace of the weekend's events. Anyway, he made some excuse and departed on the Sunday morning. By the Sunday evening, however, romance was rife, for Laurence now bestowed his amorous attention upon Serena. The two of them were Catholics, so Xenia and I regarded it as an appropriate match – while wondering just how far they took things when together. They looked quite an odd couple, with Laurence so skinny and slight of build and Serena as roundly ebullient as a bouncing ball. But they shared a bed together, wrapped in each others' arms, so Xenia and myself were not the only revellers that night. It suddenly seemed evident that so many of us were finally graduating with zeal, if belatedly, into the enjoyment of these fornicating games in which the adult world so happily indulged.

> Rapiers aloft, we **doff** our **hats** to **ladies**,
> **trad**ing **jests**, or **swing**ing from **chandeliers**,
> **fear**ing **nothing** as we **slide** a **ride** on **grand**

bannistered stairs, wearing our military buckles.
Lucky in love, we cavort the floor of the spurred
herd's stomping-ground, with wild lust
thrusting notes from formerly silent throats -
to croak, howl, bellow, roar and bay.
Displaying our fantails with rustling feathers, flicking
quickly our red coxcombs, with sperm-sacks
packed to overflowing, we offer our god-like
bodies as tools for shaping another's joy.
      Now men and women all should understand,
      we've come and joined the copulatory clan.

This was the weekend, of course, when Xenia revealed that Kerry St Johnstone had kissed her – if not more. This was about the wager between him and Nicky Gordon-Lennox as to who might score the higher number of points for sexual conquest over the course of the Hilary term. His claim that he had scored points with her implied a less innocent encounter than she had previously seen fit to indicate by letter, and the discrepancy between the two accounts bothered me. If she could dissimulate on this important detail, how was I to know that she wasn't doing so on others? So I probed a bit deeper, but Xenia merely took delight in accusing me of jealousy – without answering my questions.

I was to discover that this was quite characteristic of Xenia, for she was always willing to confess half-truths, which may have had the effect of relieving her conscience without opening herself to censure. And if the truth emerged, she could always append something to her original story in – partial – clarification. Ultimately, however, I felt confident that this episode was of a relatively trivial nature.

There were no additional meetings with Xenia before my return to Paris. But I was able to feel that enormous strides of progress had been achieved in my relationship with her over this brief period. And in fact, I now felt disquieted with some notion of guilt for my potential infidelity with Lita when I flew back to Paris.

As soon as I returned to the Sorbonne, I discovered the scene I had left behind me had been greatly disrupted during my absence. The harem of English girls who had greatly enhanced my romantic image during the previous term, had now been infiltrated by some Old Etonians just marginally younger than myself. These were Bobby Nicholl, David

Nickerson and Philip de Lazlo. They were friendly and we all got on well together. But it wasn't the same thing as having my personal harem all to myself.

There had been similar developments over on Lita's enclave in the upper gallery, for I now noticed that she was sometimes in the company of an American. She suggested that I come for a coffee with them on one occasion and the tenor of his conversation was noticeably more intellectual than my own. He was wrong-footing me on my own subject of art, where my dismissive attitude towards the great masters became almost a defensive stance against his probing enquiries as to where I stood within the wider perspectives of painting. Lita noticed my tensing up all round and concluded no doubt that the plan to make friends with us simultaneously would never work.

I'm not sure how it came about, but the American then dropped out of her life and she reverted to being my own companion for the coffee breaks. Things were never quite the same as they once had been, however. I had the feeling that, in my absence, Lita had fully found her feet in Paris. She was a popular girl and it showed all too clearly. There was an occasion when she invited me to accompany her to some ball and I saw how there were numerous young men – of all nationalities – coming up to greet her. I felt as if I was merely on the fringe of her circle… and in some ways that is indeed where I stayed.

It was at this ball that I saw Lady Diana Cooper standing by the door, watching while we danced. I made it my business to introduce Lita to her, but the greeting was cooler than I'd been anticipating. And a little later in the evening, when I asked her if she didn't find Lita to be truly beautiful, Lady Diana's distinct absence of enthusiasm made it quite clear to me that, through ambassadorial eyes, this Catholic Argentinean fell short of what might be regarded as a suitable wife for the scion of Longleat.

I had been introduced to Lita's father, a man with a striking resemblance to the film star Victor Mature. I gathered that he acquired a new Bentley to drive every year and it was evident in his lifestyle that they were an opulent family. But I was still aware of a cultural divide. There was a carelessness with which they indulged in such matters that was all so different from the character of my own upbringing – which almost went so far as stressing a need to appear rather less well off than we really were.

I should not give the impression that I saw nobody other than Lita during these weeks. I continued to see a fair amount of Camilla Crawley, for example. Camilla was always indignant about "that Argentinean girl" –

protesting not so much against my taste as against my disloyalty in looking outside the group of English girls that were available and choosing someone so foreign. She was really quite funny about it at times – clucking at me like one of my disapproving aunts. But it would have been wrong to depict our own relationship as being totally chaste. There was one occasion at any rate, after a dance, when I walked with her under the bridges of the Seine and eventually we kissed. We even sat down on the concrete and embraced in a lascivious fashion. I can remember a *clochard* walking by and staring at us with surprise in that her ball-gown and my dinner-jacket made it look as if we had found the wrong setting for our amorous encounter. But he didn't stop to discuss the matter.

Generally speaking, however, my relationship with Camilla was fraternal – and was to remain so. I think she regarded me as a romantic figure. She even managed to conceive of me as the stereotypical young artist, starving in his garret for lack of money to pay for his food. This conception arose because I always displayed an exaggerated appetite when she invited me to dinner with her family. I must have told her that I wasn't getting enough to eat at the students' restaurants I was now frequenting. Anyway, she took it into her head that she was responsible for my better nourishment and, whenever we met, she would surreptitiously hand me a paper bag in which she collected scraps of bread and cheese that had been left surplus on the de Castignac household's sideboard. I never had the heart to tell Camilla that I found these scraps to be singularly unappetising. As a matter of fact, I used to eat fairly well at these government-subsidised students' restaurants. The one I usually attended was the Restaurant des Beaux Arts. The food was surprisingly good, although I might have welcomed a larger quantity of it. But a meal cost as little as 100 francs, if my memory serves me accurately.

With regard to my relationship with Xenia, I continued to bombard her with letters. I had never lost sight of the idea that she was the girl that I really desired to seduce. I always appreciated that as far as Lita was concerned it was a hopeless case – she was the hope for infidelity that I harboured in my fantasy life. But with Xenia, I felt that I might well be on to the real thing. It was still unbeknown to me, however, that Laurence Kelly had already opened her eyes to my interest in an Argentinean girl – and exaggerated the dangers, it would seem. For she was now too ready to mistrust certain passages in my letters, though I feel sure they were innocent enough in what they sought to express.

I don't think she was ever seriously worried in her assumption of my infidelity, but I was to learn later that she used it to placate her own conscience concerning her own conduct, which over this period may have been rather more unfaithful than my own. I have never found out exactly how much of an affair she had with [M] over these weeks, but I'll be coming back to that. But it does seem that she gave [M] reason to believe that it was him that she loved and that her interest in myself was something more frivolous. All this is difficult to square, however, with the tone that she was currently adopting in her letters to myself.

I'm inclined to think that one of her friends might have hinted to her that I could be homosexual and she therefore felt it to be her duty to discourage me from such tendencies, if they existed. My guess is that I had just recounted to her how I had nearly got picked up in Luxembourg Gardens. My Velosolex was punctured and I had wheeled it into the garden to mend it away from the traffic. There was a paunchy man sitting on a bench, just behind the spot where I was conducting the repair. And obviously I had no intention to excite him sexually, but my behaviour may have titillated his fantasies: after all, it's difficult to remove a tyre, put a patch on the inner tube and then pump up the reassembled wheel, without wiggling one's arse in what might be viewed as a lascivious fashion.

Just as I was finishing the job, the paunchy man came up to have a chat with me. He was ageing, fat and slobbery, but was trying to be friendly – which I appreciated. After establishing my nationality, the talk was about English personality in contrast to French. Then he wanted to know what I was doing in Paris. "An art student? That must be a wonderful life. It's all free love among the students." I didn't want to seem lacking in virility, so I agreed. He then gave me some hints about making love, culminating in a description of *"l'amour à trois"*. He then made it a personal suggestion. "I could show you how it works. All you have to do is find a woman and bring her along to my house."

Only then had it dawned upon me that I was being accosted by a homosexual and that I was to be the party sandwiched in the middle, receiving sexual attention from both sides. The traces of astonishment must have been apparent on my face, since his advances petered out. I murmured something about being late and that I must be on my way. He must have thought that I was going to fetch a policeman as suddenly he became nervous. But I shook the hand he proffered and relief was evident upon his face as I took my leave of him.

I have no record of what I wrote to Xenia about this episode, but at a guess I suggested that if she came to Paris we might take up his offer. It seems that my jesting remark may have been ill-received... Not that this diminished the warmth in her letters.

Now that I was at a distance from Xenia, I began to prepare her for my homecoming – when I anticipated that we should rapidly become fully-fledged lovers. Not having the letters that I then wrote to her, I am unable to recount the arguments that I presented to her for the acceptance of the Existentialist attitude towards free love. As it is, I have to make do with her replies. Her sense of morality was as naïve as it was conventional – whereas mine probably displayed an excessive and immature zeal for liberating ourselves from convention, in the embrace of modern trends.

I was still endeavouring to make some headway in my relationship with Lita, however. It will be remembered how she had a superstition that the good things in her life were apt to occur on the ninth of any month. The first time that I had spoken to her was fortuitously on May 9th. Then I had made it my business to return to Paris just prior to June 9th, so that I could arrange that our re-meeting would be on that date – not that this did much good for me, when I discovered there were now others in her orbit. But the next date when I might advantage myself from her superstition was July 9th. And I was planning to invite her out to dinner, in the hope that I would then find her in the right mood for significant development in our relationship.

Lita was living with her father and mother at the Hotel Bellman in the Rue François I. When I phoned her with my invitation, she sounded as if she was already aware of the purpose that had motivated it and she made some excuse for declining. Then she suggested that she might be able to go out with me the evening prior to that – whereupon I quickly registered that it would become July 9th after the stroke of midnight. So this looked propitious.

We had dinner somewhere in Montmartre. Nothing special occurred as the hours ticked slowly by. But I waited until midnight and then suggested a nightclub. Lita declared that she had to get back home, but she looked at me with a slight smile and said, "Why, it's already tomorrow!" This was the sole indication she gave me that she realised how I was playing deliberately on her superstition. And I felt it to be a favourable sign that she was making a joke about it.

So in the taxi, while I was taking her home, I decided that the time might be opportune for me to venture a kiss. I was uncertain how best to make the initial move. My difficulty arose from the fact that our relationship lacked any element of frivolity or humour. The fault was mine rather than hers. Anything I did or said I insisted was taken literally, for I was not in the custom of clowning or making jokes. So when I moved to lay my hand on hers, it was an act of great deliberation. And she unfortunately responded in what was – to my understanding – the wrong way. In retrospect, I can almost persuade myself that she really wanted me to kiss her but that she was offering the slight resistance that might be expected of her, for modesty's sake. She gave a slight smile and withdrew her hand to her own lap. I interpreted this as meaning that she didn't want to be kissed. So I promptly desisted and we resorted to commonplace conversation for the remainder of the taxi ride. The opportunity for advancing the intimacy of our relationship had then slipped past me.

We were now into a new kind of relationship where the inhibitions had to be recognised as limitations. Inasmuch as I couldn't feel that I was really making any headway in my relationship with her, I may have hinted to Lita that I had amorous commitments back in London. So it may be that it was in response to such statements that Lita saw fit to drop some hints about her own interests elsewhere. I remember feeling deeply wounded when she asked me if I minded her telling her father that it was me who took her home from a particular ball we were both attending, because he disapproved of the man from whom she had actually received a lift. I couldn't discern whether this was a tit-for-tat retort to my own hints that my heart belonged elsewhere or whether I was truly one of her secondary flirtations.

She had in fact introduced me to the man in question – a smooth socialite with aristocratic pretensions. I never did take much of a liking to his prolonged way of smiling but, then, of course I was soured by jealousy. Nonetheless, I thought of him as Mr Smoothie. Another thing that bothered me was the way Lita sometimes seemed to be telling me that I should avail myself of the company of her girl friends at the Sorbonne. There was Martha and there was June. Martha, she hinted, was really quite enamoured of me. I should take her in my arms and kiss her, she declared – laughing as she said it. But was I to read from this that she was trying to fob me off with another – or that she was making an effort to goad me into more demonstrative acts of courtship? I simply didn't know.

On the other hand, she was urging me to come and stay with her in Biarritz that summer, declaring that her parents would make me very welcome. There was going to be a huge fancy dress ball down there at the height of the holiday season and I could join their party. But she needed a definite answer, which I wasn't prepared to give her. I simply didn't know where I stood with her – or , for that matter, even where I wanted to stand. Lita herself was on the verge of departure for Biarritz, so a decision had to be made. I wasn't going to be rushed, so it was assumed that I had declined. And Lita departed from Paris just shortly before the *quatorze juillet* celebrations.

My tardiness might almost be put down to an effort to remain faithful in spirit to Xenia. And if I fell short of that, it is evident that I was still bombarding her with love-letters of a soppy nature – if her replies are at all indicative of the tone that we adopted to one another. Xenia did have conventional views upon moral conduct: it merely served as a measure of her moral indignation. But her own behaviour was often such as to make conventional people raise their eyebrows. Her prudery sprang from naïvety, while her own bouts of daring behaviour sprang from her very genuine high spirits.

Now, I must have recounted to Xenia that I was currently having a little difficulty in dissuading a woman called Margo from developing an amorous interest in me. This was someone who came up to me in the Academie Julien – about three years older than myself and not my idea of a beauty. But she claimed that she liked my paintings, and engaged me in conversation. She mentioned that she had once been a debutante, which led me to ask if she had known my sister, Caroline Thynne. This established my identity and heightened her curiosity in me.

Margo made a couple of attempts to arouse my sexual interest in her, inviting me up to her room to see her paintings on the first occasion. Then she enquired whether I had read *The Razor's Edge* by Somerset Maugham. I hadn't. But made a point of buying it later, so that I could discover what she was talking about – after which I was able to see that she was casting me in the role of Larry, the elusive young mystic, and herself as Sophie, the soulful nymphomaniac. Margo went on to tell me that she had "almost forgotten how to behave" – as if encouraging me to take her spiritually in hand and to debauch her. But I had no such ambition in mind and announced that I must be on my way. She looked upset.

She wasn't quite through with me however. The next invitation was for me to come back and have dinner with a few of her friends – Americans for the most part. I had no suitable excuse for declining, so I went. One of the men had evidently been given the task of asking me the appropriate questions to discover if I was heterosexual. I indicated as much and he went back into the kitchen where I assume his findings were duly reported back to Margo. All of the guests were quick to make their departure after we had dined.

Then she took me to a cupboard where she showed me professional photographs of herself, for which she had modelled, while telling me there were others where she was naked. But I neglected to ask to see these and she was nonplussed as to what move she should make next. So I suggested that we go out for a drink. We moved from place to place, but at the end of the evening I dumped her – ungallantly – in a taxi, while declaring that I myself was going to walk home. I could see from the look on her face that she had now registered that I was a hopeless case.

Not that it was any worry to me that I wouldn't be seeing Margo again, for my thoughts were (principally) upon Xenia. But it seems that she was having a good time in London with [M] – as was subsequently revealed. And this infidelity was soon to reach its climax, for she was planning to invite him down to Serena's home, Stowell Park, for the weekend. It was interesting to note the breezy terms with which she acquainted me of the fact that there was going to be such a weekend party; and even more interesting that there was no mention at all of [M].

Although there were quite evidently some other options open to me, I chose to be on my own for the *quatorze juillet* celebrations, wandering round various districts in Paris, watching the bands playing outside cafés and the couples clinging together as they danced and, finally, to St Germain for more boisterous dancing. Although it had been my choice, this did not mitigate my loneliness and sense of estrangement.

The whole of Paris was now draining fast and I still hadn't made up my mind whether to follow Lita to Biarritz. Martha and June had a plan for going off on holiday together and they had urged me to come with them. I realised that there were far more favourable prospects for an instant affair with Martha than there had ever been with Lita. She was an attractive girl too, if slightly on the heavy side. (Her father worked in some small capacity at the Argentine Consulate I believe.) And we did pair up to wander round the jazz clubs on a couple of occasions. But my desire to develop the relationship with her was never truly aroused. So we just remained friends.

There was now a holiday course at the Sorbonne, which offered me a good opportunity for a rapid review of the ground we'd covered previously. None of my friends had re-enrolled but that didn't deter me. Besides, I had always treated the Salle Richelieu as the nearest thing available to a dating agency. It had solved my problem of loneliness over the earlier months of this year, so I had hopes that it might serve the same purpose now.

It wasn't quite the same, though – or perhaps I simply wasn't in attendance for long enough. I employed my previous tactics in playing the telepathy game and I had quite a number of attractive girls aware of my presence up in my gallery enclave. There was even a bunch of British undergraduates over on the far side, including an attractive girl from St Andrews, whose name I discovered to be Anne. But she had men in regular attendance – one of whom I was later to encounter at Oxford.

The method that ultimately proved successful in breaking through her defences involved the chance purchase of a gingerbread pig, with the words "*a ma pin-up*" inscribed upon it in icing sugar. I then sketched a small portrait of Anne, pinned it to the pig and left it on her seat in the auditorium for her to find when she came back from her coffee-break. It evoked laughter and a covert hand movement of recognition. Nor was I too greatly put off that the boyfriend sat there eating my gift to her. In any case, I was now in a position to speak to her in the corridors when I next ran into her. And this led to her coming for a coffee with me in the break. But it didn't go any further than that. She had her own bunch of friends and it remained that way.

Then came a letter from Xenia, in which she furnished a few vague details about the weekend party at Stowell Park – although she only dwells briefly upon [M]'s name. There is very little in this account to suggest what might really have taken place between them – although some of it was revealed to me later. Just how innocent it may all have been, I have little means of knowing, but she was always to assert that little more than kissing was involved. In any case, I am convinced that when I returned to England in late August she was still *technically* a virgin as she continued to stress her devotion to the whole cult of virginity. But I was evidently not at ease concerning her description of the weekend's hilarity and must have questioned her on the subject in my next letter. In her reply, she sought to set my fears at rest.

So much for all that – but at the same time, in her letters of late July and early August, she returned again and again to her reasons for remaining a practising virgin. I found myself having to contend with this attitude for the duration of our affair. The frustration was to make a deep impression on me, while also giving rise to a certain resentment that I was being required to tolerate such anachronistic virtue when the contemporary trend was drifting towards permissiveness. Of course, the point really to be noted is that the permissive era had not yet begun. The contraceptive pill had yet to be invented and, in Britain at least, society was still striving to re-establish its values upon the pre-war model. We regarded ourselves as the victors and somehow expected that the old order still prevailed. But I was here in Paris, which had seen the failure and destruction of that old order and where Existentialism was the language of the new spirit of individual liberty. So I was baffled by the restraints imposed on me by the one person with whom I really wanted to break free.

Yet, judging from her letters, while Xenia may have been an avowed professional virgin, it didn't sound as if she felt much reverence for the ideal of becoming a faithful wife. I have no recollection whether this was a point that I took up with her, but it would seem from the reply she sent me in August that I must then have attempted to promote a more libertine attitude towards premarital sex. Given her reply, I cannot absolve Xenia from the charge of cock-teasing. Viewed from this distance, I am inclined to suppose that it was deliberate: alternating restraint and encouragement with an even hand. She went on to discuss other matters – namely the latest gossip on the subject of Serena and Laurence – but it was chiefly to declare that in her view Laurence should now be regarded as being in love with Serena

After Xenia's letter of August 5th, there was a long gap before she next wrote – the reason being that France was paralysed by a rail strike, which meant that the letter I posted to her on about August 7th didn't actually reach her until much later in the month. She knew nothing about this strike, so concluded that my silence implied that I had decided to break off the relationship. For it seemed to her that I might have reason to do this, not only because I might be growing weary of her cock-teasing but also because I might have been informed – by the likes of Laurence – how very well she had been getting on of late with [M]. Some degree of poetic justice may therefore be discernible in the manner she now punished herself with the mistaken conviction that I had ditched her. But this was punishment of a similar kind that, as a result of my own pursuit of infidelity, I was to inflict upon myself. For this is what lay in store for me in Biarritz, where I went both to paint and to romance Lita.

The decision to travel south to Biarritz was taken quite suddenly and it had to be accelerated because of the threatened rail strike. I managed to get out of Paris on one of the last trains before the system became paralysed. But the date was also determined by my wish to make my re-meeting with Lita coincide with the 9th day of the month. So it was on August 7th that I was travelling – without giving Lita any warning of my intent and without knowing if I would find myself welcome when I got there.

As recounted, my first couple of nights were passed in great discomfort on the beach. Then, on August 9th, I went to enquire at the Hotel Miramar, which was the address Lita had given me, if the Sanchez-Cires family were still there. I was told that they had moved to a rented villa not far from the beach where I had been sleeping. I found it and rang their door-bell. Lita appeared genuinely delighted to see me. The notion that I had followed her down from Paris, then camped out on her doorstep over the past two nights, furnished me with an image that was quite romantic. Her parents promptly invited me to come and stay with them. Curiously, however, I felt that I couldn't cope with that. I didn't want to impose myself so blatantly upon their hospitality when the nature of my relationship with Lita was so indeterminate. I might find myself as a mere appendage to her scene, obliged to watch her flirting with a host of others. My moodiness would then become obsessive. And besides, I had now received this offer of the wooden shed in Prince Radziwill's garden as a beachhead for my activities: in many respects I regarded this as the preferable option, which is why I took it.

It may be that my nonchalance offended Lita. I had arrived upon her scene, but I was keeping my distance from her. I learnt that she and her friends spent most of their time at the fashionable swimming pool situated on the beach where I had been sleeping. I used to go in and join her group, but always felt myself as an intruder upon their scene. I found it impossible to mingle with them on terms of equality, for I was still acting out the fiction, within my own self-imagery, that I was some kind of artist/tramp who had been rescued from his life of dossing down on the beaches. I simply didn't feel comfortable in their presence and was far happier when getting on with my own work as a painter.

At the same time I didn't want to be rid of her. She was there in the vicinity and I kept returning to her. Yet when I saw her in the company of others, I was apt to glower at them in a manner that disrupted the friendliness of their conversation. In particular there was Mr Smoothie, the man who had sometimes escorted her to parties back in Paris. Biarritz, though, was his stamping ground. I gathered that he was the kingpin in the social whirl of the younger crowd. It was disconcerting for me to find that I was so much on his territory in this realm. And the worst part was that I simply didn't know how he might really rate in Lita's affections.

There was an occasion when Mr Smoothie invited Lita and the rest of us to come back up to his château for a drink. It was indeed a big house, and set in cultivated woodland, which reminded me of Longleat. He was forever smiling without actually addressing any remarks to me. And when we were all sitting in his drawing room, he put on records of classical music, not as background music but to be listened to and appreciated. Although I had learnt to play small pieces of classical music on the piano, ten years earlier, there had been a deplorable absence of such culture during my upbringing at Sturford. But I rose to his fly and offered my occasional comment, supposing that I might just know enough about the subject to disguise my ignorance. It didn't work out like that, however. Whenever I opened my mouth, I was aware how my naïve observances went down like a lead balloon. He would lift a furtive glance of condolence in Lita's direction, whom I could see looked ruffled. All I could do was to await the minute of our departure, slumped in what I might hope was taken as a profound contemplation of the music.

I realised that, down here in Biarritz, I wasn't making any progress with Lita. I therefore immersed myself in my painting. So it came as a great delight to me when I received an invitation from Mr Smoothie to join his table at a party he was throwing in the Casino nightclub. I had heard these parties were a regular event to which all of Lita's friends put in an attendance. Naturally I assumed that this invitation must have been sent me at her request, for I could hardly suppose that Mr Smoothie himself could regard me as a friend. I had brought my dinner-jacket for just such an occasion as this, so I turned up promptly on the appointed evening.

I should have been forewarned that there was evil intent, just as soon as I discovered that Lita herself was not in attendance at his party. Mr Smoothie informed me that she had been obliged to cancel due to unforeseen circumstances. So I was placed at his long table between girls whom I found stodgy and ill-at-ease. In fact there was no one at all at his table who displayed the slightest wish to converse with me and I decided that I would take my leave at the earliest possible opportunity. But I couldn't very well depart the instant that we had finished eating. So I was sitting there, watching the others as they danced, when Smoothie came up with an attractive girl to suggest that I should dance with her.

It still struck me that this was an act of friendliness, so I got up to dance. But we were only halfway round the floor when the music ceased and there was a roll of drums. Suddenly a spotlight came down upon me, followed by a further roll of drums, and I found myself collared by the master of ceremonies. The attractive girl who had been my companion had by now miraculously vanished. I was told how, at the moment when the music ceased, I happened to be standing upon some magic spot – known only to them – where the person who would furnish the evening's cabaret would be found. There were two other equally innocuous young men who had been singled out in the same fashion as myself. And horror was on our faces as it was announced how we were going to compete with one another.

The initial embarrassment was that we had to select a comrade from the assembled company. Mr Smoothie knew perfectly well that I had come to his party very much on my own and that I would be unlikely to be able to find such a person to support me. Or he might even have been calculating that this might oblige me to select him, which would doubtless have resulted in still worse humiliations for me, as he would then have been in greater control of the proceedings. But it so happened that I had spotted Dru Montague, a friend of mine from Eton, in the company of his girlfriend. When he saw me coming over to appoint him as my comrade he ducked under the table in an attempt to hide. But I pleaded with him to assist me in my predicament and he eventually accompanied me back under the spotlight.

Anyway, our comrades were given the task of taking us backstage and dressing us up as mannequins, with appropriate cosmetics and undergarments… in full feminine finery – whereupon each of us was thrust forward on to the dance floor, with an announcer declaring something in the vein of: "Ladies and Gentlemen, I have much pleasure in presenting to you… Mademoiselle Zizi… in her very first appearance Chez Dior." I was the first of the sacrificial victims to be pushed out for exhibition, so my anguish was appropriately heightened. To the accompaniment of much laughter, I began to blush. There were cries for me to start the fashion parade, so I began to walk – mincingly, as I assumed might be appropriate for a mannequin. And once again I was overcome with confusion – almost in tears actually. But the crowd roared its applause since my embarrassment was perfect for the act. And while I was out of my depth in all their social glee, I found that I was rising to the occasion – curtsying to the waiters and blowing kisses to all the more dashing young men.

> I'm tethered in a zoo cage, huddled fearful
> as jeering gobs thrust forward, pressing
> the bars, incessant, insistent and impatient for the slow
> show to start, while grinning toothy grimaces.
> My place is spotlit. I trot with planks as footwear,
> sooty-faced and jingling bells dripping
> from the tips of a spiked joker's hat, while I gibber

the scripted rubbish, **burb**ling to the **act's end.**
Sentenced to universal **mirth, I dig**
my ignominious grave as a hasty cachette;
dead to this scornful caste, I'll let
a better set revamp my dampened spirit.
> While somewhere out of sight, there stands the man
> who engineered my folly as his plan.

None of the others could possibly match the spontaneity of my bashful performance, so I was pronounced the winner and awarded a bottle of Izzara, the Basque liqueur, as my prize. All that I could then do was to play out the rest of the evening as if I'd been delighted to be given this opportunity to excel as a carbaret star. I even thanked Mr Smoothie profusely for his gift of the liqueur, although the mocking smile that he now bestowed upon me could be read as little other than contempt. It was a situation where I couldn't possibly hope to win. Nor could I persuade myself that Lita herself had been oblivious of the fate that awaited me when I accepted his invitation to the Casino. Yes, she had declined to attend as a witness to my humiliation – but she had also refrained from passing me any warning of what might lie in store for me.

In Biarritz I was on Mr Smoothie's territory and it was folly for me to dally here any longer in the vain hope of winning Lita's heart. I bundled up my dinner-jacket along with my painting equipment and made my way to the train – for the strike had at last been settled. I was leaving Biarritz on the eve of the great fancy-dress ball they had all been awaiting with such a heightened sense of anticipation. It was their turn now to flaunt themselves in lewd finery. But I now knew that it was no place for me. I was longing once more for the peaceful temperance of England.

I called in briefly at the Rue Falguière to bid farewell to Mme Pla and to see if there were any letters for me. There was one in particular – from Xenia, dated 22nd August. It contained an item of gossip concerning the innocuous Moyra Hamilton; plus some gossip about Serena – who had just departed for a holiday in Italy – with an indication that her affair with Laurence was foundering. There was some talk about my paintings with reference to some description of them that I had given her. But the conclusions she reaches are quite curious and I suspect were inspired by some ideas about me that had been told to her by others. And she talked about her former love for [M] – she described it as a schoolgirl's crush, while still managing to convince herself that the love was real. But she appeared anxious to reassure me that her present love for myself was something of a wholly different nature.

Whatever plans we may have had for celebrating our reunion – with a party for our friends – it seems that Xenia's parents had other ideas. For on arriving back in England I phoned her only to be told that they were leaving for their home in Scotland. However, I was invited to come and join them up there. This was near Inverness, their stately home in the Scottish baronial style, which had been built by Xenia's great-grandfather. I accepted it readily enough, and Xenia then wrote to me confirming it in a letter dated September 8th.

My visit to Inverness could not have been for much more than a week. And it was characterised by a most strained atmosphere. This accumulated largely through my exasperation at the hypocritical moral behaviour of Xenia: from the very start extolling abstinence whilst indulging, just as soon as we were out of her parents' sight, in as much sexual behaviour as we dared. I felt her parents must surely know what we were getting up to and it was simply a pretence that they were noticing nothing at all. Yet Xenia insisted that they were indeed that naïve and that our sham restraint was an essential part of the deception. I have never felt comfortable in deceit, however, and the anxiety must have been showing on my face.

On the other hand, it's quite possible that our behaviour was in reality more innocent than Xenia's parents may have feared. She did come sneaking down to my bedroom on two or three occasions. But the degree of sexual intercourse that she permitted was never sufficient to get her pregnant. There was minimal penetration and I was never permitted an orgasm inside her – whether with or without a condom. Xenia always managed to persuade herself that such activities were still quite virginal and she probably found them much more exciting than any blatantly permissive behaviour since she was playing both roles at the same time. But from my own point of view, it was merely frustrating. I remained hopeful, however, that the day when I might be permitted to make love to her without inhibition could not be far distant.

It was plain enough for me to see why her parents were feeling the strain. Xenia and myself were for ever finding pretexts for getting off alone together, when we might disappear for hours on end. On one such occasion I had borrowed Xenia's father's twelve-bore shotgun and went off with Xenia to shoot ourselves a capercaillie. During the first half-hour, I let off the occasional shot in order to keep the parents happy. Then came a long silence, after we had stripped off in the bracken. I dared not fire any shots from that place of concealment, in case it brought a gamekeeper to our love-nest in hot pursuit of what he might assume to be a poacher. But when we returned, Xenia's father remarked dryly that he hadn't heard much shooting after the first half hour.

On another occasion, we drove up the glen from Glencoe, on the pretext that I wanted to paint a landscape. I got one finished too – and it hangs today at Longleat, within a collage of some other early examples of my work. But it goes to show just how rapidly I could complete a painting in those days. I'd calculate that it was polished off within the hour – which left us a further two hours to scramble around naked together in the heather.

But the result of such misbehaviour was that Xenia was becoming increasingly keyed up mentally, anxiously supposing that detection always lurked in wait for us around the next corner. The more she worked herself up into this state of nerves, the more volatile she became and I found it quite difficult to remain on an even keel with her. We had our first quarrels in Scotland – quite a few of them. Not that they were anything serious in substance, but we were sometimes on non-speaking terms for the duration of ten minutes or so – usually with her accusing me of displaying insufficient understanding for her predicament. And what made things a lot worse was the fact that we had to keep up our act of platonic friendship whenever her parents came into the room. But I imagine they had a shrewd idea of all that was going on.

The nervous tension affected my own behaviour as well. I became increasingly irritable in my exasperation over Xenia's acts, which struck me as being childishly naïve. There is one instance I remember quite clearly. It was after dinner and the two of us were playing cards on the floor. Xenia's mother was still with us in the drawing room and the problem, as Xenia saw it, was how to persuade her to retire to her bedroom. So she became increasingly obstreperous in a manner that she knew would irritate her mother – an assumption that proved correct, for we were soon left to ourselves. We then abandoned any pretence at playing cards and started to romp around on the floor.

It was at this point that we suddenly heard someone approaching the door, so our attention was rapidly transferred to the cards. Her father was looking for his wife and Xenia seemed to think it necessary to put on an act for his benefit, explaining to me the rules of some fictional card game. To my ears, nothing could have sounded more false but, after throwing a quizzical glance in our direction, her father bade us goodnight and withdrew from the room.

Xenia then expected me to congratulate her on her cunning. But after my anxiety started to subside, I merely felt angry with her for putting on such a ridiculous charade, which could not have done other than arouse their suspicions. She was considerably offended with me and we were soon on non-speaking terms. An hour later however, we were lying naked on the sofa together – worrying again in case her father might take it into his head to come down to see what was really going on.

It was on another evening, when we had ended up lying in bed together, that Xenia confessed to me that she had "misbehaved just slightly" with [M] on that weekend at Stowell Park, while I was away in Paris. The confession was limited to an admission that she had shared his bed for part of one night and I was never told any more than that; but I was later informed by several other guests that she had created the impression that her real passion was for [M], far more so than it ever was for me. Still, as I saw it, her feelings for [M] were now anchored in some of the backwater of her life, whereas her feelings towards myself were buoyant in the very mainstream of her emotions. The suspicion lingered, however, that the restraint in what had occurred between herself and [M] had been at his insistence, rather than at hers.

One of the ways that her parents kept our minds occupied – and away from sex – was to take us on sightseeing tours. We were dependent on the use of their car, since I had travelled up to Scotland by train. But they were all too pleased to take us, it seemed, thus diminishing the likelihood that we could get up to other things. So we paid visits to John o'Groats and to Loch Ness. And there was a ball at Cawdor Castle one evening, to celebrate Hugh Emlyn's Coming-of-Age. But hard as I might endeavour to appear in her parents' eyes as the ideal potential son-in-law, I realised they harboured reservations upon this issue. I think they felt that I was hardly the right person to guide Xenia's steps on to a more stable and conventional path. Indeed, I was liable to encourage her to throw all restraint to the winds. And they wondered – without due cause – just how "honourable" I might turn out to be, if our precautions and inhibitions went awry and Xenia became pregnant.

When the time came for me to leave, I declared my hope they would permit me to repay the hospitality by letting Xenia come to stay for a short while in Cornwall, as my mother's guest. Mrs Xenia was silent for a moment before saying softly, "We'll see."

Chapter 6.3

Identity: posing under the hat of genius

It is now my concern to examine certain episodes that seem to underscore the sense of identity that was emerging in me over this period. Undoubtedly, I harboured some feeling that I was an embryonic genius – and that I expected people to recognise this. So it is a subject that I must treat seriously, whatever its absurdity.

If I had been questioned fiercely upon the grounds that I might base such an evaluation, I would have admitted straight away that I did not regard myself as more intelligent than many another student, nor even more gifted in artistic skills. It was more a question of the restless discomfort at the idea that I had to discover an identity within any ordinary stratum, which sent me swirling up into self-vaunting heights, where I was always in danger of betraying my own inner conceit. For I never doubted that I must be something closely akin to genius. I saw no necessity to define to myself what precise manner in which such excellence might ultimately be achieved – I just knew that nothing less could ever be satisfying to me. I needed such an accolade for my own inner sanity.

Such doubts as I did have fed my tendency towards melancholia: it was particularly noticeable when I first started to work as an art student. It was almost unthinkable to me that I would not eventually make the grade, but fear of what would then be in store for me, coloured my emotions, making me withdraw into a recurrent state of depression – concerning potential that remained unfulfilled – whilst I continued urging myself forwards into resilient resurgence. It could well be that my demeanour was melancholic at such times. Nor did I give free rein to the more extrovert manic tendencies that could easily take over when socially at ease in more festive company. I felt bottled up and restricted by my present sense of inadequacy – yet never doubting that I'd eventually discover my own time and my own way to establish my ultimate worth.

Sensing all this within me, Henry's reaction was to dismiss it as juvenile conceit and something that should be smothered with ridicule. It was a question of not perceiving my own place in life, in his view, and a lack of modesty in my non-alignment with the relatively mediocre degree of eminence that was expected of the Thynne family. But it may be of interest to take note how Xenia viewed his efforts to hold my ambitions in check, after I had broached this subject to her. It is clear that she was prepared to encourage me in such conceit, albeit cautiously.

Sometimes it was all too evident that I was goading Henry to pass a lowly judgment on my potential either as a painter or as a writer, so that I might fling it back at him once I had proved my worth. But the tone which I adopted in such letters was partly facetious, and partly braggadocio – almost as if I was courting the humiliation in not succeeding. For example, as I wrote in early July, when I was enquiring what Henry and Virginia might like as a wedding present:

> *I may even present you with one of my masterpieces of modern art, to mark the occasion! But as I know that it would end up in the darkest corner of some upstairs lavatory, I very much doubt if I shall be giving you one…*
> *I am now finishing the last chapter of my novel – the first of a long series of future classics. After that I shall get it typed and it should be in the publisher's appreciative hands by about October. I should be a famous young man by about my twenty-second birthday. You are lucky having such a genius for a son!*

It was as if I was trying to tell him that I was not prepared to back down in my assertion that I could succeed in both fields of art and literature, but the humour in my statements was questionable. Still, I was clearly concerned to present myself to the widest possible public in this light, and the press too came in on the act. Daphne had spoken to Nicholas Phipps, who was currently working for the Ephraim Hardcastle column on the Sunday Express, to tell him about some of my recent exploits in Paris. An item duly appeared on July 19th, under the heading "The Viscount startles the Left Bank".

> *Dark aquiline good looks of Viscount Weymouth, 21, heir to the Marquess of Bath, have created something of a flurry in the Left Bank bop-shops of Paris, where he is an art student. So of course has his title. Weymouth has been working in two well known studios since February. He is sufficiently talented to have been solemnly warned against the dangers of dilettantism by his professors. He paints somewhat in the style of Matthew Smith. His behaviour frankly puzzles fellow students. There he is in a cheap sixth-floor room near the slaughter-house, eating in student restaurants, bicycling round Paris with huge canvases strapped to his back. And yet why for instance should he refuse to carry them as a parcel through the streets? The answer is plain to me. As a former subaltern of the Life Guards, he is still fettered by the curious, but stern social code of his regiment.*

The gist of what was being put over to the public, perhaps, was that I was an eccentric personality, far more than that I might be a talented artist. As gossip items go, it was not unflattering. But it did gall me to find that I was just fodder for the gossip columnist's mill, rather than making my debut on the art pages. And it worried me, too, that it would be impossible to blend in with the life of other art students if I was to be singled out so conspicuously as a subject for people's attention. I was discovering how hard anonymity was to preserve for someone from my kind of background. I was irritated to find that this flattered me, while at the same time being unnerved in anticipation of all the intrusions into my privacy that I guessed life might have in store. Not that this discouraged me too greatly. It was after all some manner of beginning to the ultimate need that others should start reading about me in the papers. I just hoped that I'd find the right way of upgrading the level of their interest as time went by.

While I had now dedicated the best part of a year displaying the zeal that was necessary to become an artist, and learning a great deal about painting in the process, I was still painfully aware of my inadequate appreciation of culture as a whole. I could never hope to conceal how little I knew when it came to discussion on the directions that art, literature or

An exhibition, which included some of my works,
at the British council, St. Giles, after returning from Paris

music were taking. My vulnerability had been spotted all too quickly by the likes of that smoothie from Biarritz, for example. But it was worse than that. There was a lack of sophistication in evidence whenever I opened my mouth on these subjects. From beginning to end of such conversations, I was hoping to get by on minimal utterances of specious profundity. And in my awareness of this vacuum in my knowledge, I often wriggled in embarrassment at what I heard myself saying.

This deficiency had come very much to my notice when I mingled with Laurence Fleming and his friends – John, Jane, Eve and David. He was my fellow lodger in Mme Pla's apartments in the Rue Falguière, and his friends were Cambridge graduates like himself. A couple of them were holding a small dinner party one evening to which Laurie invited me. I think he had previously enthused to them about some paintings that he had seen of mine, so I was being introduced to them as someone whose career they should watch. And I certainly liked the deferential tone of their enquiries as to my influences and the methods I used to construct my paintings. But it sank home to me that evening just how wide a gap existed between what I had already absorbed about Western culture and the level at which they were discussing these matters. I perceived all too clearly that what I still so badly lacked was the finesse of a university polish to my education. And until I had acquired it, I would remain an intellectually impoverished ignoramus. I felt impatient to get the Oxford experience behind me, for I was now at long last ready for it.

The enthusiasm I had acquired for painting had by now unsettled my former intent to become a diplomat. There was always the precedent set by Rubens who had managed to combine such two careers successfully… but it wasn't very likely in this day and age that one would have the time to develop both activities simultaneously. I was now realising that if I was going to be serious about my painting, I'd best drop any idea of applying to join the Foreign Office. Besides I was becoming aware I would require a good honours degree before they might even consider such an application. As a diplomat, it was dubious whether I was of the right material. But as an artist, I might be just what was required, with sufficient intelligence for originality, an intensity in my temperament and a soaring ambition to attain the highest peaks of achievement – plus all the perseverance and stamina that might prove necessary as additional assets.

Nor would the careers of painter and writer conflict badly. It might even work out that they complemented one another – living the life of an artist, and then writing about it at the same time. And Duff Cooper's advice to me that I should start keeping a journal, as a tool of the writer, had struck me as being my best possible approach to that profession – in the light of my scant knowledge concerning what the rest of English literature might already have covered.

Equally, I had uncomfortable doubts that I didn't really have the right background to be an artist. There might be a long tradition of contribution to English literature from the British aristocracy, but this hardly held true in the world of art: where painting was concerned, aristocrats had made a mere dilettante contribution. And the same might be said if one assessed the contribution to art of people who had been educated at Eton. There was evidently something in an upper class upbringing that didn't quite lend itself to bohemian excellence. Or that, at any rate, was the obvious deduction to be made from any present examination of our cultural heritage.

Despite the general parsimony of Henry's own attitude – which rubbed off to some extent upon all of his offspring – I felt cluttered and inhibited by the sheer opulence of my background, but at the same time in two minds as to whether I *ought* to keep it hidden or thrust it forward on display. It wasn't that I was consciously employing subterfuge; it was simply that I had been brought up to consider myself as belonging to an impoverished aristocracy that was having the greatest difficulty surviving in the harsh modern world.

I had constantly heard Henry declaiming upon the injustices of the British system of taxation and how, nowadays, we had no money to spare upon luxuries. Not having any personal knowledge of comparative incomes, I accepted too readily that his pronouncements on the subject were accurate. I was well aware that, like Lita's father, he drove round in a Bentley that his chauffeur kept spotlessly clean. But it was also noticeable that he wore his sports jackets until the cuffs began to fray. And I could remember him declining to let us have some magazine sent regularly to the house in order to economise upon the stationers' bill.

I have mentioned previously how Lita's family were dwelling at the Hotel Bellman in the Rue François I. But when my father was to pass through Paris – I will come to this shortly – he booked in at a relatively banal hotel in the Rue de Rivoli. I noted when Lita then enquired where he was staying that her expression denoted that she was unimpressed at his choice. She had also indicated previously how – on a visit that she herself had made to London several years ago – she had been recommended what she had found to be a terrible old-fashioned hotel. It turned out that this was the Cavendish, which my own parents' aristocratic circle had revered for its Edwardian eccentricity. It was this kind of difference in our values that made me aware of the cultural divide between us; it also brought home to me how I had been raised to revere a crusty, more threadbare kind of elegance, where impoverished lifestyles were something you could admire and even hope to emulate.

There were also some more personal psychological aspects to the development of my attitude in these matters, as I have touched upon previously. It was almost as if I disliked spending money because I felt as if I was unworthy of luxury. The general squalor that I was apt to cultivate was also a symbol of revolt against Henry's standards. There was a rejection of all that easy comfort in my upbringing – which may have been linked to some notion that I had been tainted with a dandified tendency towards homosexuality in my youth. Living rough seemed the antithesis of all that. I couldn't stand the idea of looking like a neatly groomed Nancy-boy, nor even like a rich man's son. It was from a combination of all these factors that the full complexity of my behaviour emerged.

But from the viewpoint of anyone like Lita, it must have seemed a trifle curious, for the credibility of my impoverished image had long been undermined by her discovery that I was the heir to one of Britain's most illustrious stately homes. She could forgive me for confusing Bach with Beethoven but my deliberate uncleanliness – when I could well afford the soap – was something that she found difficult to discuss with any equanimity. In fact we never really discussed it at all, although it was perfectly obvious that the subject was in both of our minds. And I'm sure that she never regarded my grubbiness as enhancing my bohemian image in any way at all: in her mind, the concepts of dirt and genius had never been linked together.

Sometimes I did ask myself how I could make so bold as to venture into this territory, vaunting myself as a potential genius, when the likelihood of such success was statistically minimal. I needed to *feel* that I was different from that crowd. They were the clean, well-manicured set, and I somehow identified these concepts quite closely with my father. I needed to break away from all that and to become instantly identifiable as a bohemian – unwashed in appearance and shabbily attired.

To some extent however, it may be that I was simply romanticising such imagery. It is true that I didn't have money to spare, nor would I have until the transfer of capital had been fully implemented by the family lawyers. But I might question whether I really needed to economise on my restaurant expenses to the extent that I actually did. The meagreness of my diet was in fact indicative of my attempt to achieve the lean and hungry look. And I enjoyed letting my friends know that my belly was empty.

Nor was it just a voraciously unkempt *appearance* that I was cultivating. It was the aroma too. Now that no one any longer shared my company within their family embrace, I began to miss out on my baths until I had reduced them to one per week. And on such occasions, I was apt to take all of my clothes that were in need of a wash into the bath with me, so that I could launder them at the same time. I managed to persuade myself that these were good bohemian habits and that the more I benefited in spirit the greater the distance I managed to put between my present way of living and all those superfluous refineries of my upbringing.

The parsimony in my outlook had perhaps long been there, but it certainly wasn't diminishing now that I was out here in Paris. I was trying to do everything on the cheap. It was as if, psychologically, I wanted to feel that I could crack the problems of life from the meanest of depths; that I didn't need any manner of cosseting from others and I certainly didn't offer it to myself. I'd win through to my goals, regardless

It might have been anticipated that, politically, I would veer to the left over this period. But this was not the case. Various episodes come to mind which may be indicative of the complexion of my bias at this time.

I remember the hostility I felt when a German youth at the Alliance Française, which I attended briefly to see if my grasp of the French language might improve, was occupying the discussion floor in speculation as to how different a place the world might now be if Germany had won the war. He had been hogging the floor the previous day, as well. And I felt there was an arrogant contempt for others in the way all the discussion was centred upon him. He was conversing with the French teacher (an attractive young woman) and with his fellow nationals. But the rest of us weren't making much of a contribution – until I was suddenly smitten by his idea of a "Germany calling" and telling us how unfortunate it was for the world that they had lost the war. If anyone was going to stand up to him, indicating that this gathering of Europeans had no intention of following where he led, then that role must fall to myself.

These were tense moments, with only a minimum of remarks actually uttered. But I took a firm line and said that the outcome of the war was never in serious doubt, because Germany was gradually over-extending its authority to the point where it could no longer control the areas which it had over-run. He found this dismissive attitude to his nation's war effort irksome and we were sitting there for several seconds glaring daggers at each other, while the teacher stirred uneasily. *"Vous croyez ça, vraiment?"* he enquired. *"Oui, je crois ça, vraiment,"* I repeated. Then the tension was released by someone contributing to the discussion in a lighter vein. But I was aware that a Yugoslav student in the row behind mine took the trouble to lean forward and to pat me on the back.

It may only have been for a brief period, but a consciousness of all that Nazi Germany had stood for and all that democratic Britain had stood for were encapsulated in the hatred in our glaring faces. We were never to clash again – in fact, I don't think I put in more than a couple of further attendances at the Alliance Française. But the incident made me strangely aware how the two of us represented different trends within the same European culture.

Even if I was aware of the distinction, however, I was not yet fully distanced from all the fascist views that Henry had preached to me over the course of my upbringing. My gut reaction to Jews, Arabs or Negroes was still faintly hostile and irrational. Instances come to mind. There was the youth who came up to sit in the portion of the Salle Richelieu at the Sorbonne, which I regarded as the territory for my harem. He promptly introduced himself as "a Jew from Liverpool" and followed this with a lot of talk with crude expletives, such as 'fucking' thrown in for good measure.

The language itself didn't encourage me to feel at ease with him. But I was also conscious of the thought that he – a Jew – was attempting to break in on my harem. The lack of warmth in my response quickly persuaded him that I was a racist and he never came back.

There was another instance when Lita had introduced me to an Arab friend who had accosted her while she had been waiting at the café. He was full of talk about us going on together – with Martha, June and some others – to a jazz club. But my expression displayed how I uncomfortable I was with the idea that such a man should be chatting in an intimate vein with a girl whom I regarded as my own. I realised at the time my hostility towards him wasn't rational and owed something to him being an Arab.

The worst instance of all arose just after this. Having managed to lose the Arab, I accompanied both Lita and Martha to *Le Vieux Colombier*, where we spent the afternoon dancing to a jazz band. While I was dancing with Lita however, Martha was approached by a Negro whom she must have given offence by her manner of declining to dance with him. Anyway, the first thing that we knew about it was that he was slapping her around the face and calling her *"Salope!"* I stepped between them and demanded to know what the matter might be, indicating that Martha was with me. He was shouting abuse at her now for being English – as he had understood from my own accent. And this led to others explaining that she was Argentinean. In the meantime Lita had hustled Martha out into the street, so it was now wisest for me just to follow them. Martha claimed later that the Negro had touched her breast when asking her to dance. I felt a fury of indignation against such behaviour – and it was his colour that had made the act seem so foul.

I think it does need to be registered that I was still of a racist disposition in all such matters. But I would stress that I had yet to meet anyone whom I could regard as a friend who was of a different race to my own. Such widening of my acquaintance was yet to come.

The Rosenbergs were executed in America during this summer. And there was strong feeling amongst Parisian students against the Americans for not commuting the sentences to terms of imprisonment. They had been offered their lives in exchange for revealing all details about the spy ring in which they had played a relatively small part. With considerable bravery, they had refused to inform on their accomplices – so were executed. The Communist party was highly active over these days, collecting signatures for their reprieve. And I was asked for my signature on more than one occasion, but I declined.

At this distance in time, it strikes me as curious that I should appear to have been *in favour* of their death sentence. And I really don't think that my reluctance to participate in the campaign was concerned with the fact that the Rosenbergs were Jewish. I think it was just that I wanted no part in a campaign that was so evidently organised by the Communists, who were as authoritarian in their outlook as ever the Fascists had been.

I think that those who ran the student restaurant at the Beaux-Arts may have regarded me as suspiciously right wing – as an informer for the CIA or some such group. I was someone who was nearly always on his own, seldom mingling or conversing with any of the other students – seeming perhaps as if I had been planted there to observe who mixed with whom, or who the politically active young students might be. Anyway, that might explain the fact that I observed one of their staff taking photographs of me one day, as I carried my tray from the food counter. He was snapping me with an air of insolence on his face, as if he wanted me to notice what he was doing. For if I was such an informer, I might take fright. As it was, my snapshot probably just circulated round such restaurants, which the Communists regarded as their recruiting-ground, with a query as to whether anyone had evidence of any suspicious behaviour by the likes of me.

The way I didn't readily make friends – withdrawing from others whose motivations I neither knew nor trusted – combined with my conscious efforts to cultivate a unique individualistic style meant that I did strike people as being eccentric. This was mainly because of my determination to be my own kind of person – without the aid of any others to assist me in discovering what that might entail. It wasn't that my behaviour was *really* that odd – but there were instances when I saw that other did.

There was an occasion, for example, when I had left a number of the canvases I had painted rolled up together behind the counter of a café, while I went off on some errand. I had been careful to see that the canvases were rolled with the painted surface on the outer side, in the manner that I'd learnt was necessary, to avoid any cracking of the pigment. Yet by the time I returned, the scroll had been reversed, so that the painted surfaces were now on the inside. And because this might cause the paint at a later date to crack, I had become angry with the proprietor of the café for opening the scroll without my permission. But the crosser I became, the broader grew the smiles on the faces of the proprietor and his family. In their eyes my anger was absurd from start to finish. And I suddenly perceived how I was seen by them as the stereotype of a mad young artist, giving vent to an irrational anger that simply would not arise in more normal people. I realised I was getting nowhere at all with such irascibility, so picked up my roll of paintings and flounced off.

There was another occasion when I became aware how the attractive Norwegian girl I had badgered at the Sorbonne – and taken to have a coffee with me – had soon decided that I was far too inelegant and absorbed in myself to qualify as an agreeable companion. I had, in fact, met her before – she had modelled at the Academie Julien for some sketching sessions. So I was delighted to observe her in attendance at some of the lectures in the holiday course at the Sorbonne. But I had no realistic understanding of how to bridge the communication gap, as we sat in a café, exploring if we wanted to know one another any better.

As we were sitting there, a fight broke out between a couple of men some way down, over on the far side of the road. I stood up from a genuine curiosity to see if I could discern what might have been the cause of their antagonism. And, since I regarded boxing as one of my specialist subjects, I was hoping that my observations on this street brawl might produce an interesting area of conversation. But I suddenly realised I had taken a wrong step. She was irritated by my desire to observe two men brawling and was muttering that I should sit down – which I chose to ignore. And when I informed her that neither of the contestants knew how to box, she exclaimed softly enough that if I thought I could do better, then I ought to take it up with them.

I was always utterly useless at discreetly conveying whatever prowess might be attributable to me – invariably I came over crass or, as in this case, frankly incredible. I ended up, not enhanced in her eyes, but as someone whose boastfulness was without foundation and quite simply absurd. The Norwegian girl terminated our incipient romance by getting up to leave. And on a subsequent occasion when I suggested she might like to come and have a coffee with me, she merely shook her head and walked away.

I was indeed aware how other people sometimes judged that there was something fraudulent in the image I presented. For example, while pursuing my career as an artist, some of the English people who were at the Sorbonne with me evidently supposed that my pose as an art student was a mere sham. I learnt this many years later when re-encountering Sarah Jewson – after she had married David Nickerson. They were both in attendance at the *Cours de Civilisation Française*, but Sarah was to tell me that her particular friends supposed that the paint smears upon my grey flannels and Tweed jacket were placed there with a sense of deliberation so as to give people the impression that I was painting in my spare time. It seems to me that no one would ever have attributed such a laborious deception to me, if it wasn't for the fact that they knew about my aristocratic background. It was that much of a disadvantage, coming from a stately home, that people should regard it as incongruous that I might sincerely be striving to emerge as an artist of merit.

On the other hand, that wasn't always the image that I gave to people. I have described previously how Margo identified me with the elusive young mystic Larry in *The Razor's Edge*. In any case her regard for me was certainly romanticised. Romantic or phoney, both images were held of me at this time and yet neither were strictly engineered by me. Those who perceived the naïvety in me were perhaps getting somewhere nearer the truth. But I can remember feeling mortally offended when I was trying to convey to Martha and June, who were sitting in a café with an Italian male friend of theirs, that kissing nowadays in Britain was regarded as quite permissible during first encounters. He murmured world-wearily to the others, "Once I inhaled a cigarette!" It had the effect of reminding me that I was still only a juvenile in an adults' world.

In my own way, however, I was gearing myself up towards the formation of an attitude to life. In philosophical terms, I was endeavouring to acquaint myself with the Existentialism of the Parisian Left Bank. Not that this was really in evidence in any of the circles that I frequented – but it was a fashionable talking point, which represented many of the subjects in life where I appreciated that my own more traditional ideas needed to evolve. So, in terms of literature for example, I had now read several books by the likes of Henry Miller and Jean-Paul Sartre.

It might be said that I had already broken away from the naivety of Henry and Daphne's positions – which might be summarised as a post-war reversion to the pre-war values of gentlemanly gallantry towards flapper individualism. I supposed that there must be a definite rationale to be unearthed, which could justify all the current trends – in whose origin they themselves had been participants – towards an effervescent enjoyment of life, even if their staidly friends might regard such behaviour as libertine or even promiscuous. If such concepts were to be applied, I myself felt critical of such conduct, but there remained a strong desire in my heart to find my place in a society that had been loosened up from the rigours of such definitions. And I was aware how Britain – perhaps through the experience of winning rather than losing the recent war – was now lagging behind France in the exploration of such new positions.

Chapter 6.4

Parents: a fresh start

We now entered what was a very good period for my relationship with each of my parents. While the divorce had been still pending, they had both been under considerable strain as to how things might finally be resolved. More than ever before, they needed the moral support of their children as they separately rediscovered their positions in life. They wanted our acceptance of their new marital status as they wanted our silent confirmation that there were bonds of continuity in a surviving family spirit on both sides of the divide. We all gave them this.

There was also the idea that Henry had now initiated what might be regarded as the start to the gradual transfer of the Longleat estate into the hands of his heir. Seen from his point of view, he felt confident that I would soon outgrow this arty phase through which I was passing... it would be like all that butterfly-collecting when I was sixteen. I would grow to appreciate there were more important concerns for me in life. Oxford would take care of that for me; so he was now beginning to feel pleased that I would be going there.

And the fact that I'd be reading Philosophy, Politics and Economics might well turn out to have been a good choice – well, not the philosophy perhaps, for that was too abstruse a subject for the Thynnes. But the economics might infuse me with the beginnings of a business sense. And the politics too might come in handy, so long as it didn't turn me into a socialist – which was an outcome that his friends from Whites' Club always deemed was the possible risk of permitting a son the experience of an Oxbridge education. But he didn't really see that kind of deviation in me. And if I did ever take it into my head to go into politics, then he knew from the past that I had leadership qualities. He was really quite proud of his son and heir.

Christopher and Valentine were all right but neither of them had really made their mark upon school in the way that I had. Valentine might be doing better at Eton than Christopher had done, but there was a stubborn streak in him that was appreciated neither by Henry nor by his schoolmasters. In some ways there might be greater bonds of identity between Christopher and himself – in the way that they had both had difficulty in coping with their educational curriculum. And they were closer in personality, too, with their capacity to shrug off any rebukes or setbacks that they might receive in life. Christopher was doing all right now, having just passed out from Mons – with a low grading, but one a little better than the one I had been awarded. Despite Henry's affection for Christopher, he never really set him quite in the same category as myself – or not in terms of being an appropriate heir to Longleat. He always felt that I had the makings of an excellent Marquess.

Henry had been curiously reserved about arranging for us to meet Virginia – but perhaps the reserve had been more on her side than his. She probably wanted to feel that their marital status was firmly established before having to contend with us since, in her naturally timid disposition, she might otherwise have felt at a disadvantage within the existing family relationships.

With Daphne it had always been different, in that she had never concealed Xan from our acquaintance. After all, he had been with her in Paris when I first arrived back there, after the Coronation. Before they returned to London, we all had dinner together one evening, in the company of Louise de Vilmorin, the French novelist, who was a long-standing friend of Daphne's. The part I remember most about the evening was the sense of irritation that Xan later declared he felt at the way Louise "made a spectacle of herself" in condescending to my level – almost patronising me, in effect – explaining to me how I should learn to *tutoyer* my elders once they had given me such permission. She had been crooking her arm round mine so that we could toast each other simultaneously with champagne.

I sensed Xan's irritation – possibly with both of us. But precisely what offence we were committing remained obscure to me. Was it that I was treading on his preserves from a previous sexual relationship? Was she deliberately seeking to anger him? Or was the coyness in such pseudo-intimacy an abomination in his Anglo-Saxon eyes? I grew aware

My mother Daphne, my youngest brother Valentine and Xan

Xan at Cowrie

that Daphne's relationship with Xan now exposed me to a new set of values to which my behaviour would need to address itself.

There was another snippet from the dinner conversation that comes to mind. Louise was saying that she really didn't understand why Daphne and Xan should trouble themselves with the formalisation of their relationship in a marriage contract. Why not quite simply enjoy each other's company for what it was worth, without assuming all the legal responsibilities that followed on from the official ceremony? I noted that Xan sat looking into space not commenting. But it was Daphne who appeared thrown by the suggestion. She tried to justify their mariage by saying that to do otherwise would make things difficult for Valentine. He was still at school and might found it embarrasing if his mother remained unmarried.

But she was beginning to fluster in her argument and suddenly turned to me for support: "Oh, do tell her Alexander! Surely you see that we've got to get married?"

The truth of the matter is that I was easy with whatever course they might take. But I did see how Daphne's own sense of security depended upon people not being able to single her out as the divorced – and now unmarried – woman. So I hastened to endorse her conceit, saying, "Yes, definitely." I noted out of the corner of my eye Louise smiling with a sense of irony over the hypocritical prudery of her British friends.

Even with Daphne back in Britain, there was always a sense in which her presence remained with me, far more than was the case with Henry. This was partly because she took the trouble to put me in contact with her special friends. There was Lady Diana Cooper, as previously indicated, though I only ran into her on the rare occasion. Someone whom I saw rather more frequently was Oonagh – Lady Oranmore, one of the Guinness sisters who had been so prominent in London society, shortly after Daphne's own emergence upon the social scene. She currently had apartments in the Rue St Honoré and had written to me during my earlier days in Paris, inviting me to come round and have tea with her. And once this contact had been established, the visits continued. She was a sympathetic and caring lady, whom I identified quite closely with Daphne. She enjoyed the company of younger people and I warmed to her. It was a friendship that was to endure over the years.

It may well be that Daphne was still uncertain of herself in her recent transition of identity. It had yet to be worked what way her life might now be run. There were still doubts whether it would all come to pass as had been planned. And it was against this background that Xenia had a sighting of her in London, at the dance given for Juliet Fitzwilliam. She wrote to me about it in June. Daphne's own account of the dance came in a letter a week later – although there is no indication that she was aware that Xenia had been observing her.

> I went to a deb dance when staying with Caroline – the Fitzwilliams'. We stayed until the end and then went back with Oonagh to drink with her at her hotel before she caught a morning plane back to Dublin. We returned to Caroline's house at 11 o'clock in the morning, in full evening dress, to meet my grandson and his nanny on the doorstep, leaving for his morning outing in the park. Nanny didn't half raise her eyebrows at Granny!!

Daphne was the first of my parents to remarry. The ceremony was a realtively quiet one in Cornwall and I was relieved that she and Xan didn't deem it necessary to drag me all the way back from Paris for the celebration. Yet there were many old friends at the reception – including Nicholas Phipps, who had then obtained enough details about my current life in Paris to write that item in the *Sunday Express*.

Henry and Virginia were quick to follow suit – in another very quiet ceremony. But they passed through Paris on their honeymoon and Henry used the occasion to reintroduce me to his new wife. I went to have lunch with them at the Hotel Brighton on the Rue de Rivoli. I had been aware of Virginia's attractiveness from our occasional encounters while I was still at Eton and that impression was now reaffirmed. There was a shy coyness about her which I found most attractive; it was quite evident that she was determined that our relationship was going to be positive from the very start. We both wanted to like one another and we found that to be easy. And Henry was being charming to me throughout.

I did make one false step, however, in that I had been calculating on demonstrating to Virginia how Henry's obsession with cleanliness was exaggerated, with little foundation in olfactory discernment. In anticipation of their visit, I had been careful to refrain from any baths during a whole week prior to their arrival. So when I went to lunch with them, I was hoping to take them by surprise, at the end of the meal, with my proud proclamation that I had in fact gone many days unwashed – and then to rib Henry on his failure to notice any difference from the standard he expected of me. Well I made my boast, but it was followed by an embarrassed silence. Then Henry declared sheepishly, "I think I'd better confess that, when Virginia first came downstairs, I whispered her a warning that you were smelling a bit musty!" And it was clear from Virginia's apologetic expression that he was telling me the truth.

They both came round to my room to have a look at my recent paintings and here, too, I was disappointed. Virginia herself had been a talented art student in younger days and I'd been hoping that her appreciation of my work would serve to persuade Henry of my potential as an artist. But it was quite evident to me from the start that she was deliberately holding herself in tactful restraint – not actually coming out with any criticism of my work, but not expressing any appreciation of it either. I suspected that her judgment had been formed prior to her arrival in Paris and was the product of what she discerned as the necessary lines of alliance within our emergent family. I could not expect her to take over Daphne's established role in championing my right to become a painter. She had appreciated just how important it was to Henry that I should grow out of this interest in art and my own wishes on this issue were tactfully subordinated to his.

The next occasion that I saw them both was after my return to England in September. It had been a tedious journey by train, carting all of my painting equipment and the precious roll of completed canvases back from Paris and down to Longleat. Henry had prepared the Dowager suite at Longleat for my use, which was really just a matter of transferring some essential furniture from the top passage where it had been stored and supplying the room at the end with a small electric stove. This was only intended as a gadget on which I could cook myself a breakfast each morning.

Henry, who had never himself been self-sufficient when it came to basic cooking, had supposed that I would need Mrs Chapman's assistance for such a task and was surprised to hear that this wouldn't be necessary. Since my National Service, I was of course quite capable of dealing with such matters on my own. And for the rest of the meals, I was to drive over to Job's Mill where Henry and Virginia had now set up their home – with Sturford Mead still up for sale, on a market where there wasn't much demand in evidence for large houses.

Press cutting from the **Daily Express** "The Viscount Sets up a Bridgehead" by John Ralph:

The lonely young man of Longleat descends the grand staircase, kettle in one hand, teapot in the other, watched by his painted ancestors.

What is he doing there, living alone and unattended, in the house of 365 windows?

He is the Marquess of Bath's heir and he is there, he says, "to establish a bridgehead."

Many great houses of England like this have emptied. Other old families, milched of their means in each succeeding generation, have dispersed.

Now the undergraduate Viscount Weymouth is reversing the process of time and taxation. Why? Why go back to rough it under the Gothic ceilings among the ghosts?

Not one servant.

You might say, accurately, that this picture shows 400 years of inherited attachment to a home working in a young man's blood. – It is a little more than that.

Maybe the Thynnes in their frames dating back to 1566 in the 100 rooms understand it as they watch him go to brew his tea in the pantry. Where, 50 years ago, there were 37 servants, male and female, now there is none.

His grandfather died there in 1946 and the present sixth Marquess, with death duties to pay, housed himself and his family in a cottage on the estate. "I never once slept in the house before" says Lord Weymouth. But his father – he understands and applauds this move – used to bring him often to see the "Treasure House of the West." "I always intended one day to live in it." The lovely old house "has to earn her own living these days." She grosses around £8,000 a year from tourists' half crowns.

"It takes all of £5,000 to maintain her, even if she is unoccupied. But I want my children to grow up here in this atmosphere, to feel about it as my father and I feel."

"It's our duty"
Why? Why not for that matter sell off some of these art
or antique treasures (said to be worth millions), get
himself a car to fit a nobleman? It would be natural
enough to a young man.
The Viscount smiles, shakes his head. "Maybe it's
hard to understand but it seems important to me to
preserve everything. It is a sort of duty we've been
left ..."
A House doesn't live if it doesn't belong to someone. A
family loses its own traditions and character if it loses
its roots.
So the Marquess' son with his sense of destiny and
purpose is roughing it meantime with his ancestors.
But soon, he hopes, the bridgehead will be widened; a
small wing will be opened and serviced. Life will flow
back into the great house.
Does it matter to you and me who pass by? Maybe not
a great deal. But something that is uniquely British
will be preserved.

Georgia and Sabrina – or Biblet, as she preferred to be called – were
the two members of Virginia's family whom I hadn't previously met.
But I saw no threat of potential discord from that direction. They
were a mere eight and six years old, so for them I could be very much
the big brother. And there was always Valentine, who was now back
home from Eton on holiday, to reinforce my own sense of former
family identity. But Virginia's whole influence from the very start was
to make sure that we all got on well with one another. These were
good times for everyone, in that from the start things ran very
smoothly.

I only enjoyed a few days of this before I departed upon my visit
up to Scotland to stay with Xenia. But I was soon back again, after
which we had a few more weeks to nurture the promising start we had
all made to our new relationship. The line Virginia took with me was
to suggest that there was really far more love than discord in my
relationship with Henry. And despite the fact that he might be rather
more ready to criticise me than either of my brothers, she assured me
that he really had the highest opinion of me.

In my own heart, however, I was fretting over my failure in one crucial test to prove to him that he had underrated my abilities. For I still hadn't fully digested Xan's judgment that my novel was unfit for publication, with virtually no prospect of me improving the material sufficiently to attain that end. I had in fact given Henry the manuscript to read for himself, before setting out for Scotland, hoping that he might discern some merit in it – that would have made abandoning the idea of publication that much easier for me. But on my return, he handed it back saying that he found it too heavy-going to read any further. There was a painful evening when I tried to argue that Xan, in his letter to me, had been trying to praise the novel. But when I showed it to him, Henry stated all too realistically that the letter was just a polite way of telling me that the novel was no good.

He certainly wasn't going to make things easy for me. Not that I had to face the humiliation of admitting my failure just yet, since there had been a time span of some five years on the betting slip that had been lodged in his safe. Here I think I had best take the opportunity to inform readers of the sequel. I waited for a couple of years until I hoped that the subject of the bet had temporarily been forgotten. Then I mentioned one evening, as casually as I could, that I owed him £1 – which I promptly paid. To his query concerning what it might represent, I was just vague, telling him that it didn't really matter, but that I owed it to him. And that was that – for a year or two! The day of retribution still caught up with me when Henry did finally produce the betting slip from his safe, requesting payment. He accepted my assurance that I had already paid him and the matter was then closed.

At the time when I had left Xenia up in Scotland, there had been some tentative arrangement that she would join me down in Cornwall to come and stay with Daphne and Xan – provided that her parents could be persuaded to agree to this. But for a while it seemed that such agreement couldn't be obtained. So I set out for Cowrie on my own, and spent a few days coming to terms with the novelty of having Xan there in residence with my mother. Much as I was grateful to him for the chore he had taken on in reading my novel, I was feeling so depressed by the outcome that I preferred not to discuss it any further with him. He took note of this reluctance for what it was and refrained from mentioning it.

Daphne, too, made but the briefest reference to it – which indicated to me that, in deference to Xan's opinions, she had modified her own optimism concerning the rapidity with which I might be expected to emerge as a novelist. And there was less certainty too in her praise for my art work. Indeed, it struck me that Xan's influence might be resulting in a reduced faith in me all round. I was softly aware of that loss, but I was determined that it would not diminish the sense of artistic drive that I had been at pains to generate. Yet, I was becoming more hesitant now in feeling that Xan would ever be a wholesome influence upon our own very special relationship in life.

Waste no tears on the fearful pile the worrying
hurricane splintered in its wake, as you make grand
plans for new homes, sprucely tidied
with pride – in quest for neat domestic bliss.
A kiss whispered from behind a muslin yashmak
hushes restraint like a chosen posy of flowers,
her lowered lids coyly lifting to suggest
the best intentions – a bland panacea.
Sheer-edged and unsmiling, his lips
are clipped for sparse communication with eyes -
in the guise of a hawk – which no affections seek;
he speaks direct, informed, inflexible substance.
A mother's husband and a father's wife,
as such, must integrate within my life.

I was restless during those first few days at Cowrie, though this was also due to the uncertainty over whether Xenia was going to be allowed to come and stay with us. The initial soundings had evidently revealed a considerable reluctance by her parents. And there was another anxiety besides: Xenia's period had failed to appear on time. We had exchanged anxious letters on this subject – in the latest of which I had assured her that, if it really did turn out that she was pregnant, then we'd simply have to get married. Yet the prospect couldn't really be on the cards since no semen had ever been permitted to enter her womb. Or that is what we believed in any case.

During the anxiety of waiting, we had agreed upon a specific code-phrase for her to tell me over the telephone when her period did finally arrive – this was to say: "I've got spots!" (Which were apt to break out on her face at such times.) Of course, I hardly think that the intention of keeping our communication secret could really have succeeded in the event. If any of her family were in the room when she did phone to break the good news, screaming out ecstatically that she had spots, they must surely have appreciated that some coded message was being conveyed.

Anyway, we discovered we were in the clear and Xenia was able to negotiate a visit to Cowrie with greater determination. And she did eventually arrive to spend just a few days with us. I had been dreaming that here at last we should be enabled to develop a realistic sexual togetherness. For I knew Daphne and Xan well enough to feel confident that they could accept the idea of us sharing the same bed at nights with equanimity – if only Xenia herself could have felt comfortable in her own mind upon the issue. What was all so frustrating for me was that she could not.

Much as I loved Xenia, I found the situation ridiculous. Just to hear her making public comments that were designed to hide from them what was taking place made me cringe in shame. A remark to me on the stairs as we went up to bed – even as insignificant as "Well I'll see you in the morning" – was enough to reveal the falsity of the moral façade that Xenia always contrived to uphold. The creaks at night in the passage, as I crept from my room to hers and back again later, were all too painfully audible. Indeed, Daphne commented on them privately, virtually as a rebuke to me for participating in such deception. But that wasn't the way Xenia saw it. There was a morally correct code of conduct in her own mind's eye and even if you couldn't actually do things that way, you should keep up the appearance that you were.

In other respects, and especially in the reciprocal warmth of their humour, it seemed to me that Xenia got on very well with Daphne, who commented that she seemed well able to keep me in my place: this followed an episode when Xenia had managed to tease me back into a good humour, after I had started to become argumentative about something. But it seems that Xan had formed a less favourable impression and, in her reassessment of our visit, Daphne adopted the viewpoint of Xan, who was currently the dominant male for which ever since the days of her childhood she had been seeking. This was later to be revealed in the second volume of her autobiography – The Nearest Way Home – in which she wrote about Xan's dislike of anyone interfering with his desk.

Daphne and Xan at Olympia, holding hands

...Here his typewriter sat enthroned, ancient and majestic, kept in a caul of silk when not in use... A girlfriend of one of my sons, who thoughtlessly left a half-eaten apple on the keyboard, was not asked to Cowrie again.

I recall the episode. In fact, Xenia had deliberately perched the apple core there as a tease – because he had been going on so determinedly about not wanting us to touch any of the things on his desk. She took it as a declaration of suspicion that we might have been reading what he was in the process of writing – when we had not. So the apple core was deposited there to taunt him, after he and Daphne had gone up to bed. No comment was passed upon the incident but evidently he was not amused.

What mattered rather more, however, was that Daphne was now not to perform the service that might otherwise have been on offer of putting in a good word with Henry about Xenia's suitability as a prospective Marchioness. Not that such an arrangement was precisely being negotiated – but such an event would have taken few people by surprise.

We were now into the final weeks before I was due to take up my place at Oxford. But there was still this question of wanting to embark upon this new phase in my life in the knowledge that Henry did approve of my girlfriend. So when I got back to Longleat, I took the step of inviting Xenia to come over to lunch with us at Job's Mill – her own home near Chippenham being conveniently close. The encounter cannot be regarded as a success.

There was a cool reserve on either side from the very start – which I think can be attributed to the fact that neither Henry nor Xenia's mother had (on long-previous encounters) got on well together. And Henry seemed determined to perceive in Xenia the full list of faults that he attributed to her relations. She would be as "boring" as the father, as "simple-minded" as the mother and as "flighty" as the grandmother. And there may now have been a few other unsatisfactory epithets conveyed to him from Xan via Daphne. Nor was Xenia herself free from such bias, in that she had decided before she met him that Henry was an unprincipled philistine. All of these ill impressions of each other were ingrained in their expressions, as they attempted to maintain a civilised conversation throughout the course of luncheon. And I could see that Virginia was merely trying to preserve an aura of hospitality, with the shy reticence of her habitual attitude.

Well, I didn't permit any of this to trouble me too greatly. These were early days – there was time enough for all of them to revise their opinions of one another during the three years ahead of me at Oxford. Besides which, I was quite clear in my own mind that it would be best to remain single until after these studies were completed.

It had been the pre-war custom, and was soon to become so again, to go up to university straight from school. And there were many people who continued to do so even then. But during this period, while there were two years of compulsory National Service to perform, it was more usual to get that intrusive period over and done with, before getting back to the further education that would supposedly be preparing us for the career of our choice.

I was by no means unhappy that I had chosen to do things this way round. Being a schoolboy had been just a prelude to what really went on in the world. I had now experienced a taste of two ways of living that were as much in contrast to each other as I might hope to find. The careers of soldier and artist could hardly be more different and, regardless of whether I might ultimately choose either for myself, I felt that I had taken two large bites from the big apple of adult life. And it was good that I now had something under my belt before embarking upon my studies at Oxford and tasting the delights of whatever extra-curricula activities might come my way.

To be continued

All Artnik titles can be ordered from major bookshops
or in case of difficulty contact
Gazelle Distribution
Falcon House
Queen Square
Lancaster
LA11RN
Telephone + 44 (0) 1524 68765
Fax: + 44 (0) 1524 68232
E-mail: trevorw.gazelle@talk21.com

For further information about titles published
by Artnik contact
26 Pont Street
London
SW1X 0AB

The Artnik Media Foundation (Reg. no. 8490/2001) was established in 2000 to promote
literary exchange between Eastern Europe and the West. We publish our books in
English, Russian and Bulgarian.

Other titles published by
Artnik

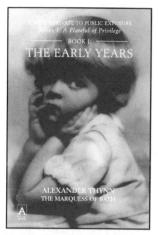

Book I: The Early Years
ISBN 1-903906-24-5
November 2002
Glossy Paperback
240mm x 160mm
202pp
£9.99

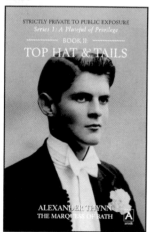

Book II: Top Hat & Tails
ISBN 1-903906-24-5
February 2003
Glossy Paperback
8 pp photographs
240mm x 160mm
240pp
£12.99

Strictly Private to Public Exposure
SERIES 1 : A PLATEFUL OF PRIVILEGE
Alexander Thynn
Foreword by Nigel Dempster

Alexander Thynn, as the Marquess insists on being called, is now 71 years old. Throughout his life he has kept a journal and his prodigious autobiography, **Strictly Private to Public Exposure**, is based on those journals. In all it is over 5 million words long but Alexander has decided that most of it will only be published after his death. He has allowed Artnik to publish the first three books of the autobiography and all are available.

They all stand alone as books in their own right as he has written them as self-contained accounts of different periods of his life. **The Early Years** covers the establishment of Longleat Estate, his title and his early childhood.

Top Hat & Tails deals with his years at Eton and the period up to his conscription into the Life Guards, which is described in **Two Bites of the Apple**.

This trilogy of books - called **A Plateful of Privilege** - Artnik will later make available as a box set in Autumn 2003. Both **Top Hat & Tails** and **Two Bites of the Apple** are richly illustrated with photographs from Alexander's own personal albums.

All three are both highly readable and enjoyable works - as Nigel Dempster notes in his foreword, "His style is elegant, light and, in the best English tradition, gently ironical. It is a rare page that will not draw a wry smile from the reader." But they are also valuable historical documents of the 20th century.

Artnik
26 Pont Street
SW1X 0AB   UK
www.artnik.org
ArtnikBooks@dsl.pipex.com
+44 (0)20 7622 5469

Other titles published by
Artnik

PRINCESS STEPHANIE
Inside the life and mind of Monaco's wild child
Jim Parton

Princess Stephanie charts the story of the Monaco's celebrated enfant terrible or, as The Sun dubbed her, "the trailer-trash princess". It begins with the tragedy that proved the turning point in her life: the death of her mother, Grace Kelly, in September 13, 1982 when the car they were in crashed. Badly injured, Stephanie had to clamber out over the unconscious body of her mother, who had suffered a mild stroke at the wheel. She had the presence of mind to put on the Rover 3500's handbrake and move the automatic shift to park.

For two decades Stephanie has denied persistent rumours that she was the driver. Since the accident, she has lived it up as only a rich, headstrong and some would say disturbed royal can. She inherited her mother's powerful sex drive and has had a string of highly-publicised affairs with *bad boys* like Anthony Delon (convicted of car theft and gun possession).and Jean-Yves Le Feur (imprisoned for fraud and theft) and"below the stairs" men such as bodyguards and palace staff. These have corroded her relationship with her father and sister. It has also led to her being labelled as suffering from the "Lady Chatterley syndrome".

While Parton documents the well-known scandals in her life, he always does so with an eye not to sensationalise but to paint a human portrait of this complex, turbulent, fiercely independent female hellraiser.

Jim Parton was a stockbroker in the '80s and used this experience to write the highly successful **The Bucks Stop Here** [1993]. He is divorced with one son, Gen, who lives with his Japanese mother in Osaka.

ISBN 1-903906-34-2
Autumn 2003
Glossy paperback
8-pp colour photographs
200mm x 130mm
260pp
£12.99

Other books by Parton include **Unreasonable Behaviour** (Simon and Schuster, 1997) a ghosted biog for Robbie Williams and also, **Playing Footsie** (Artnik, 2003).

Artnik
26 Pont Street
SW1X 0AB   UK
www.artnik.org
ArtnikBooks@dsl.pipex.com
+44 (0)20 7622 5469

Other titles published by

Artnik

An ex-minister s journey from the Treasury to opening a Cuban restaurant

Join the Party!

Phillip Oppenheim

ISBN 1-903906-32-6
Autumn 2003
Glossy Paperback
24 photographs
210mm x 160mm
304pp
£9.99

When he was unexpectedly elected to the mining seat of Amber Valley in 1983 with an unprecedented swing, Phillip Oppenheim became the youngest Tory MP. He then became parliamentary private secretary to Kenneth Clarke before being made Employment Minister in 1994 under Michael Portillo. His other books include **The New Masters** (1990 Macmillan) and **Trade Wars** (1992 Weidenfeld)

JOIN THE PARTY
An ex-Minister's journey from the Treasury to opening a Cuban restaurant in London

Phillip Oppenheim

Join the Party is an intriguing and hilarious account of how Phillip Oppenheim lost his parliamentary seat and his job at the Treasury in 1997. He then went on a journey that took him to Cuba where he became fascinated with what will happen when one of the last socialist economies turns back to capitalism... He concluded that it will never happen until Fidel Castro dies.

He was struck by how a command economy such as Cuba's could not even grow enough food to feed its population despite a rich agricultural heritage. Indeed, the cuisine itself was so bad that he began to investigate what Cubans ate before Fidel. He hunted down old recipe books and decided to open the first Cuban restaurant in London. **Cubana** in Waterloo was an instant success and Oppenheim followed by opening another one in Notting Hill. He appends a sample of some of his favourite dishes.

Join the Party is his account of this extraordinary career move but it is written with such verve and humour that it reads like a novel.

Artnik
26 Pont Street
SW1X 0AB   UK
www.artnik.org
ArtnikBooks@dsl.pipex.com
+44 (0)20 7622 5469